Dad! Wanna be our Manager?

WHAT WOULD YOU DO WITH A MULTI-MILLION DOLLAR LOTTERY WIN?

J. B. ERRICO

QUOHOG
a division of typestorm

Dad, wanna be our Manager? / John B. Errico — 2nd ed.
Quohog, a division of BytesPress
ISBN 978-0-9974709-4-9

Contents

To Maria and Abby

who didn't think I was crazy for writing this

To my father, Johnny

who really was the best manager I ever had

I'd like to thank my family and friends, who have been there from the first sentence of this amazing journey.

David Hess, who encouraged me to give this story a second chance, Candy Zulkosky, who reached out and helped me refine my story, and to the 1984 Schautz Teener League V.F.W. team, the best bunch of guys I ever played baseball with.

[1]

PROLOGUE

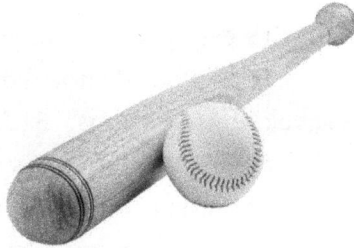

"COME ON, BERNIE, ASK! Double-dog dare you!" Derek, whose voice was deeper than it should have been for a 13-year-old, spoke with a slight lisp. He pushed his finger repeatedly into Bernie's chest as he spoke.

Bernie was intimidated by none of his peers despite his diminutive size. He stepped back, only to be stopped by Ricky and Mark's outstretched arms.

"Yeah. Come on, Bernie," Ricky said. His voice was going through the change and was mostly a squeak these days. This time, maybe because he really had something important to say, the volume and deepness of his voice increased with each word until he practically shouted in Bernie's ear. "Wha cho afraid of? If you don't ask your Dad, we're screwed! You know your Dad's our only chance of getting to play another year."

Mark, the youngest of the friends and the tallest, spoke up, "I wish I was back in Little League. Who made that stupid rule anyway? So what if we'll be 13 before the end of the season? At least I'd be playing. Bernie, if your Dad says no we have no league to play in! It's bad enough we can't play Little League all because of when our birthdays fall, but it's really not fair that we have to miss out on a whole year of baseball, too."

Greg grabbed Bernie's shoulder and spun him around, face-to-chest as he squinted, looking up into his friend's eyes. "I like playing ball with you jackholes, so get it done, Bern. He's it. We ain't got no more options. It's get up a Pony League team, this year or nothing. And besides, my Dad won't do it without your Dad."

Bernie shook off their hands, "Back off you guys!" He backed up a step, looking down at the four pairs of dirty white and red-striped converse sneaks pointing in his direction. He put his hands to his temples and blinked hard, willing himself not to let a tear drop.

He scuffed at a patch of loose dirt under foot and sighed heavily before speaking in a low tone, a quiet hiccup evidence in his voice of the deep concern he felt. "You don't get it. I gotta pick the right time. Dad works third shift and he still tends bar two weekends a month, there's a whole lot going on."

He sighed again and shrugged. "I'll ask him tonight, if he's home. Promise. Come on. Let's get going."

Bernie looked around at his four friends as they walked slightly ahead and to the side, spanning the empty street. The town's construction of sidewalks and new sewers was just starting here, so there were all kinds of interesting stuff along the curb that would normally cause all four to dawdle and be late for dinner. Not today. Bernie thought they all looked as worried as he felt. As if to bolster his promise to get them a coach, he mentally matched each with their ball playing skills as if he was the coach deciding who would play and when.

Ricky was the burly catcher with the cannon arm and thunderous bat. Mark was the infielder with the soft hands and smooth glove. Greg was the speedy outfielder with the impeccable bat control. Derek was the natural hitter with the swing as sweet as cotton candy. All deserved to play this season. They had the potential to be special.

How could Bernie let them down? The boys walked on in silence, dejection evident in their shuffling steps and lackluster energy.

"What if he says no?" Bernie spoke up at last, expressing his greatest fear, only realizing at that moment that he was talking to himself, the other boys having split off to go to their separate homes. He paused in front of the modest ranch house his family called home. Typical of Northeastern Pennsylvania in the Spring, little purple flowers and tall daffodils spurted out of the brown dirt that would soon be the solid patch of green grass his father mowed faithfully every Saturday morning.

Slowly he moved forward, up the three steps to open the front door.

"Dad?" He called out as he entered.

"In here, Bern! How'd practice go?" Johnny hollered back.

Bernie turned toward the card room, a converted small bedroom in the back corner of the house. On the rare occasions when he wasn't working, Johnny could usually be found here, where his father brought work home from the office—something that happened way to frequently in Bernie's opinion. He took a breath, stood up tall, and squared his shoulders.

He knew his friends were right. A yes from his father was their only hope of playing baseball this year and making an easy transition to the JV teams next year. He walked into the room as if the floor were covered in broken glass, hoping his voice didn't break.

"Dad."

His voice had a waver in it, but he asked the question anyway.

"Wanna manage our team?"

[2]

THE COAL BARONS & PONY LEAGUE

"POP, I'M HERE! READY to go?" Bernie yelled into the hallway as he entered his parents' house.

Bernie's mom Catherine yelled back, "He's in the card room, Bernie! He'll be out in a minute."

Ah...the card room. Bernie smiled as he jogged down the hall and entered Johnny's personal sports and memorabilia-filled sanctuary. It had grown so much since Bernie was a kid. Autographed balls, bats and hats filled the shelves. Pictures and collectible figurines never taken out of the packaging adorn the walls. Albums and boxes stuffed with trading cards in cabinets surrounded the room. It's a collection that had taken him decades to amass and next to his family, it was his pride and joy.

On a special spot on the wall hung two pictures of Pony League baseball teams. To the left, Bernie knew without looking, hung the team photo from thirteen years ago, the first team Johnny ever managed.

Johnny got up from his chair, looked at the two pictures, and touched the frame as he always did. He crossed the room and smiled at his oldest child. Bernie saw his father almost every day but always felt the joy of a son seeing his father for the first time in years.

"Dad, do you ever miss it?"

"Miss what?"

"Managing." Bernie spread his arms in a broad wave to encompass the pictures.

Johnny grabbed his favorite baseball cap and adjusted it on his head. He said, "Yeah, sometimes. It was a hell of a lot of fun."

Bernie asked, "Would you ever do it again?"

Johnny, silent for a moment, studied the picture of the final championship baseball team he led. He said, "It would have to be the right circumstance, but yeah, I think I'd give it another go." He turned toward the door, motioning for Bernie to go ahead and said, "But today, we have a game to get to. Let's go. I want to catch batting practice!"

It was a beautiful Friday night for the last game of the season. Not a cloud in the sky with a warm, late August breeze blowing to keep it from getting too hot. Not that the fans would notice the weather. It was another sparse crowd.

The stadium showed signs of age. Water stains were scattered on the exterior walls and the sidewalk had holes that would double as wading pools after a good rain. Even the gate attendant seemed depressing as he scanned their tickets half-heartedly.

"Welcome to Penn Mountains Field, home of the Coal Barons. Enjoy the game," the attendant said, his voice a mechanical monotone that clearly echoed the dismal status of the minor league franchise that employed him.

Johnny and Bernie took their traditional pre-game stroll around the concourse. It was dark and uninviting. At least half of the posters on the wall were torn or covered in graffiti; the condiment counters dented with old ketchup and mustard stains dotting them. The whole concourse resembled a prison hallway and with the way the team was playing; their stroll might as well be a walk towards the electric chair.

Things really needed an upgrade, but there was no way the Mantids, the team's big league affiliate who also owned the stadium, were going to put money into a franchise that couldn't draw fans. The Coal Barons were languishing in last place, a spot they'd held for the better part of the past three years.

Johnny and Bernie had aisle seats right behind the Coal Barons dugout on the third base side.

Bernie, continuing a conversation begun during the 15-minute drive to the stadium, said, "...all I'm saying is that Mickey Dowdell just doesn't get through to the players and when the manager hardly seems to care anymore, the players can't possibly do any better."

"Yeah," his father replied. "But it's more than mismanagement. This roster is filled with players who are just hanging on. They don't want to give up the dream, but they've got no passion left and have no idea what else to do. They are wasting their talent because nobody is teaching them, nobody is helping them get to the next level! In short, apathy rules."

"I hear you, dad. Look at Hank Rundle at third base." Bernie pointed towards the field where the players were warming up. "No question that by far he's the best player on this team. He's got power, a great glove, and both speed and size going for him, but his attitude stinks."

"That's my point, Bern. He's good and at 23, Rundle has the potential to lead this team. Hell, if I saw 215 pounds of 6'3" muscle looming over me, I'd follow his lead. So why can't Dowdell fix that attitude? We'd have a completely different team. Instead, that worthless manager lets Rundle trash talk publicly about being in Triple-A and how he hates Northeastern Pennsylvania. I'd fine him and then I'd bench him for telling reporters that all he wants from this season is to be traded."

Both men settled in to watch as the Coal Barons' starters headed to the field and took their positions. The game's tone was set early and not in a good way for the Coal Barons. In the top of the second inning with two outs and runners on second and third base, a ground ball was hit to the Coal Barons' 21-year-old Venezuelan second baseman, Miguel Beniquez. He fielded the ball cleanly as he regularly did then promptly threw it five rows into the seats along the first base line, as he also regularly did. This quickly put the Coal Barons behind 2-0.

The top of the fourth inning was when the bottom really fell out. Coal Barons' starting pitcher, 22-year-old left-hander Jake Williams had a live fastball, a hard-breaking curveball and a potentially mesmerizing changeup. Problem was, Jake had trouble throwing strikes. He started the inning by walking the first batter on four pitches, none of which were anywhere near the strike zone. He duplicated this to the next batter, prompting a heckler from the stands to shout,

"Hey Williams, you need a GPS to find home plate!"

Johnny turned to Bernie. "This kid actually has talent. I can see what he's doing wrong from here. Why the Hell isn't Dowdell going out to talk with this kid?"

Williams was more economical with the next batter, hitting him in the ribs with the first pitch, loading the bases.

After throwing two more balls out of the strike zone, Williams finally threw a perfect strike, which got tattooed over the left-field fence for a grand slam and a 6-0 deficit for the Coal Barons.

Despite the calamity unfolding, Dowdell sat stoically in the dugout. Johnny couldn't take it anymore. Rising from his seat he screamed, "Hey, someone better call 9-1-1! I think Dowdell's dead in there!"

Laughter ensued from the few fans scattered in Bernie and Johnny's section, but Mickey Dowdell wasn't chuckling. He made his way out of the dugout to talk to Williams, making sure to give Bernie and Johnny a long glare on his way to the pitcher's mound.

As for the offense, the Coal Barons got their first and only hit of the game with two outs in the sixth inning. Rundle went hitless in his four at-bats and struck out three times, each of them coming with the bat sitting on his shoulder like he was more of a marble statue than a ballplayer.

Johnny said, "Man's already on vacation, Bernie."

Bernie said, "Yeah. I'll bet his locker is squeaky clean and his ride to the airport is outside with the engine running."

The game ended in a 12-0 Coal Barons loss. Bernie and Johnny were two of a handful of fans who stayed for the final out, not like many were there to start.

Keeping to their traditions, Bernie and Johnny waited outside the Coal Barons' clubhouse to say thanks to the players for their efforts. Some of the players' gave half-smiles and said, "Thanks," but most left with their heads down and all too ready to put another miserable season in their rear-view mirror.

Manager, Mickey Dowdell, was the last one out. Johnny spotted him and refused to let him get away without one more comment.

"Dowdell, you're embarrassing. Why don't you just quit and give us all a break?"

Dowdell stopped dead in his tracks and made a bee-line for Johnny, his face an unhealthy, glowing red. The muscle in his left jaw twitched and his voice was a low growl as he said, "You think this is so easy? You think getting your ass handed to you almost every night for the last three years is fun? I'm sick of guys like you telling me what a terrible job I'm doing. I don't need this shit any more. Well guess what, wise ass, you got your wish. They just fired me."

Dowdell balled his hand into a fist and was ready to lay into Johnny. Bernie knew that Dowdell had received a lot of negative press in the last few months. Throwing a punch at Johnny wasn't going to help him. Thankfully Dowdell didn't deck Johnny. He pulled back at the last second, and with momentum instead of a closed fist, pushed Johnny out of his way.

Bernie caught his father, stumbling as he struggled to keep them both from falling to the ground.

Johnny said, "I'm OK, Bern. He didn't hurt me." He patted Bernie's arm and watched the embittered ex-manager stride aggressively across the parking lot.

The ride home for Bernie and Johnny was quiet. Both men were rattled by their encounter with Mickey Dowdell.

A few minutes before Bernie dropped his father off, he said, "Do you feel bad about blowing up at Dowdell?"

Johnny said, "Yeah. I do. I shouldn't have lost it like that. Not even he deserved to be blindsided right after getting that kind of news."

"Don't beat yourself up, Pop. He earned that firing. It was way overdue."

Bernie turned the car into his father's driveway and parked. Turning to face Johnny, he continued, "I wonder who's going to take over for next season?"

"That's the million-dollar question, Bern. Maybe next year we'll get out of the cellar, or at least have a better season."

"Maybe. I guess we'll see. Talk to you tomorrow, Pop."

Neither of them had any idea just how close a view they would have in only a few weeks.

[3]

A Weekend Like No Other

IT WAS A TYPICAL Saturday morning for Bernie: Up before the family, get to the gym, then a stop by the doughnut shop for his coffee (a medium with cream and sugar) and doughnuts or muffins to take home. As he walked out of the doughnut shop, he chuckled quietly thinking, If I didn't stop for the doughnuts I wouldn't have to work out every Saturday.

Bernie had no idea this would be the last routine Saturday morning for a long while. He munched his doughnut and sipped his coffee and, before putting the car into gear to head home, tucked away the five dollars' worth of lottery tickets he'd gotten after topping off the gas tank.

He hummed along with a song on the radio and thought again about his Saturday routine. He wanted to do something else with his life but the job market wasn't exactly thriving in his area. With a wife and two daughters to support, seemed like buying those lottery tickets was as close to a retirement plan as he was ever going to get. He figured by now he's paid for an entire retirement home wing with all the tickets he's bought.

The rest of the weekend was as uneventful as watching a raindrop rolling down the window. Not unpleasant, simply not memorable.

Chores around the house. Picnic his wife Rachel and daughters Anna and Lizzie. Hustle and bustle to get everyone gathered up for Church. Daydreaming about baseball instead of listening to the sermon. The kind of weekend you know happened but at the same time aren't quite sure you were there for it.

That changed Sunday night, after the girls were in bed and he and Rachel were finally taking time to read the paper and have a snack. Bernie was reading an article about the local high school football teams while Rachel poured through the coupons looking for every bargain she could find.

Yes. Bernie would always remember that Sunday evening.

"Hey, did you get lottery tickets yesterday?" Rachel asked, glancing up briefly from making her food shopping list.

Bernie said, "Oh yeah, I totally forgot."

Bernie took the tickets out of his wallet. The first ticket didn't match a single number.

"Wow! Won two bucks on this ticket, Rae." He grinned and waved it around as if it was a million-dollar winner.

"Don't spend it all in one place, B." Rachel's response was part of their routine and given absentmindedly without really looking away from her shopping list.

Bernie, still grinning and humming the Heart of a Champion, suddenly stopped humming. His grin spread into a dropped open jaw as he rechecked the lottery numbers in the newspaper.

It had to be a mistake. He read it wrong.

His hand shook so hard, he had to put the ticket down on the arm of his chair so that he could read the number again, then he meticulously checked each individual number twice and backwards a third time just to be sure.

Not a mistake.

"Rachel?" His voice was intense and quiet and for the first time since he was 12 years old, it broke and he croaked out the rest, "You won't believe this!"

There they were. Seven numbers in the newspaper exactly matching the seven numbers on the lottery ticket in Bernie's hand. A $260 million jackpot, $92 million if they took the lump sum payout.

The Endinos were rich beyond anything they could ever have imagined.

Rachel put down her scissors. "Once more. Please."

Bernie handed the winning ticket to his awe-stricken wife. His eyes locked on hers for a moment and he picked up the now-worn newspaper page and read off the numbers slowly. They looked at each other, smiles so big they could feel the tightness in their skin. Bernie jumped out of his chair and broke into a dance move straight out of the disco era.

Rachel burst into tears of the happiest kind. Wiping her eyes saying, "What do we do now, B?"

"I guess first get in touch with a lawyer or a finance guy—I'll call Derek, he'll know how this all has to be verified and can advise us on how to take the money. We'll have to use vacation time to go to Harrisburg and get the money, so we may not have enough time left over for that Orlando trip you wanted to take..."

Bernie stopped speaking and started to laugh, delighted by their amazing luck, and suddenly aware of how much life was about to change. "Rae... we are never going to trade hours for dollars again. From now on, we are permanently on vacation!"

Rachel joined in the laughter as Bernie again spun her around in a long unused dance move. Out of breath finally, she clung to him and turned sober as the laughfest ebbed away. "Bern, we have to use some of this to help others. Who can we donate some of our good fortune to?"

Bernie sat back in his chair and thought for a second.

"Rachel, what if you created your own foundation and had some volunteers to help you run it? You can donate to whoever you feel needs the help." Bernie grabbed her hand to spin her again. "Decisions can wait," he whispered in her ear. "Let's enjoy the moment and just dance."

"Hey man, come on in!" Bernie opened the door and stepped aside to let his childhood friend, Derek Figlione walk past. Calling Derek for financial advice about the money was the first thing he had done this sunny Monday morning, after a sleepless night filled with hushed discussions and pillow talk about the reality of dreams they'd never dared dream before.

Derek had long since traded in his bat and glove for a calculator and computer and was an extremely respected financial advisor. "It's been a while, Bernie. How are you?"

"Doing okay. I work for a bank, got married, had two girls oh, and I just won $92 million in the lottery."

Derek laughed, then realized his friend was serious and blurted out. "No shit!" His face turned beet red and he stuttered an apology to Rachel and the girls.

Bernie laughed too, clapping his friend on the back and guiding him toward the kitchen table. "Don't worry about it. I'd probably have done the same thing."

Bernie and Derek sat down with some coffees and chocolate chip cookies that Rachel had made with daughter Anna's help. They were always better when Anna helped because she put in extra chocolate chips. After a few hours of discussions, they worked out a plan where Bernie and his family could live off the interest from the winnings.

Derek pocketed his cell phone and stood up, stretching his 220-pound frame past its 6 foot 2 inch height to tag the crown molding decorating the ceiling and wall join. "Not used to sitting quite this long a stretch. I use a stand up desk at work. Keeps me limber." He returned to the table and put his papers together, speaking all the while. "We're set for now. We'll meet again tomorrow at the attorney's office. Meanwhile, he's already started the ball rolling to claim your winnings. Now we follow the process and wait for the payout."

"Thanks, Pal. We had no idea how to handle this. Here, have another cookie. Hey, I was wondering, do you still play baseball?"

Derek paused. "I played in some local leagues for a while, but work got too busy. I haven't picked up a bat in two years."

"But you like your job, right?"

Derek put some notes into his briefcase. "It's a good living. Yeah, I guess so."

Bernie shook Derek's hand and walked him out.

Rachel asked, "Everything okay?"

Bernie wasn't quite thrilled about the meeting and he guessed Rachel could sense it.

"What? Oh yeah, I'm fine. Just thinking about something." He quickly redirected Rachel's attention saying, "Hey, I guess we should call our families to share the good news, huh?"

Rachel said, "Oh wow! We never told them!"

Bernie looked into the eyes of his life-partner and felt a wave of happiness as he saw Rachel's joy and excitement. He grinned and laughed out loud as each of them grabbed their cell phones at the same time to call family and share their news.

It had been a wild time for the Endinos. They hired a lawyer, a friend of Johnny, to help them with the mountain of paperwork needed to claim the prize. Picking up the check was a chaotic scene with cameras and reporters on hand. Bernie and Rachel handled it like old pros, cordially answering questions without revealing too much detail. Slowly the hype wore down and the newly-retired

Endinos took the opportunity to schedule a trip to the beach to regain sanity.

They hit the road early in the morning. During a stop for lunch, Bernie took the newspaper from the back seat. As he read a concerned look appeared on his face.

Rachel asked, "Something wrong?"

Bernie shook the paper hard. "The Mantids are going to move the Coal Barons unless they can find a buyer."

"That stinks."

Bernie glanced up at his wife. He knew that she honestly didn't care much either way about baseball. He rustled the paper again, lifting it to hide the appreciative smile on his face. *I picked a good one,* he thought, recognizing that she pretended to care about the Coal Barons only because she knew how much having the team in the area meant to her husband and his dad.

"I hope they find a buyer that keeps the team in our area."

Suddenly the wheels in Bernie's head spun. He couldn't believe it took him even this long. "Hey, I wonder how much they're asking."

As Rachel grabbed a bag of rounded oats cereal to give to Anna her eyes narrowed. "Bernie, I hope you aren't thinking about buying that team."

"But what if they only want something like eighteen or twenty million? We'd still have plenty of money---"

Rachel cut in, "What about the costs of running the team? That eighteen to twenty million wouldn't include that, right? Anyway, what do you know about running a baseball team?"

Bernie nodded, admitting those were very good questions. "I don't know anything about running a team, but I can learn. I'll just make sure there are people on staff to help me. As far as expenses go, a lot of those get paid by the big-league team and we'd get money from tickets and concessions sales."

Bernie now wanted this to happen and was damned determined to do whatever it took to make it so.

"Tell you what, I'll call Derek when we get to the beach. I'll have him do some research and we can talk to him about it when we get home from the trip. Fair?"

Rachel wiped Lizzie's runny nose then said, "After you call him, no more talk about it for the rest of our vacation. I want us to enjoy this trip."

Bernie gave Rachel a salute. "Yes, Ma'am." He had a smile from ear to ear.

They got back on the road with their next stop being the beach. Even though Bernie had just promised not to talk about it, there's no way he could help but think about the possibility of owning the Coal Barons.

As soon as they checked into their hotel, Bernie grabbed his phone.

"Hey Derek, it's Bernie. Sorry to bug you on a Saturday, but I'm hoping you can do something for me."

Derek said, "No problem, Bernie. What's up?"

"I heard the Coal Barons are up for sale and I was wondering if you'd look into the asking price and income potential for the new owner."

"You want to bid on the team, don't you?"

"Maybe...but I want the details first."

"Let me see what I can dig up."

Bernie looked around like an informant about to rat on a suspect then said, "Thanks. Rachel doesn't want me obsessing over this while we're on vacation so just email me what you find out I can read it later."

The girls were all sleeping by nine o'clock but Bernie was wide awake. He checked his email. Nothing from Derek. It actually took a few days before Bernie finally got the email. His heart beat just a bit faster as he waited for the email to open. And suddenly he felt deflated like a leaky beach ball. It wasn't really bad news, just no news.

> *"Bernie,*
> *Sorry but nothing from my contacts. Hope to have something by tomorrow.*
> *Derek."*

Bernie did his best but try as he might, he couldn't stop thinking about owning the Coal Barons. At breakfast, he reached into his pocket.

Rachel noticed and said, "What are you checking? Did you bring your phone with you?"

Bernie thought fast. "Oh yeah, just checking the scores from last night. Pennant race is heating up, you know."

Ah sports! Always there when an excuse was needed. A dirty diaper from Lizzie later that afternoon gave Bernie's his next chance to check his mail.

Rachel said, "Bernie, I have to find a ladies' room to change Lizzie. Would you stay right here and keep an eye on Anna?"

Bernie said, "Sure, no problem. We'll meet you here."

Once Rachel and Lizzie were out of sight Bernie found a bench and sat down with Anna, grabbing his phone to check his email.

Anna asked, "Daddy, whatch'a doin'?"

Bernie said, "Oh, just checking to see if Nana and Poppie tried to call." Lying to his 3-year-old wasn't a high point in his life but Bernie felt it necessary to keep questions to a minimum.

Bernie got what he'd been hoping for, an email from Derek. As Bernie read, Anna asked, "Did Nana and Poppie send a message? What does it say?"

"Oh, they didn't send one, honey."

"Well what are you looking at?" Anna was far too smart for her age.

He decided putting the phone away was his best option. He could read Derek's email later. He answered Anna, "It was nothing. Just a wrong number." He hoped this would put an end to the questions.

Rachel and Lizzie returned from the ladies' room. "Oh man that was a bad one! Good thing I packed an extra outfit! So, what did you two do while I was gone?"

Anna, without taking a breath, said, "Daddy checked to see if Nana and Poppie left a message, mommy, but they didn't but someone with a wrong number sent him one."

A puzzled look crossed Rachel's face. She said, "Wrong number? Who were they looking for?"

"Ah it was just one of those junk sales calls trying to sell me insurance on my phone. I deleted it."

Another bullet had been temporarily dodged.

Bernie was dying to read the message from Derek. He feared an opportunity might be slipping away; that someone else might have been making a bid right at that moment and move the team. He couldn't let that happen.

"Rachel, I need to stop at the men's room. I'll meet you. Where's a good spot?"

Rachel surveyed the area. "By the ice cream shop?"

"Perfect. I'll be there in a little bit." Bernie found an empty stall and quickly opened the email from Derek. He smiled as he read:

Bernie,
Finally got some financial information for you. Jerry Benjamin is the principal owner. Word is he wants $25 million for the team. The Mantids will pay the player salaries but that's it. Hope this helps.
Derek

Bernie quickly replied:

Derek,
Thanks for getting the information to me. I think we can make this work. Hopefully, they won't sell before I get back. Now I just need to convince Rachel.
Bernie

Convince Rachel? That was going to be interesting. Bernie needed a plan and at that moment didn't have a clue. He had two days to come up with one but at that moment, he needed a good excuse for why he was in the men's room for so long. This vacation was getting extremely stressful!

Rachel and the girls had finished their ice cream treat and she backtracked to catch up with him as he walked out of the men's room. "What happened? Are you all right? You were gone forever."

Bernie picked up his elder daughter, spinning her around in the air just to hear her delighted scream, and replied, "I'm fine. I guess I overdid it a bit at breakfast."

"Are you sure? We can head back to the hotel if you aren't feeling well."

"No really, I'm fine. Let's explore what else there is to see here."

Later on, Bernie saw an opportunity to lay ground work for his plan to buy the Coal Barons as they strolled the board walk peering in shop windows and stopping to take silly pictures of their heads inserted into plywood cutouts. "Nice day, wasn't it?"

Rachel pulled a piece of cotton candy from the cone in her hand. "Beautiful. It's still like a dream that we have all of this money now."

Bernie took a cinnamon almond out of the bag he was carrying. He loved those things. "It is, isn't it? More than we could ever imagine spending in a lifetime. Is there anything big that you want to buy? You know something you've always wanted but thought we could never afford?"

Rachel thought for a minute. "You know I've always wanted a summer home at the beach."

Perfect! They could get a summer home at the beach. It would make Rachel happy and maybe, just maybe, more open to Bernie buying the Coal Barons.

Bernie said, "Let's look for one. We're here now. Let's go take a serious look at those real estate listing we passed a while back on the window of that agency storefront."

Rachel stopped dead in her tracks. "No, really? Should we?"

Bernie smiled, "Why not? Let's take care of that dream."

Rachel gave her husband a big hug. "Oh my God! I can't believe this. We are going to have a summer home!"

And with that, Bernie was another step closer to his dream.

[4]

CHASING DREAMS

BRIBERY HOUSE

IN NO TIME, RACHEL found a house at the shore that she absolutely loved with a large deck and stairs leading directly to the beach. It was close enough to the boardwalk to see the lights from the master bedroom window but far enough away to avoid the noise and confusion during tourist season. It was everything she wanted in her dream summer home.

Now Bernie could concentrate on his dream.

He started researching the team. First, he studied Jerry Benjamin, the financial data about minor league baseball teams, and other general information about running a minor league team.

Jerry made his money in the pizza business with franchises all throughout the northeastern United States. Jerry was also a huge baseball fan who also has a dream of owning a team. When Major League baseball elected to expand four years ago, Jerry jumped at the chance and the Connecticut Mantids were born. Jerry bought the Coal Barons as a feeder, giving him an existing team and stadium available to stock his upstart Major League team. Unfortunately, things with the Coal Barons hadn't worked out quite as he'd hoped and he was ready to dump them.

Bernie hoped to take advantage of the situation. Now that Rachel had her home, Bernie was ready to make Jerry an offer, but first he had more groundwork to lay with Rachel.

He went into the kitchen where Rachel was making a salad at the center island. "So Rachel, happy?"

Rachel tore lettuce and put it into a large, wooden bowl. "Very much. I can't believe we bought a beach home."

Bernie kissed Rachel's forehead then looked at his watch. He said, "Derek should be here any minute."

"We're going with his investment plan, right?"

"Well yeah, I think so." Bernie wasn't thinking about Derek's investment plan. He said, "I wonder what Derek found out about the Coal Barons."

Rachel stopped cutting a cucumber and looked at her husband. "Bernie, you aren't seriously considering that are you?" Her smile quickly disappeared.

Bernie opened his arms. "I just want to hear what he found out."

Rachel rolled her eyes, saying nothing as a loud knock and shouted Hey! announced Derek's arrival.

"Hey Bernie, how was the vacation?"

"Great! Nice weather, great food, oh and we bought a house on the beach."

Derek chuckled. "Good luck with it. So, are we ready to move on the paperwork?"

Rachel walked into the living room. "Hi Derek. Can I get you anything?"

"Oh hi Rachel. No thanks. Just want to get these papers signed and then I have to see another client. So, Bernie on page two..."

"Derek before we look at that, what do you think about me buying the Coal Barons? How feasible is it?"

Bernie kept his eyes on his friend, pretending not to see Rachel as she stood with crossed arms.

Derek looked at the sky then at Bernie. "Well it's not a bad idea, but I wouldn't expect to make a lot of money on it. Of course, if things don't work out you could always sell the team. Normally, there's money to be made there."

Bernie conveniently edited Derek's assessment to help his own cause, "Hear that, Rae? There's money to be made!"

Rachel didn't bite. "That's not what I heard."

Bernie felt Rachel's stare, without even having to look at her. It sent a chill up his spine. "Rachel, we don't need to make a lot of money from the team. We have a lot of money. Heck, even if we break even every year, we'd still be all right. Right, Derek?"

Derek came to the aid of his friend, saying, "Yeah, you'd still have a lot of money left from the lottery winnings even after you pay the twenty-five million."

Rachel didn't let that slip by. "Twenty-five million dollars for the team?"

Bernie said, "That's only the opening price. We can talk it down."

"How much can you talk that down? That is a lot of money."

Bernie needed to nip things in the bud. He could tell that she was getting more irritated by the second.

"Rachel, if things don't work out, we can sell the team. Even if, and it's a big if, we took a loss on the sale, we'd still have plenty of the lottery winnings left to live on."

Bernie almost had her. Then he blurted out a most damaging blurt.

"And we did just buy your dream house."

As the words came from his mouth, Bernie wished he could stuff them all back.

Rachel stood straight up. "Wait, did we buy a summer home so you could buy the baseball team?"

Bernie fumbled over his words. "What? No! That's got nothing to do with this. I wanted you to have something nice, that's all."

Even he didn't believe this line of bullshit.

Rachel looked at Bernie with a face normally reserved for Anna after she'd just colored on the walls. "Bernie, we are not buying the team."

Bernie made one last-ditch effort.

"Rachel, I've always dreamed of doing something in baseball. Now I have a chance. I know it's a lot of money but it's money we have now, more than we've ever had or expected to have in our lifetime. Let's do this. Please? If it doesn't work out, I'll sell the team. I promise. Come on."

Bernie stopped just short of dropping to his hands and knees.

Rachel sighed, looking back and forth between her anguished husband and his embarrassed friend. "All right. We'll buy the team."

Bernie took Rachel's hand and plopped a sloppy kiss on her forehead. "We'll make it work, Rachel. Promise. All right Derek, let's set up a meeting with Jerry Benjamin."

"Will do. I'll call you later with the time and place."

Bernie wasn't sure Rachel was truly on board, but he knew that she understood what it was to finally have the means to chase a dream.

HELLO JERRY

A few days later, Bernie was hopeful as his new cell phone's caller ID rang with Derek's tone. "What's up, Derek? Do we have our meeting?"

"Just getting in touch with Jerry took some doing but yep, we have our meeting. Can you make a trip to Connecticut next week?"

Bernie was opening a cup of peaches for Anna and switched to speakerphone to multitask. "My schedule is pretty booked but I think

I can make it." Bernie had never been one to let an opportunity to be a smart ass get away.

Bernie was going to Connecticut to meet with the owner of not just the Coal Barons but the Mantids, a Major League team! The wheels in Bernie's head began spinning. He needed to form a plan of attack and began working on a proposal. He typed up a document detailing a list of negotiating points, not quite sure any of them were standard. After two hours of work, he was ready. Bernie emailed Derek a copy to review. It wasn't long before Bernie's phone again played Derek's ring tone.

"Hey Bernie, it's Derek. I looked at your proposal. It's, uh, interesting."

"I know it's unconventional, but that's what I want."

Derek hit the speakerphone button and picked up Bernie's proposal. Thumbing through it again, he began pacing around his office. "I get that. But, Bernie, I don't know that Jerry is going to give it to you."

"If he says no, he says no. If he's really interested in selling the team, he'll consider it." Bernie was obviously trying to sound like a tough businessman but in reality, Derek felt certain that he was scared to death. Derek knew that this proposal was so outrageous that it would either get them thrown out of Jerry's office or be the most amazing deal he'd ever been a part of.

The day had come for the trip to Bristol. Bernie and Derek arrived and checked into their rooms. Bernie decided to run through his proposal one more time. It was more of an act of nerves than anything. It was well after midnight before Bernie was finally ready to get some sleep. He didn't know what was in store for the morning meeting, but he was going to have some fun, no matter what.

After a night where sleep continued to be elusive, Bernie gave up about dawn and popped open his laptop to check the sports news back home. The headline read:

"Still No Buyer for Coal Barons"

He thought to himself, *Soon folks...soon.*

Upon arriving at Jerry's office, they were met by the man himself at the door with a booming, "Good morning, gentlemen!"

Jerry looked like you'd expect a pizza mogul to look. He was tall and to be nice, let's say 'well-fed.' He wore cowboy boots with his suit pants; although he'd never been south of New Jersey nor had he ever been near a ranch. He was known for having a plethora of outrageously colorful dress shirts, wearing a mint green one on this day, and only wore a tie when absolutely necessary.

Jerry's office was almost as large as Bernie's hotel room. There were pizza and baseball memorabilia items everywhere as well as a collection of civic awards he had received.

Pleasantries where short lived as Jerry soon said, "Let's get down to business. I understand you're interested in buying my baseball team."

Bernie felt his heart rate settle down, surprised it hadn't popped out of his chest yet, as he replied, "I might be, depending on the asking price." He leaned back in the leather office chair, facing the big man across his desk.

Jerry echoed Bernie's action and leaned back in his big black chair. "What are you thinking?"

Bernie saw Jerry's game but he wasn't playing.

"I'm thinking I'd like to know what a man like you is asking as a purchase price for his AAA baseball franchise."

A smile, more like a sneer, appeared upon Jerry's face. Bernie kept his own face poker-straight, making sure that Jerry realized negotiations weren't going to be as simple as he first thought.

"All right, Endino. I'm asking $25 million."

"That's a bit high, isn't it? I'm a fan and I live there. I see who isn't showing up at the ballpark. I think you can do better."

Now Jerry leaned forward. He grabbed the unlit cigar sitting in his ash tray and began chewing on it. "How much better?"

Bernie sat back and put his hands behind his head. "I'm thinking $7 million better."

Now Jerry took the cigar out of his mouth. "$18 million? Don't insult my intelligence, Endino. I can get at least $25 million for that team."

Bernie stayed cocky. "And yet here you sit talking to me, a guy who lucked into money. I'm guessing you don't have a single decent offer. I'm here right now offering you $18 million for a team I know you don't want. Do you really want to take a chance and wait?"

The chess match wasn't over yet. Jerry grabbed another cigar from the humidor on his desk.

"$20 million. You want the team, that's what it's going to take."

"Let me talk to my advisor for a minute, please."

Jerry stood up. "Fine. I've got to take a leak anyway. I'll be back in a few minutes for your answer."

Once Jerry was out of earshot, Bernie and Derek talked.

Bernie said, "What do you think?"

Derek said, "I don't know, Bernie. It still seems high."

Bernie got up and began to pace the office. "Derek, I'm going to make changes to this franchise. Big ones."

Derek folded his hands. "It's obvious that I can't stop you."

Bernie just grinned and patted his friend on the back.

Jerry returned tucking in his shirt. "All right gentlemen, what are we going to do?"

Bernie said, "Jerry, you're a tough negotiator but I'll take your offer. $20 million it is."

Jerry pulled up his pants, which immediately dropped below his stomach. "Well, all right! I'll get the papers drawn up." He was obviously pleased, but Bernie intended to quickly steal some of Jerry's thunder.

Bernie stood up and began strolling around the office. "Let me review a few conditions first."

Jerry's face turned the color of his pizza sauce. "Conditions? What kind of conditions?"

Derek could barely contain his laughter.

Bernie had a copy of his conditions and pulled it from his coat pocket. "Just a few minor ones, really."

Jerry again leaned back in his chair and folded his hands, preparing himself for the conditions.

"First, our stadium needs a major upgrade before next season starts. We estimate the costs of this upgrade at $20 million, which includes a nursery. You'll pay for the upgrades. However, I will pay you $600,000 per year in rent for the first three years with a five percent increase every three years for the next thirty-six years."

Jerry put both hands on his desk. "You want me to spend $20 million to upgrade the stadium? Are you nuts?"

"Jerry, you can depreciate the cost of the stadium over thirty-nine years. In the end, you'll make over $6 million here."

Jerry bit hard on his cigar. "It'll take thirty-nine years to turn that profit, Endino! I'll be dead before then!"

"So, your heirs will get some of it. You can put your name on the stadium, you know."

Jerry thought it over. "All right, Endino. You have your renovations."

Bernie's confidence grew. He continued pacing.

"Second, I want some say in player personnel. Of our 25-man roster, I'd like as many as four of them to be players of my choice."

The redness returned to Jerry's face. "A say in the players? That's ridiculous!"

Bernie put his hands together. "Hear me out, Jerry. Every roster at this level ends up with a bunch of players who aren't really prospects. You have no intention of bringing these guys to the Major Leagues. I'd guess that at least four guys on a team fit this description and probably more. I'm just taking something you don't want to own off your hands and have just come up with a way for you to look good while making money from the stadium upgrades. I don't think this is an unreasonable request."

"Edino, I'm paying for these guys."

"That's right, Jerry, but my choices will be cheaper than your own. Again, money you don't have to spend."

Jerry stared back at Bernie almost squinting. "Fair point, Endino. You have your players but I don't want any circus side-shows. They have to be legitimate baseball players, got it?"

Bernie said, "Absolutely. Continuing..."

"There's more?"

Bernie considered his words, taking another stroll around the office.

"Get on with it, kid! What else is in that screwball head of yours? Let's hear it."

Bernie, turned toward the red-faced owner. "I get to pick the new manager and he picks his own coaching staff."

Jerry popped out of his chair. "Now I know you're nuts!"

"Jerry, just listen. Dowdell and his staff were a disaster. Those guys didn't care anymore. You need coaches who have fire in their bellies and who can teach guys how to play at the next level. You need fresh faces. I think I have the perfect manager for you."

Jerry placed both hands flat on the desk between them. His cigar dropped a layer of ash with the sudden movement. Ignoring the charcoal dust and potential fire hazard, he leaned forward. "Who?!"

Bernie let out a big exhale and resisted taking a step back. "I have a guy in mind, but I want to wait until he accepts the job before I tell you who it is."

Jerry pointed his cigar at Bernie. "Now you listen. I am not signing off on your manager unless I know who he is!"

Bernie began surveying the room for defibrillator paddles in case Jerry suddenly went into cardiac arrest. He looked Jerry in the eye. "Johnny Endino, my dad."

"Your...dad?" He couldn't believe his ears.

"Yep. He's the best manager I've ever played for. He knows the game as well as anyone and I know he can do the job."

Jerry just shook his head. "Your dad."

Bernie walked over to Jerry, reached up to the burly owner, and put his arm around his shoulder. He noticed Derek hide behind his briefcase to cover his laughter.

"Jerry, I'll tell you what. Give him one season. If you don't think he's done a good job, I'll fire him. I won't even make you do the dirty work and I'll reimburse you for his entire year's salary. So, do we have a deal?"

Jerry removed Bernie's arm and took his turn strolling around the office. "$20 million, I pay for renovations, you get a say in the roster, and the manager is your dad." He shook his head again then continued, "And if your father doesn't pan out, you'll fire him and pick up the cost of his salary?"

Bernie put his hands down flat on Jerry's desk, leaning forward, forgetting about the ashen mess. "Those are my conditions."

Jerry moved back to the desk, this time on the other side. He pulled the ashtray toward himself and mashed out his cigar, splitting what was left of the chewed, tobacco-stuffed cylinder down the middle. "I can't believe I'm doing this. Okay, Endino, you've got a deal."

Bernie shook Jerry's hand. "I can make this work. Trust me."

Jerry smiled a real smile for the first time since he'd met Derek and Bernie.

"Well son, I sure hope so. I'll have the paperwork sent to you next week."

Bernie and Derek left the office. As soon as they got to the lobby they gave each other a big hug.

Bernie said, "We did it."

Derek said, "You did it, Bernie. I was just watching it happen."

"The main thing is, it got done. Can't wait to tell Rachel the news."

Derek gave Bernie a handshake and headed off to do some sightseeing and shopping for gifts to take back to his family.

Bernie got back to his hotel room barely able to contain his excitement. He called Rachel. "Hey, Rae. It's your husband."

"So, what happened?"

Bernie began to take off his tie. "Jerry's office was huge! He had all kinds of sports stuff everywhere. There was a full bar in it too. He asked Derek and me if we wanted a drink..."

Rachel cut in. "Bernie you sound like your mother. What about the baseball team?"

He plopped onto the bed. "Oh that. We got that." He answered as if he had just picked up milk from the grocery store.

"So, how much did it cost us?"

Bernie paused before answering. Nothing like a blunt question to take the starch out of a good day. "I had to pay a little bit more than I'd hoped. It cost us $20 million."

The silence on the other end of the phone was broken by a loud thump.

"Rae? You OK?"

"Yes. Dropped the baby's bottle. I thought you said it would only cost $18 million!"

Bernie sensed Rachel's growing annoyance and spoke quickly to diffuse the situation. "Yeah but I figure getting a nursery room for the kids is worth the extra two million."

The silence was longer this time, broken with a quiet query, "A nursery?"

Bernie leaned back on a pillow. "Yep. You and the girls need a place to hang out when you're at the stadium." After many years of marriage, Bernie knew when to shut up and let his wife's thought process engage.

"Thanks for thinking of us. I guess the extra $2 million isn't a big deal. Did you tell your dad the news yet?"

"I haven't really asked him yet."

What if he says no?"

Bernie sat up. "He won't say no." Bernie wasn't as sure as he made it sound to Rachel. "I've gotta go. I need to call my new manager."

Rachel corrected him. "You mean your possible new manager."

Bernie hung up and immediately dialed his dad who thankfully answered, sparing Bernie one of his mom's stories.

"Hey, Dad, it's Bernie. Just wanted to check in. I'm in Connecticut."

"Oh hey, Bern. Just organizing the baseballs in my shrine. I wondered why I hadn't heard from you in a few days."

"Sorry about that. I'm here on business."

"What business?"

Bernie grabbed a diet root beer from the mini fridge in his room and sat on the side of the bed. He took a quick sip from the cold can and said, "I bought the Coal Barons."

"You bought the Coal Barons?"

Bernie poured the rest of his root beer into the plastic cup supplied by the hotel. "Yep, they belong to me now."

"You bought the Coal Barons."

Bernie heard wonder and maybe confusion in his father's voice as he wrapped his head around this unexpected news.

"You bought the Coal Barons! That's great, Bern. If I can help with anything just let me know."

Bernie seized the opportunity.

"Actually, that's why I'm calling you."

Bernie hesitated, realized his voice would crack if he spoke right now. He flashed back to his Pony League days suddenly feeling like that kid, both hopeful and uncertain. He stood up and moved to lean against the window, looking out but not seeing the view from the hotel room.

"Dad, wanna be our manager?"

Dead silence took over on the other end.

Bernie asked, "Dad, did you hear me?"

Johnny answered almost in a whisper, "Yeah, I heard you."

"Will you do it?" Bernie had all kinds of arguments lined up to convince his father and realized that he couldn't speak a single one. Even though he'd just spent $20 million to make this dream a reality for both of them, this decision was one he could not, would not, influence.

Johnny sighed. "I don't know, Bern. I'll need to think about this."

"Okay. We can talk about it in a few days when I get home."

Not how Bernie had hoped the conversation would have gone. But he hadn't said no, so Bernie continued to be hopeful. If his father said no, Bernie had no Plan B in place for the new manager. How would he convince Johnny to take the job? Bernie hoped he could find a way to negotiate with his dad as well as he'd negotiated with Jerry.

A PROPOSAL FOR POPPIE

Bernie was home watching television, sipping his morning coffee and contemplating what it would take to convince his dad to manage the Coal Barons.

Anna bounded down the stairs to join him. She plopped down in the chair next to him and rubbed the sleep from her eyes. Bernie was not surprised that she was be the first one up. They both treasured this together time while the rest of the house slept. Something to be said for both being morning people.

"Daddy, can I have some juice?"

"Sure, kiddo. Let's get you some juice."

Anna twirled her hair. "And a cookie too? Please?"

Bernie smiled. "Yes, Miss Anna. I can give you a cookie too."

Anna had a way of asking for things that made it hard to say no. Bernie really loved that about Anna. Everybody found it hard to say no to her.

Bernie handed Anna a chocolate chip cookie, her favorite, and a brilliant idea struck him. "Anna, want to visit Poppie with daddy today?"

Anna almost dropped her juice. "Yeah! Let's go see Poppie!"

Anna could convince his father to take the manager's job. Johnny couldn't say no to her...well at least he never had before. The trick was not making things too obvious. He chatted with Anna, keeping his exuberant daughter quiet until Rachel, with Lizzie in tow, joined them.

"Mommy, daddy's taking me to see Poppie today!" Anna couldn't contain her joy.

Rachel looked suspiciously at Bernie. "So, you're taking Anna over when you talk to your father?"

Bernie rocked side to side a bit. "Yeah. She hasn't seen my parents in a little while and I thought..."

Rachel interrupted. "You thought you'd use our daughter to do your dirty work."

Bernie looked sheepishly at Rachel. "No, but if she does happen to bring it up..."

Rachel broke in again. "I'm not sure I like this idea, you using our daughter and all, but a visit with her grandparents is a good idea, so go ahead."

"Great! I hope it works...I mean I hope they have a nice visit."

Bernie and Anna arrived at his parents' house. Anna quickly headed to the kitchen with her Nana while Bernie talked with his father.

"So, Dad, have you thought about my question?"

Johnny sat back in his oversized recliner, sort of his own throne. "Yeah, Bern. It would be amazing. I still can't believe any of this. I'm barely over the news of your windfall lottery win and now you buy the Coal Barons AND you want me as manager? It's a little overwhelming. Look, Bern, I'm not a professional manager. I don't know if I can do it."

"Dad, I know you can."

"Yeah? How?"

Bernie leaned forward in his chair. "I've seen you manage. No one gets more out of a player than you."

"Good of you to think that. And flattering to my ego," Johnny flashed his son a wry smile and continued, "I know you're not just feeding me a line to get me to say yes."

Bernie flushed. His father knew him well and recognized attempted manipulation when he saw it.

"But Bernie, you guys were kids and managing kids is way different than managing pros, even semi-pros."

Bernie persisted. "Dad, they're ball players and you know ball players."

Johnny shook his head. "Those guys won't listen to me."

"Dad, just show them what you know."

Johnny got out of his recliner, pacing the living room and not sure what to do.

In a whirlwind of activity, Anna entered the room to deliver a monstrous hug for Johnny.

Johnny returned the hug and said, "Hey, Anna Banana!"

Bernie had his opening.

"Hey Anna, did you know Poppie used to be a baseball coach?"

"He was?" Bernie could have said Johnny was once a unicorn and gotten the same response.

"Yep. He was really good at it, too."

Johnny's eyes narrowed in suspicion as he looked into Bernie's, but before he could say anything, Anna asked, "Why don't you coach any more, Poppie?"

Johnny picked up his granddaughter. "The boys I coached grew up and don't play anymore."

Anna innocently said, "Just find some new boys."

He kissed Anna's forehead. "I don't think I can coach new boys."

Bernie chimed in, ready to play his hole card. "What about coaching some of your old boys?"

"What the hell are you talking about?" Johnny had forgotten that Anna was still in his arms.

Bernie took Anna from his dad. "What if we can get a few of your old players onto the Coal Barons roster?"

A puzzled look crossed Johnny's face as Bernie continued. "Dad, the terms of the purchase give me roster spots to fill with players I choose. If we get your old Pony League kids, will you manage the Coal Barons?"

"Bern, this whole idea is crazy. Taking a bunch of guys who were great thirteen years ago as kids and making professionals out of them is absurd." John thought for a moment then sat back in his chair. "Tell you what. If you get my guys back, I'll take the job."

Bernie extended his hand. "Great! It's a deal!"

Johnny, however, didn't extend his hand back. "You have one month."

A month to assemble guys who may or may not still be playing baseball and to get them to drop whatever they were doing to be Coal Barons. It seemed like a long shot but what else could Bernie do? "Okay, a month. If I can't get the guys to agree to play in a month, I'll find someone else to manage."

This time Johnny put out his hand, "You have a deal then."

As Bernie got up to leave he said one last thing to Johnny.

"You know, you get to pick your own coaching staff."

Johnny looked towards the ceiling and rubbed his chin. "My own staff, huh? "Tell you what. The two of us will see if we can find the guys together."

Johnny gave Anna a goodbye hug and a kiss and Bernie and Anna headed home, both content with their morning with Poppie.

The two arrived home to find Rachel feeding Lizzie mashed bananas. She said, "How did you make out?"

"Dad agreed to take the job under a few conditions."

Rachel wiped Lizzie's chin. "What conditions?"

Bernie let out a heavy sigh. "I need to get some of his old Pony League guys to play before he takes the job."

Rachel picked Lizzie up from her high chair. "Can you do that?"

Bernie shrugged. "I'll do my best." He just hoped his best would be good enough.

[5]

BUILDING THE DREAM TEAM

DEREK FIGLIONE

FIRST ON THE LIST was Derek. Bernie wiped a bead of sweat from his nose with the towel he had brought with him. He could barely find a dry spot. Bernie bumped the difficulty level on the elliptical machine back to begin his warm down.

He reached for the cell phone resting on the machine's dashboard and punched up Derek's number but held off on hitting the call icon as he thought about his approach. Bernie had already been working with him for several weeks, but this conversation would be different.

Derek was Johnny's first baseman in Pony League. He was as smooth as double-churned ice cream when fielding the baseball. If you got a ball by him, you'd really earned your way on base. As for hitting, Derek could hit just about anything you threw at him to anywhere on the field. He could get three hits immediately after jumping out of bed while still wearing his pajamas.

Bernie slowed his pace on the elliptical and hit the call button with his thumb.

Derek searched for a pen and notepad on his desk, muttering under his breath as he always did about needing to organize his stuff. He had financial reports strewn everywhere along with highlighters of every shape and color. The pictures of his wife and new baby barely had a place. His walls were crammed with pictures of him with various professional athletes and celebrities he'd met over the years at business conferences and dinners.

He jumped when his "Play Ball" ring tone loudly broke the silence in his empty, early Saturday morning office. He found both cell phone and notepad at the same time and touched his pal's smiling face to answer. "Oh hey, Bernie. What's up?"

"Derek, you still play a little ball?"

"Well I did play but..."

"Derek, I'd like you to try out for the Coal Barons."

There was a long pause, filled by laughter that abruptly changed back to silence as Derek realized Bernie had not joined in the mirth. "Bern, you're joking, right?"

"Dead serious. My dad said he'd manage the team but only if I could get you and a few other guys to play."

Derek spotted his errant pen sticking out of a pile of folders and plucked it out. Holding it like a drumstick, he tapped out a staccato rhythm on his desk that even he couldn't place. "Bernie," he said at last, "I've got a great job. I can't give it up to give baseball a shot."

Bernie countered and said, "Tell you what. Give it a try. If it doesn't work out, I'll hire you to be a financial consultant for the Coal Barons at your current salary, plus a five percent raise."

Derek chuckled, still half believing this entire conversation to be the setup for a joke. "Bernie, you're nuts. You know that, right?"

"Yeah, maybe, but I've got nothing to lose. So, what's it gonna be?"

The silence stretched as he thought hard about Bernie's proposal. Sure his job was steady and challenging but he did so love those days on the baseball field. He also missed his old coach. Numbers and spreadsheets would always be there. The years for playing baseball wouldn't.

Finally, Derek chuckled again, both in appreciation of Bernie's salesmanship in knowing when to shut up and admiration of the size of his big brass ones for coming up with the idea in the first place. "I guess we're both nuts. Okay, I'm in."

Bernie let out the breath he had been holding for what seemed like forever and let loose a loud "HA!" then promptly remembered where he was.

He nodded his apology to the trainer next to him who was working with a client then headed to the locker room. The grin on his face felt permanent, even though he knew Derek was the easiest of his old pals to bring into this crazy venture.

One down, three to go.

GREG JEFFERS

Greg was on deck. He'd graduated college with a physical education degree and stayed close to home taking the gym teacher's job at a local high school. It had been a few years since they had spoken. In his Pony League days, Greg played centerfield. If he were a puppy, he'd be the runt of the litter, but there was a lot of talent in this little player. He was easily the fastest kid on the team. If a fly ball was hit anywhere to the outfield, you expected Greg to catch it. He wasn't going to hit with power, but he knew how to work counts and bunt. If you put a dime anywhere on the infield, Greg could bunt the ball within six inches of it. He was that good.

Bernie sent a text and arranged to meet Greg at his school's cafeteria for lunch on Monday.

"All that security stuff is real important, Bernie. Remember how it was when we were in school? Anybody could, and did, just walk in." Greg walked with his old friend toward the cafeteria after having signed away both of their first-born kids to get Bernie a 2-hour pass to be on campus and in Greg's custody.

"Sad to say that while the security has improved, school lunches haven't improved much since we were in high school. Grab what you want, and I'll snag one of the small tables for us."

Once both were seated, he said, "Damn, Bernie, how have you been?"

"Doing great. I've had quite a ride these past few weeks."

"You won a bunch of money in the lottery, right?"

Bernie shrugged his shoulders. His face turned a rosy red as he replied, "$92 million, but that's not why I want to talk to you..."

Greg looked over the school-lunch-sized milk carton he'd just lifted to his lips and paused in his drinking to interrupt, "Yeah I was wondering about that myself." He finished his drink, eyes locked on Bernie, and waited. His friend appeared uncomfortable, an action he'd rarely ever seen in Bernie.

He watched closely as Bernie picked up a French fry from his lunch tray, chewed slowly, then seemed to come to terms with his struggle. Greg smiled. The calm attitude he expected to see spread over Bernie's entire body as leaned forward and spoke, "Greg, I bought the Coal Barons and I'm looking to hire a new manager."

Greg's left eyebrow lifted, a poker tell he'd never learned to control when surprised. "Well, that's certainly not even remotely what I expected to hear. Bernie, I still play on weekends. I'm not ready to manage just yet."

"I don't want you to manage. I'd like you to try out for the Coal Barons. Derek already said yes. If you and a couple of the other guys agree, my dad says he'll manage."

Greg said, "You want me to try out for the Coal Barons? Wow, I don't know what to say."

Bernie grabbed another fry and dipped it into his chocolate pudding. "Say you'll give it a shot."

Greg poked at his spaghetti and meatballs. A career in baseball had really never crossed his mind. He was good as a kid but this was something altogether different.

"Wait, did you say your Dad is gonna manage the Barons?"

"That's the plan." Bernie grinned and lifted a messy pork barbeque spilling out of its hamburger bun to his face.

"Wow. Best coach I ever had..." His words trailed off and the next few minutes the friends ate quietly as he ran through pros and cons in his head.

"Bernie, how can I just quit my job? I don't know that I can even play pro baseball."

"Can you take a sabbatical or something?

Greg was quiet again, thinking over Bernie's proposal and calculating his accumulated leave time as he finished the last of his milk.

He looked up, smile gone, and locked gazes with Bernie. Decision made.

Surely someone else could handle handing out the basketballs in his absence.

"What the hell, why not? I'll do it."

RICKY BONETTO

Bernie was half way home, pleased to have his second player, when he detoured and headed to his dad's house to check on his progress tracking down the other players.

"How's it going, Dad?"

"Depends. I know where Ricky and Mark are, but they're both out of town. Ricky works for a prison in Chicago and Mark's a stunt double for a movie studio out in California."

The distance was not an insurmountable challenge in Bernie's mind. "Let's see if we can reach Ricky."

Bernie sat down on the opposite side of Johnny's desk and pulled the laptop over to find a phone number for the prison. Luck was on their side as Ricky was on duty. They waited for the call to be connected to him.

Bernie pictured Ricky in his mind. His friend was a big catcher with a rifle for an arm and a powerful swing. Infielders would put extra padding in their gloves to protect against the sting from one of Ricky's throws. When his bat made contact with the baseball, the 'oohs and aahs' from the bleachers sounded like firework watchers on the Fourth of July—and no one wanted to try catching one of his line drives.

Ricky's supervisor called him away from overseeing the inmates' breakfast. He grabbed the phone and heard, "Hey, Ricky, it's Johnny Endino, your old Pony League coach. How've you been?"

"Pretty good, Mr. E. Had a little problem with an inmate last week. He tried to stab me with a shank, but I took care of him. He'll think twice before trying that again."

Johnny had no response. How would anyone respond to that?

"Sorry, Mr. Endino. Too much information. I'm surprised to hear from you. Why did you call me?"

"Well Ricky, Bernie had some good fortune and, long story short, he bought our minor league team, the Coal Barons. He wants me to manage, but I'll only do it if I can bring in some of my guys. I want you to try out for the team."

Ricky paused. The sounds coming from the prisoners' metal dining trays in the background sounded loud in his ears. Had he really heard that? Play ball for the Coal Barons? "Wow. Mr. Endino, that's really nice but I don't think you want me."

"Ricky, you have one of the best throwing arms on a catcher I've ever seen and when you hit a baseball, it's one of the sweetest sounds anyone could ever hear. I'll bet you've still got it and I want to find out."

Ricky thought hard about it. He wasn't thrilled with the dangers of working at a prison. He also wasn't thrilled with the idea of being unemployed if this doesn't work out.

"Mr. Endino, what if I don't still have it?"

The sound of the call changed and Ricky heard Bernie's voice as he jumped into the conversation, "Ricky! Tell you what. If for some reason it doesn't work out, you can head up our stadium security. No more dealing with getting shanked. At worst, maybe an unruly drunk. What do you say?"

Ricky looked down at the freshly stitched wound on his arm and didn't think about it any longer. "Where and when do you need me?"

MARK BENFANTI

Three down and only one left. Bernie said, "We're on a roll, Pop! Let's get in touch with Mark!"

In Pony League, Mark was a good all-around player. He played just about anywhere he was needed but shortstop was where he played best.

After several false starts, they had tracked Mark to his California office. Johnny dialed the number and on the other end he heard, "Cali Studios, Deanna speaking. May I help you?"

"My name is Johnny Endino. I'm a friend of Mark's father."

"I'm sorry, Mr. Endino, but Mark is on location in Anaheim for the next four weeks."

Johnny hit the button to mute the cell phone. "What now, Bern?"

"Just make sure she gives him the message and lets him know we're coming to visit him...oh and give her my cell phone number."

After conveying Bernie's message, Johnny gave Bernie a puzzled look. "Bernie, what did you mean about us going to visit Mark?"

Without blinking an eye Bernie said, "We're going to Anaheim."

Johnny put both of his hands on the table and stood up. "Maybe you are, but I'm not."

Now Bernie got up. "Dad, you have to come to convince Mark to play."

Johnny gave his son a long stare. "Fine. I'll go to Anaheim, but this had better work."

Bernie had no idea if they'd even see Mark. He hadn't thought that far ahead. His just hoped Mark would call him.

Bernie changed subjects. "Pop, what do you think about our roster?"

Johnny's long face brightened into a broad smile as he put in his two cents, knuckling down to talk shop with Bernie. He had ideas about moving Beniquez to shortstop and Williams' potential as a pitcher. He also spoke frankly about the team's star.

"Someone really needs to give Rundle a kick in the ass. His attitude sucks." Johnny may not have taken the job yet, but he sounded a lot like the manager.

"Well Pop, if you take the job, you can kick it for him."

Arriving in Anaheim, Bernie spotted a chauffeur-capped woman holding a sign that read: ENDINOS. They approached and Bernie said, "Excuse me, our name is Endino. Did someone send you for us?"

"Cali Studios sent me to drive you to your hotel."

The limo ride from the airport was a relaxing surprise to Bernie who expected to either rent a car and fight traffic or wait in line for a taxi and pay as much for one ride as for a week of the car rental. The hotel was also a surprise as they found out their reserved double bed room had been upgraded to a suite. Bernie was about to call the desk to ask if it was an error when Johnny handed him the card attached to the basket of fruit on his bed.

Mr. E.,
Was surprised to hear you were coming. Hope you enjoyed the limo ride. If you and Bernie don't have any plans, how about me taking you on a tour of the studio tomorrow? Our driver will pick you up at 10 AM. See you there!
Mark

Bernie put the phone down as his father dove into the fruit and cheese selection. They settled into the luxurious couch and searched for a ballgame on the cinematic-sized television. The Endinos would have their chance to convince Mark to play.

Mark was waiting for them when the same driver opened the limo door and they stepped out onto the studio's driveway.

"Hey, Mr. Endino! Hey, Bernie! How have you been?"

Johnny grabbed Mark's hand with both of his. "Doin' great. Thanks for showing us around today."

Mark put his arm on Johnny's shoulder. "It's good to see you guys. I'll take you on a tour of the place, then we can grab some lunch."

After a morning meeting actors and seeing live sets, the three men sat down to lunch.

Mark asked, "So what brings you across the country?"

Bernie explained how good fortune had come upon him. Mark was happy for him, but still had a question, "That's fantastic, but you didn't fly all the way to California just to tell me you won the lottery."

Bernie took a forkful of his penne pasta. "Not exactly. I used some of the money to buy the Coal Barons and one of my first decisions was to hire my dad to manage the team. Thing is, he'll only take the job if Ricky, Derek, Greg and you play for him."

Mark nearly choked as he took a sip of his energy drink. "Why would you do that? You don't need us. You can coach anyone."

"I want to coach my guys. You guys understand me. I won't do it unless you all come back."

Mark sighed. "Guys, I've got a good living here. I know some amazing people. California is my home now. How can I drop this to chase a pipe dream?"

Bernie knew there was no good reason for Mark to leave this life behind, but Johnny made one last plea.

"Mark, you've got it great here. You're living a dream. I have a dream too...it's managing a professional baseball team with players I know can help us win. Your dream is being fulfilled. I've been waiting over thirty years for this chance, and I may never get it again."

Mark played with his napkin.

"I'm sorry but I just can't."

The three men finished lunch and left. Johnny shook Mark's hand and then hugged him. "Great seeing you again, Mark. Take care of yourself."

Bernie and Johnny settled into the back of the limo for the ride back to the airport. Just as the driver started to pull away, Bernie noticed Mark running toward them, yelling and waving his arms.

Mark caught the limo. Even after running half the length of a football field he was not winded. He leaned against the car door, head in the open window. "Mr. Endino, take the job. You're the best manager I ever had. Take the job and teach those guys how to win, okay?"

Tears formed in the corners of Johnny's eyes. "I'll think about it, Mark. Thanks."

The ride to the airport began in silence. Bernie couldn't hold his tongue for long. "You know, Mark is right. You don't really need him to do this job. You can lead these guys, Dad."

Johnny was looking out his window. "Bernie, I'll be honest with you. I'm scared. I'm 56 years old and I'm shit-scared of this. What if I really can't do it?"

"Is that why you didn't say yes right away?"

Johnny stopped looking out the window and now turned to Bernie. "Yeah, but I couldn't tell you that."

Bernie put his hand on his father's shoulder. "Why not?"

Johnny turned to look out the window again. "Because I'm your father. I'm not supposed to be scared."

"Dad, it's okay. There's nothing wrong with being a little scared. I was scared about buying this team, but you know what? I wanted this so badly that nothing was going to stop me. I know this is right and I know you are the only person I want managing this team. You have to at least try."

Johnny looked away from the window, this time with the corners of his mouth turned up. "What the hell...I'll do it."

They'd fly home without Mark, but in the end, he was probably the most important player they'd talked to during the whole thing. Bernie was glad to see his father finally excited, but something was still on his mind. "Dad, do you think you would have said yes if we hadn't talked to Ricky, Derek, Greg, and Mark?"

Johnny shrugged. "Maybe, but they sure made it easier to say yes. Coaching Ricky, Derek, and Greg again will be great. I just hope I enjoy coaching everyone else."

It was late when Bernie got home. Rachel was still up and watching some turn-of-the century English show on PBS.

She whispered, "How was the trip?"

Bernie whispered back, "Very productive. Mark isn't playing, but he talked my dad into managing."

Rachel fluffed her pillow. "I'm glad it worked out and that you're home. Are you coming to bed soon?"

Bernie put on his pajama bottoms and an old concert t-shirt he always wore to bed. "In a little bit. I'm kind of hungry. I think I'll grab something to eat and then maybe I'll watch some TV."

Rachel patted Bernie's pillow. "Instead of watching TV, why don't you come back upstairs when you're done?"

Bernie knew exactly what she meant and honestly, Rachel's idea was far better than watching anything TV had to offer.

THE COACHES

The Coal Barons had three new players and a new manager. Now that he was officially the manager, Johnny's thoughts moved to his coaching staff. He would handle the hitting coach duties and hoped that Art Jeffers and Phil Figlione would sign on as base coaches. Only one position was troubling him. Who would handle pitching coach duties? The guys Bernie had mentioned already had jobs either in the Major Leagues or the Minor League ranks. They had to come up with someone soon.

Phil Figlione was first on his list. Phil had been Johnny's barber for what seemed like forever. He figured it was time for a trim and some conversation.

Phil said, "Hey, Johnny! What's up?" Johnny sat down for his haircut.

He talked to Phil about Bernie's lottery win and his purchase. Phil was hopeful that Bernie could breathe some new life into the team and was glad that Dowdell had been fired. He got so involved in the conversation that he narrowly missed taking a piece of Johnny's ear with the last snip of the scissors.

Phil asked, "Hey, any idea who they're getting to replace Dowdell?"

"Funny you should ask. Bernie hired me."

"No shit!" He narrowly missed clipping Johnny's other ear.

Johnny seized his opportunity.

"Phil, Bernie's letting me put together my own coaching staff. How'd you like to be my third base coach?"

Phil dropped his scissors.

"You want me to help you coach the Coal Barons?"

"Yeah. I want you and Art to come and help me."

Phil grabbed some shaving cream and put it on Johnny's neck. "Johnny, why us?"

Johnny closed his eyes. The warm shaving cream was relaxing. "Phil, we built something great once. I think we can do it again."

"Johnny, this isn't Pony League."

"It's still baseball, isn't it?"

Phil took the straight razor to the back of Johnny's neck. "Yeah but Johnny..."

Johnny interrupted, causing Phil's hand to slip. "Shit, Phil that hurt! Phil, we can do it. Derek, Ricky, and Greg agreed to play."

Phil took a piece of tissue to help with the cut he'd made. "Derek's playing? He's been busy, and we haven't talked in a few weeks."

Phil paused a moment and locked eyes with his long-time friend in the mirror. "Wow, Derek's playing." He spoke softly, his eyes never leaving Johnny's.

Phil, like Johnny, had truly loved coaching his son. It was fun coaching all of the boys, but coaching had forged a special bond between father and son.

Johnny realized that Phil got it; that he felt the potential being offered. Coaching Derek again made the idea more interesting to Phil. Question was, would it be interesting enough?

Johnny asked, "So are you in?"

"I'll have to close up the shop for a while but okay, Johnny, you've got me."

Johnny grinned. "Glad to have you aboard. Now, can you finish my hair cut? I've got to talk to Art." The two men laughed and a few minutes later Johnny headed to the diner for his lunch meeting with Art, sporting a fresh haircut, both ears intact, and his first base coach.

Art called, "Hey Johnny! Over here!" He was a pleasant guy with salt and pepper hair. Most people smiled when they saw him because he could make them laugh without even trying.

"How are you, Art? Thanks for meeting me."

The two men caught up on what was happening with each other's families. Art had heard about Bernie's good fortune through conversations with his son, Greg.

"Art, I have something to ask you."

Art looked up from his menu. "Shoot."

Before Johnny could say anything more, the waitress appeared to take orders. After she'd left Johnny continued, "Bernie asked me to manage the Coal Barons. He's letting me put together my own coaching staff. I'd like you to be my first base coach."

Art was sipping his water and spat it out. "Geez, glad that was only water. Are you nuts? You want me to coach first base for the Coal Barons?"

"Can't think of a better choice."

Art quipped, "Then you aren't trying."

"Art, you have to say yes. I've already got Phil on board. It'll be like old times."

Just then their meals came out. It gave Art a second to think. He swallowed a French fry. "Johnny, I already have a job at the market. This coaching thing...I just don't know."

Johnny finished one of his onion rings. "Don't you want the chance to coach your son again?"

Art smiled, obviously recalling how special it was coaching Greg with Johnny and Phil. "Yeah, I don't remember many times where I was happier." He thought it over while downing one more French fry.

"All right, I'll do it. I hope you're right about this, because if not, my wife will be calling a divorce attorney."

The two old friends finished their lunch catching up and swapping stories. As they shook hands and went their separate ways, Johnny's thoughts again turned to the Barons. He was satisfied. He had the core of his coaching staff onboard. Now all Johnny had left was a pitching coach. He hoped Bernie had someone in mind.

Art's doorbell rang. He opened it to Greg standing on the porch. "You busy, Dad?"

"No, just watching the news. Nothing important. What's up?"

Greg shook his head. "Can you believe they want me to play ball again?"

Art smiled. "Yeah and Johnny wants me to coach. Are these guys crazy or what?"

Greg's face went blank for a second. "I'm scared, Dad."

"Scared of what?"

Greg looked his father in the eyes. "Failing."

Art rocked in his recliner. "Greg, you won't fail. Just go out and have fun. Remember how to do that?"

Greg's eyes lit up. "It was fun back then, wasn't it?"

"Some of the best days of my life."

"Maybe it can be fun again, Dad."

"Yeah maybe. Guess we'll find out, huh?"

Bernie had been busting his brain thinking about options for a pitching coach. He decided to head to the gym to clear his mind for a while. While there, he ran into an old high school friend who had finished his workout and was dressing for home.

"Hey, Bernie!"

It was Jimmy McConnell. Like Bernie, Jimmy was an accountant. He worked for a small company that dealt primarily with online merchandise sales.

Jimmy had been a great high school pitcher. He had a blazing fastball, nasty slider, and just when you thought you'd figured him out, he'd drop a devastating curveball in that could completely ruin your day.

During their senior year, a batter sent a line drive whistling towards Jimmy. He deflected the ball slightly with his glove, but still took a glancing blow to the side of his head. The psychological damage was greater than the physical and his pitching career came to an abrupt halt.

"Jimmy! How've you been?"

"Fantastic, Bernie! My wife had a baby boy a few months ago and I was just promoted to the head of my department, but I'll bet I'm not doing as well as you."

Bernie tied his sneakers. "Yeah, we still can't believe it. You read about things like that happening but never figure it will happen to you."

Jimmy rooted through his gym bag for deodorant. "I hear you bought the Coal Barons. Nice toy, huh?"

That was when the idea hit Bernie.

"Jimmy, can I ask you something?"

"What's up?"

"Have you ever considered a career change?"

Jimmy raised an eyebrow. "What are you getting at, Bern?"

"Would you consider being the Coal Barons pitching coach? I think you're just what we need."

Jimmy shook his head while he put on his jeans. "How so?"

"You know pitching, and I think you can relate to these guys." Bernie ran possibilities through his mind to figure out what would get Jimmy to bite on this offer. He realized that Jimmy's choice would have been much easier if he wasn't married and hadn't just become a father. *Security*, Bernie thought, *That's going to be his key.*

"If the coaching job doesn't work out, you can work in the accounting department for the team. Same salary and benefits package you have right now."

Jimmy put on his loafers. "I'll have to talk it over with my wife. Can I have a few days?"

"Take your time. It's a big decision."

Jimmy didn't say yes, but he didn't say no either. Bernie hoped that his search for a pitching coach was over and pulled out his cell phone to call Johnny.

Bernie was playing with Anna when the house phone rang. He wondered why he hadn't gotten rid of it yet since everyone had cell phones.

Rachel answered and called out, "Bernie, it's Jimmy McConnell."

Bernie took the phone from Rachel. "Hey, Jimmy!"

"Hey Bern. You did say if it didn't work out that you could give me a job in your accounting department at the same pay and benefits that I'm getting now, right?"

He could tell from Jimmy's voice that he was nervous. "You have my word. Heck, I'll write it into the contract, too!"

"OK. In that case, you have your pitching coach."

Bernie, phone still in hand, began to do his 'happy dance' in the kitchen but quickly gathered himself as the phone cord twisted around his body.

"Thanks, Jimmy. We'll get together soon to hammer out the details."

Bernie hung up and immediately punched in his father's number, counting the rings until Johnny answered. "Hey Dad, it's me."

"Hey Bern, what's up? Just looking through some vintage cards I picked up at a yard sale."

"I've got your pitching coach. Jimmy McConnell is taking the job."

"I kind of hoped for someone with pro experience."

"Dad, Jimmy will be great. He can relate to the young guys and he was an awesome pitcher."

"All right, Bern, you sold me. I've trusted your crazy vision and instincts so far, why not now? I'm sure Jimmy's going to fit in just fine."

TAKE PRIDE IN THE NAME

Changes were happening with the Coal Barons on the field. Now Bernie decided he'd like to make changes elsewhere. He'd never really liked the Coal Barons moniker. It reminded him of a depressing time in the area's history, not a joyous one. He sat down at his computer and began typing names. After a while, he had a bunch but none that stood out. It was late and he decided maybe a good night's rest would help. His rest didn't last long. Renaming the team consumed him. He went back downstairs and again worked on the list. Sometime around 2:30 AM, Rachel came down stairs and put her arms around Bernie.

"Bernie, what are you doing up?"

Bernie just stared at the computer screen. "I can't sleep. I'm working on a new name for the team."

Rachel rubbed Bernie's hair. "You're changing the name?"

"Coal Barons is kind of a downer. I've wracked my brain but so far, nothing."

Rachel kissed Bernie's cheek. "Why don't you try to get some sleep? You'll come up with something and no matter what, we're all proud of you."

Bernie had an epiphany from the last thing Rachel said before they headed up the stairs. Suddenly, he knew he had his team name but decided to think on it and share it with Jerry after a good night's sleep. Even though Jerry had sold the team to Bernie, he still held some of the rights to merchandise sales and player movements and could be a hard sell to make a change if it affected his bottom line financially.

Bernie waited as long as he could before calling Jerry the next morning. Before Jerry could even say hello Bernie said, "Hey Jerry, I've been thinking. It's time to change the team's name. Personally, I think it sucks."

"What the Hell do you mean by that?"

"It sucks, Jerry. It truly sucks. It's depressing and it's boring."

Bernie heard the humidor opening as Jerry reached for his morning cigar. His voice was slightly muffled as he inserted the trademark stogie and continued speaking, "Well then, Mr. Big Ideas, what do you want to call the team?"

Bernie said, "The Pride. Think about it, Jerry. Pride, as in pride in the team, pride in the area, pride in what we're doing here. I think it works. How 'bout it, Jerry?"

Bernie waited, listening to the silence broken by the snapping sound as Jerry adjusted and clipped the end off his cigar. Jerry said, "You know something, Endino? I think I like it."

Bernie couldn't be happier. He said, "Good, Jerry. I'll make sure you get a hat and jersey once we get the logo designed."

Jerry said, "Let's hope that new name of yours can help sell some shit too."

Things were taking shape. Bernie hoped things on the field would take shape in the same fashion.

[6]

Beginning of a New Era

IT WAS TIME FOR spring training. Johnny was grateful that Bernie decided to rent a house in Florida so he could be there to keep an eye on things. It was even better that he brought his family along. He got to play with his grandkids every night. But today his thoughts were elsewhere. He stood behind home plate and looked out, appreciating a view of the playing field that had always been a favorite, and one he wasn't sure he'd ever really experience again—until his son made this happen.

"Mornin' coach!" Bernie was perched on the railing in front of the dugout and waved.

Johnny waved back. He was glad his son had come to his first spring training. Johnny waited for his hopefuls to come from the clubhouse to start stretching drills.

Bernie watched as the players and assistant coaches filed onto the field and to gather in front of their coach. He immediately recognized Ricky, Derek, and Greg. Then he noticed Miguel Beniquez and Jake Williams, the second baseman and left-handed pitcher from last season. Bernie wasn't familiar with most of the other players, but did notice the absence of one. Where was Hank Rundle?

61

Still in a state of wonder, Bernie heard a voice behind him, "Morning, Endino! Sleep all right?"

Jerry had made the trip to Florida as well. Bernie seized an opportunity to get some information and climbed up to the bleachers to sit beside the big man.

"Jerry, let's talk about some of the guys out there and one of the guys I don't see."

"Sure. Who don't you see?"

"Where's Rundle?"

Jerry took a sip of coffee from his stainless steel cup. "Rundle? He's doing some kind of promotional thing today. He'll be here tomorrow." Jerry pulled a cigar from his pocket with no intention of lighting it.

"He belongs here. Special treatment like that causes problems."

Jerry leaned forward from his seat and waved his cigar at Bernie. "Listen, Endio. he's my bonus baby. I have to take care of him." The decibel levels in his voice increased with seemingly every word.

Bernie stood up. "Do it now and he's going to expect it all of the time. That happens, and no one will control him."

Bernie paced the bleachers, his face burning from more than the Florida sun. While he paced he glanced back at Jerry once in a while with eyes that could pierce steel. Finally, Bernie calmed himself and sat down. Taking a deep breath, he continued.

"Fill me in on a few of these other guys. Who's number four over there?"

"Malcolm Jackson. Just up from Double-A ball. Kid can run like a deer but strikes out a hell of a lot."

Bernie felt sure that his father could fix Malcolm's batting issues. Surveying the field, Bernie spotted another interesting-looking player. "Who's the tall, skinny guy over there wearing number 26?"

Jerry took another sip of coffee. "Charlie Vanholdt, one of our pitchers. Decent stuff but not much of a fastball. He has the tools, but I don't think he's getting any better. No idea what the Hell his problem is."

"That guy wearing number 35. Who's he? He looks more like a coach than a player."

"Oh, that's Frank Carlson. He's been playing Independent League ball for the last ten years. Met him on a cruise. We got to talking and I liked him, so I offered him a tryout. He's 37 but he can hit. Put up 32 home runs last year and had 256 overall for his old team."

Frank was the type of player Bernie talked about with Jerry when they negotiated the deal for the team. "Maybe he can be sort of a player/coach."

Bernie got his answers. Jerry turned the tables.

"So Endino, which of those fellas are your boys?"

"Number 28 there is Ricky Bonetto. He catches and he swings a heck of a bat... well he did anyway." Bernie realized he'd unintentionally said that loud enough for Jerry to hear. The repercussion was immediate.

Jerry chomped down on his cigar. Each of his next words came through gritted teeth. "What do you mean he did?"

Bernie looked back at Jerry, squinting into the sun. "I haven't seen him play in a little while."

Jerry grimaced. "Where did he play last year?"

"The ICL."

Jerry nodded. "Independent Coastal League? Impressive. They've got some talented players there."

Bernie looked at the bleacher step below him. "Uh, actually Illinois Corrections League."

Jerry almost broke his cigar. "Wait, what the hell did you just say? Was this guy in jail?"

"Relax, Jerry. He was a prison guard."

Jerry shook his head.

Bernie continued, "Okay, see number two over there? That's Greg Jeffers, centerfielder. Really quick and a great bunter."

Jerry said, "Where was he last year?"

"Oh. he's in great shape, Jerry. Spends a lot of time in the gym."

Jerry just gave a skeptical nod.

Bernie pointed towards the field. "Over there, number 14, is Derek Figlione. Smooth glove and hits to all fields."

Jerry wiped his brow. "What position does he play?"

"Derek's a first baseman, Jerry, and a damn good one."

"I guess if he's any good, we can always use a backup."

Bernie leaned back on the bleachers. "That's true. I'm sure Carlson will be a more than adequate backup."

Jerry removed the cigar from his mouth. "Funny guy, Endino. Who else have you got?"

With tension still in the air, right before Bernie could answer he heard, "How about me?"

It was Mark Benfanti. Bernie greeted Mark with a fist bump.

"Mark, you made it! Why the change of heart?"

"We wrapped shooting early. I'm free until October so I figure I'll use my time wisely."

Bernie brought Mark to where Jerry sat. "Jerry, this is Mark Benfanti. He can play anywhere we need him."

Jerry put out his hand. "Nice meeting you, Benfanti. Might want to get down there. They've already started."

Once Mark was safely out of ear shot Jerry asked, "What was that stuff about films?"

"Oh, he does some stunt work."

"Holy shit, Endino, you really are turning this into a circus act, aren't you?"

Bernie just turned away and hollered to the field, "Hey coach, late addition to camp coming down!"

Johnny saw Mark and smiled.

Bernie's smile matched that of his father. He had them all now. It was time to build a team that would make everyone proud.

Drills began with no Rundle. Johnny decided to try Derek out at third. While he fielded the ball surprisingly well, throwing was a different story and having Frank Carlson at first base didn't help. Frank had the flexibility of tempered steel to go with the fielding range the approximate size of a postage stamp.

Jerry grumbled the entire time and finally Bernie spoke out.

"Jerry, Derek's played first his whole life. He's just filling in until your 'darling' graces us with his presence."

All Jerry could do was sneer.

At shortstop, Mark was still as smooth as Bernie remembered, making play after play followed by chest-high throws just about every time. Bernie swore he noticed a smile on Jerry's face.

Bernie said, "Not too shabby, is he?"

Jerry said, "Let's see if he can hit."

Bernie hoped something had clicked for Miguel during the off season. Sadly, it hadn't. Of the first ten ground balls hit to him, Miguel managed to throw six into the fifth row of the bleachers and two more into the tarp between first base and right field.

Bernie said, "Well at least two throws were in Carlson's area code."

Yet another grumble from Jerry.

The two men turned their attention to the outfield. After a few minutes, both men were pleased with what they saw. Malcolm and Greg looked like early shoo-ins for starting spots. Almost nothing seemed uncatchable if hit in their vicinity.

Satisfied with the outfield play, Bernie and Jerry focused on Ricky. Johnny dropped down a few bunts and dribblers in front of the plate. Every one of Ricky's throws was hard and accurate. Bernie couldn't have been happier.

Bernie said, "Pretty good, huh Jerry?"

Jerry said, "We'll see if he can do it in a game."

Bernie spit hard to the ground. He'd grown tired of Jerry's negativity and ended discussion of his players for the rest of the day. He moved away from Jerry to focus on practice field to watch the pitchers.

Jimmy was deep into his work with the pitchers and as Bernie watched, he mentally reviewed the coaching discussion from the day before about what was expected from the pitchers.

Jake Williams had potential but was obviously having a tough day. He threw hard but was inconsistent. His slider had a lot of break to it, but Jake clearly had no idea where the ball was going when he released it.

Charlie Vanholdt was right-handed, but he pitched like a left-handed junk baller. His breaking pitches were fine, but his fastball could be timed with a sun dial. Jimmy thought Charlie's best chance for success was deception yet how he'd accomplish that was yet to be determined.

Jimmy saw potential in the pitching staff but also saw a lot of work ahead. They were a bunch of young pitchers with live arms who had no idea how to use them, with one exception.

Clark Gresham was at the end of a great baseball career that included nine years in the Major Leagues. At one time he threw hard...really hard. Couple that with a devastating curveball and when he was on, it wasn't a fair fight.

Bernie recalled an interview he watched where Clark talked about his injury from two years ago.

Clark was cruising along in a game, blowing hitters away with his blazing fastball or freezing them with his curve. In the seventh inning he threw a pitch and felt a pop—the pop that every pitcher fears hearing. The pain that shot through him was more excruciating than anything he'd ever felt in his life. It took everything he had to keep from crying on the mound. Clark's rotator cuff was torn.

Rotator cuff injuries to pitchers happen. Sometimes they aren't that bad. Clark wasn't that lucky. His tear was a bad one, "one of the worst I've ever seen" according the specialist who examined him. It took extensive surgery to repair the damage. The prognosis for him to ever pitch again was poor. The docs agreed that even if he did return to pitching, regaining his power on the mound was highly unlikely.

34-year-old Clark was unwilling to have his career end like that.

The interviewer, while admiring Clark's unmatched determination (he was throwing 10 months after the surgery), noted that his velocity topped out at 65 miles per hour and speculated on how unlikely it was that determination alone would give Clark the comeback he wanted and deserved.

No matter what the medicos told him, Clark wouldn't quit and Jerry was the only person who would give him a chance. This was Clark's first spring training in two seasons. He was now a 36-year-old pitcher with a fastball topping out at 81 miles per hour and the bite on his curveball almost nonexistent.

Bernie hoped, with the right coaching and more work, he could get Clark back to top form.

By home plate, Malcolm was up for batting practice. Swing after swing resulted in little contact being made. Johnny watched without saying a word. Bernie wished Jerry would be as silent, but no luck.

"What the Hell is he doing?"

"Looks like swinging and missing a lot."

Jerry again bit down hard on the cigar hanging from the corner of his mouth and wiped his brow. "Not him, smart ass...your father."

Bernie turned around. "Observing, Jerry. It's what he does."

Jerry stuck his handkerchief back into his pocket. "It looks like standing around and doing Jack shit."

Frank Carlson was next into the cage. He hit several long, towering blasts over the left field scoreboard.

"Told you he can hit," said Jerry, almost cocky.

Bernie said, "Yep, he's a menace with the bat and the glove."

Jerry grabbed another cigar from his shirt pocket. "Screw you, Endino."

Bernie was anxious. He wanted to see what his Pony League buddies had to offer up against professional pitching. Ricky hit first. Early on it was easy to see Ricky's timing wasn't there. He missed badly on several swings and when he did make contact, the ball barely made the outfield grass.

Jerry tapped Bernie on the shoulder then pointed to the batting cage. "Your boy seems to have some issues."

"Just needs to get the rust off, Jerry. He'll hit."

Greg looked better than Ricky, slapping ground balls the opposite way to left field. Bernie was pleased until Jerry opened his mouth.

"You brought me a Punch and Judy hitter, Endino?"

Bernie turned, madder than a hornet. "He hits the ball on the ground and gets on base, Jerry!"

"Once the other teams find out he has no power, they'll take that away from him."

Bernie turned away, disgusted at Jerry's lack of faith. As Bernie watched Derek hit, he saw some of what he remembered from their younger days. Line drive after line drive jumped from his bat.

Jerry said, "Finally, a hitter."

Oddly enough, it was Bernie who wasn't quite as impressed with Derek's session. He noticed Derek hadn't pulled one pitch against batting-practice-speed fastballs. If he couldn't pull those, how could he do it to real pitching?

Mark was the last of the former Pony Leaguers to hit. It was evident that curveballs at that point were giving him fits.

Jerry said, "I hope these guys get better, Endino. They sure don't look like they'll help much."

For Bernie, that was the last straw.

He slammed his fist on the bleachers, stood up and said, "Dammit, Jerry, back off, all right? It's the first day of practice! I didn't see your guys lighting it up much today either. Give them a damn chance!"

Jerry dropped what was left of his cigar.

"Fine, Endino. I'll back off for now. I just hope these guys can pull it together." He wiped his brow again then headed for the exit.

After practice, Bernie met his father outside of the clubhouse. He didn't look happy.

Johnny said, "I must be nuts for taking this job."

Bernie said, "It's only the first day, Dad. Give it time."

The second day of spring training started and Hank was again a no show. Jerry and Bernie were back in their spots on the bleachers.

"Jerry, where's your boy, Rundle?"

"They needed him for one more day at the commercial shoot. Film issues."

Bernie tapped his fingers nervously on the bleachers. "Do you think he'll be gracing us with his presence tomorrow?"

Jerry didn't like Bernie's tone. "Day after tomorrow. Don't get your panties in a bunch."

"Fine. I just hope the film is okay." At this point he wasn't worried about offending Jerry.

Coach Johnny glanced into the stands and waved at the watching owners.

Bernie bet the freezing cold tension between was evident even from the field and hoped only the coaching staff noticed.

He waved back to Johnny, but noticed that the coach had already turned his focus back to working Carlson at third base and Derek at first. Derek looked great showing range and soft hands. Frank was just a body at third. He fielded what was hit right at him but nothing else. Rundle needed to get his ass to camp. Johnny was deep in conversation with Miguel at second. Both owners watched in riveted silence as Johnny brought about a major change and success for the infielder.

Johnny noticed something about Miguel. On balls not hit right at him, Miguel looked smooth and his throws were strong and accurate. On routine grounders hit right at him, Miguel's throws were abysmal.

Johnny yelled, "Hold up a minute!" He made his way out to second base.

"Miguel, what's going through your head when you field balls hit up the middle or to your left?"

With his Spanish accent he answered, "Nothing, Coach. I just field it, then I throw to first."

Johnny began to sense something. He asked his next question.

"Okay. When you field the ball hit right to you, what goes through your head?"

Miguel pounded a fist into his glove. "I think that I better not screw this up.'"

Johnny got an idea. He yelled, "Mark, come here for a second!"

Mark ran over from the shortstop position.

"Mark, take over at second. Miguel, go to shortstop."

Miguel furrowed his brow. "Coach, I've never played shortstop."

Johnny walked to the position with Miguel. "It's just like second base, only on the other side you have less time to think."

Miguel raised an eyebrow. "No time to think?"

Johnny smiled. "None."

Miguel moved to shortstop. The move seemed to work as he continued to make plays with his glove but also his throws were crisp and accurate.

Somewhat smugly, Bernie still watching from up high, turned to Jerry. "I wonder why Dowdell never thought of that?"

Next up for Coach Johnny's attention was Malcolm who was in the batter's box taking swings. He continued taking big cuts with no results. Johnny yelled, "All right hold up! I've seen enough of this!"

He pulled Malcolm aside. "Malcolm, have you ever considered hitting from the left side?"

Malcolm said, "The left side, Coach?" He reacted as if Johnny had asked him the Theory of Relativity.

"Yeah. You're damn fast and that extra step would make you even faster. It's not like you're tearing the cover off the ball from the right side. Why not try it?"

Malcolm was still not sure he heard his coach right but took his stance in the left-handed hitter's box for the first time in his life. His first few swings were awkward with no contact.

A frustrated Malcolm stepped out of the box. He dropped his bat to the ground. "Coach, I can't do this."

Johnny stood with crossed arms. "You weren't doing it from the other side, either. We'll keep working on it."

After several more nonproductive swings, Malcolm fired his bat into the screen and stormed away from the cage. Johnny stopped him. "Don't take it out on the equipment. This is going to take time."

Malcolm just gave Johnny a disapproving look and headed to the outfield to shag fly balls.

Jerry stood up from his seat, almost ready to charge the field. "What in hell is your father doing now?"

Bernie just shrugged as he honestly didn't understand the move either. He was fascinated to watch his father work from this perspective. It was eye-opening to say the least. And both perplexing and fun trying to figure out what Johnny saw and how he came up with his solutions for the players' challenges.

Ricky was next up to take his cuts and Bernie was especially curious to see what would happen with his old friend.

Ricky's timing was still off and Johnny noticed something. He yelled, "Hold up!"

Ricky, visibly frustrated, asked, "What am I doing wrong, Coach?"

Johnny, almost fatherly, offered his advice. "Listen to what I tell you. Watch the ball hit the bat."

Ricky gave Johnny a look like a puppy trying to understand a new command.

"Watch the ball hit the bat?"

Johnny nodded. "Yep."

Ricky stepped back in.

Watch the ball hit the bat. It was apparent to his coach that this thought was repeating in Ricky's mind as the ball approached the plate, since his lips were moving, chanting the words silently.

Ricky's eyes focused on the barrel of the bat as the ball hit it. He finished his swing knowing he'd made solid contact. Johnny didn't need to see. He heard it. The sound was loud and strong. The ball hit the centerfield wall on one hop.

Ricky turned to Johnny. "Watched the ball hit the bat, Coach."

Johnny pointed to his own head. "Just remember that every time!"

With Ricky's success, Johnny's mantra for the day was set.

"Watch the ball hit the bat," he said again as Mark stepped in to take his cuts.

Mark hit line drive after line drive, eyes fixed on the bat barrel.

This coaching stuff is easy, thought Johnny. Reality set in when Greg took his swings. Contact wasn't his problem. Solid contact was. Johnny knew this wouldn't be an easy fix.

When Derek took his turn, he still wasn't pulling the baseball.

Johnny hollered, "Derek, come here for a minute!" He grabbed the bat from Derek and took a few swings with it. Johnny looked at the bat. "36 inches and 36 ounces, huh?"

Derek said, "That's what I've always used, Coach."

Johnny walked over to the bat rack then returned with a different one for Derek. "Try this one."

Derek inspected the piece of lumber.

"Coach, this is only 32 inches and 28 ounces. How am I supposed to hit with this?"

Coach Phil had been watching and came to join the discussion.

"What's up, Johnny?"

"Nothing, Coach. Just suggesting to Derek that he use a shorter, lighter bat for a little while."

Derek held up the bat for his father. "Dad, this thing's like a toothpick. I can't hit with this!"

Coach Phil took the bat from Derek's hand. "First off, Derek, here I'm 'Coach,' not 'Dad'. Second, do what your manager tells you and don't argue."

Derek took back the bat. "All right Dad, uh Coach, I'll listen."

It took Derek a few swings to get used to the new piece of lumber but in no time he was hitting the ball hard to all parts of the field.

Some solid progress had been made. It was a big mountain to climb though and Johnny had barely begun his ascent. Next on the horizon was the pitching staff.

Jerry was back in Connecticut, apparently satisfied that he didn't need to hang around training camp any more. With Jerry gone, Bernie was in the bullpen with Coach Jimmy.

"Morning, Jimmy. Figured I'd hang out here for a while today. So, how's Gresham?"

Jimmy was hesitant to answer.

Bernie said, "What's up with him, Jimmy? Talk to me."

The pitching coach opened up. "First, I don't think he likes me, and I know he doesn't respect me. Second, he's got nothing on his fastball and won't admit it."

Bernie had been taking his cleats and glove with him every day. He finally saw the opportunity to use them. "Send him over with me for a bit."

Second day of camp and Clark's mood was no less foul. When he had seen Coach Jimmy for the first time, he considered walking out the gate and back to his home in Austin, Texas. Only his desire to prove something to himself kept him from leaving.

"Clark Gresham," he said, introducing himself. Clark could see that Jimmy was thrilled to meet him, almost to the point of being awed. "Guess we should get to work."

Coach Jimmy said, " How about some light tossing today?"

Clark stared him down. "Listen, don't coddle me. I don't like it and I don't need it. I'm ready to do whatever the hell the rest of these guys do today."

"Fine. Give me twenty-five pitches from the mound. Let's see what you've got."

Clark threw his pitches. His velocity topped out at 78 and his curveball had all the bite of a toothless dachshund.

Coach Jimmy tried some reassurance. "It's the first day. We'll work on it."

Clark wasn't in a smiling mood. What he really wanted to do was throw a baseball as hard as he could into Coach Jimmy's chest, but he figured that the way he'd thrown, Jimmy probably wouldn't even feel it.

And now this morning, he's been sent to the crazy owner for 'pointers'.

With an extended hand, Bernie greeted Clark. "Hello, Clark. Bernie Endino. I'm a big fan."

Clark looked at Bernie then looked at his hand without shaking it.

Bernie was undaunted. "Hey, let's play a little catch. I've always wanted to play catch with a pro."

Clark remained stationary like he was waiting for someone to say, 'Simon Says'.

Bernie smiled a little. "All right, I guess I'll have to try it this way. As the owner of this team, I'm telling you to get your ass over there and to play a little catch."

Clark reluctantly began to toss with Bernie. He had a very easy style about his throwing. Bernie tried again to start a conversation.

"Jimmy tells me things went pretty well yesterday."

Clark said nothing while he continued throwing. Bernie felt the tosses getting stronger. Bernie got louder.

"I said Jimmy tells me things went pretty well!"

The next throw stung Bernie's hand. There wasn't much padding left in his old glove so even Clark's less-than-stellar fastball made him wince.

While Bernie shook out the sting, Clark came up to him with gritted teeth. "Listen, yesterday was shitty. I sucked. I couldn't break glass with the shit I was throwing. It was an embarrassment to me and this game, so no, things didn't go okay at all. Got it, Sir?"

Bernie swallowed hard. "Good. You're mad. Now let me tell you something, Mr. Gresham. If you want to stay in this game and on this team, you need to learn how to pitch differently. See that guy over there? He's your pitching coach and despite what you may think, he knows pitching. Now I'm not asking you to listen to what he says, I'm telling you. Got it, Sir?"

Bernie figured he would get punched. He wondered where the nearest hospital was and if they could reconstruct his face. Thankfully, the punch never came.

Clark said, "Fine. I'll see what he has to say."

Bernie breathed a sigh of relief. Rachel wouldn't have to identify him in the morgue. And if Clark would give him a chance, Bernie was certain that Jimmy's coaching really would give Gresham the chance to continue his career as a ball player.

"Great. Now get back over to your coach and see what he wants you do to today. Oh, and you owe him an apology for your lousy attitude and lack of respect."

Coach Jimmy watched as Gresham left Bernie and headed his way. The player walked slowly, head down, then appeared to come to a decision as his step became purposeful. He looked around to find Jimmy's eye on him.

"Coach? Got a minute?"

Jimmy nodded and waited. The man obviously had something to say.

"I was out of line, Coach. No excuses. You know my story and history. Bernie put me straight. I want to play and he says you know your stuff. Won't guarantee I'll be easy to get along with, I'm pretty surly most of the time. But if you'll let me, I'd like to start over." Clark held out his hand.

Jimmy smiled and took the player's hand firmly in his own. He recognized what it took for this proud player to ask for help and only hoped he was up to the job.

"Let's put you to work, then. Go warm up while I work a bit with Jake."

Coach Jimmy had been watching Jake closely. His control was erratic and his changeup continued to be miserable. Jimmy took him to the side.

"Jake, why do you insist on throwing that changeup?"

Jake, with a wad of bubble gum in his mouth, said, "They said if I want to start in the Big Leagues, I need three pitches, so I picked the changeup. Seemed to be the easiest choice."

Coach Jimmy crossed his arms. "Easiest, huh?"

Jake immediately understood how dumb his answer sounded. "Yeah I guess it probably isn't so easy."

Jimmy slapped Jake on the back. "I think we can get you fixed. First, we need to decide if you're going to be a guy with two really good pitches or a guy with three mediocre ones. Which one is it?"

With the obvious answer given, they got to work.

Jimmy said, "I see part of the problem with your fastball. When you go into your wind up, your head is all over the place. You probably see half the people in the stands before each pitch. Focus on the catcher. Zero in on that target and don't lose it. How can you throw the ball consistently if you aren't looking at the place where it's supposed to go?"

Jake nodded, anxious to pitch. He wound up and fired a 95 miles per hour fastball directly to the backstop. Jimmy responded, "Which row of seats did you see first?"

Jake got his coach's point. He was determined but his next three fastballs resulted in one skipping in, one crossing through the right hand hitter's batter's box and one more to the backstop. He was visibly frustrated. He turned to Jimmy with a suggestion.

"Maybe if we work on my slider…"

Jimmy stopped him. "We can't work on the slider until we get the fastball right."

Jake paced the mound for a few seconds before toeing the pitching rubber. He took his place and focused hard on Ricky's target, firing another fastball. It nestled into Ricky's mitt without him needing to move it an inch. Jimmy said, "Nice but let's see if you can do it again."

Jake's next pitch bounced six feet in front of home plate then hit the backstop.

Jimmy responded with one word.

"Consistency."

After several more pitches, some nearly perfect and some not, Jimmy gave Jake the rest of the day off. He knew they were a long way from finished but it was time to work with Charlie Vanholdt. Talking with Charlie, Jimmy's critique was blunt. "Charlie you have pretty good breaking and off speed stuff, but without a decent fastball to go with it, you're in trouble. At the lower levels, you can get away with what you're doing. That's not going to fly here or in the Bigs."

Charlie took the criticism without response. He shrugged his shoulders and looked away, as if to say, "What did this guy know anyway? I've done pretty well so far." He threw a few more pitches.

Coach Jimmy watched silently then said, "That's enough."

"What? Am I done for the day already?"

"Not a chance," Jimmy replied then turned to one of the watching players. "Hey, Frank! Grab a bat and helmet and come over here!"

Charlie asked, "What's this about?"

Jimmy pointed at Frank. "You're going to pitch to him."

Frank stepped into the batter's box. Jimmy instructed Charlie to pitch as if it was a real game while he umpired from out by the mound. Charlie's first pitch was a curveball near the outside corner.

Jimmy yelled, "Ball one!"

Charlie took the ball back from Ricky, unhappy with the call. It seemed to affect his next pitch, which also missed the plate. Not wanting to fall further behind, he threw his fastball. It was 85 miles per hour and belt high. Frank hit a towering drive that landed in the parking lot beyond the left field wall.

Coach Jimmy flipped Charlie a new baseball and said, "Hope no one had their cars out there."

Charlie rubbed up the new ball and said, "Got lucky."

Charlie started Frank's next at bat with a beautiful changeup, which Frank watched for strike one. It may have worked once but it didn't work again. Frank took a cut and deposited the ball over the centerfield fence.

Jimmy seized the opportunity to 'improve' Charlie's attitude saying, "Wow, they'll need an air traffic controller to land that baby!"

Charlie was steaming. He took another ball from Jimmy, reared back and threw a first pitch fastball right down the middle. Frank ripped it into right field for a single.

Coach Jimmy was enjoying himself now. "Almost had the batter guessing there."

Charlie had just about enough. His next pitch was a chin-high fastball that sent Frank sprawling to the dirt. Without dusting himself off, Frank headed for the mound ready to disassemble Charlie.

Jimmy got between the two before any damage got done. "All right...enough gentlemen! This is over, hear me?"

Frank stared at Charlie, pointing his bat towards the mound. "You'd better control yourself, kid, or someone is going to kill you!"

Charlie pointed back to Frank. "Screw you, old man!"

Jimmy pointed to the dugout. "Frank, get the hell out of here now!" Frank headed for the clubhouse. Jimmy now reprimanded Charlie.

"And you, don't ever throw at anyone because you're having a bad day...got it?"

Charlie didn't answer. Jimmy reiterated. "I said got it?"

Charlie finally looked his coach in the eye. "Yeah, coach...got it."

Jimmy growled, "Good. Now, if you listen to me, I think I can help you, but it's going to take a fairly drastic change."

Charlie folded his arms. "How drastic?"

Jimmy put a hand on Charlie's shoulder. "We'll talk about it tomorrow. For now you need to think about how badly you want to make this team, 'cause I can't use anybody who can't control his temper and deliver the pitch every time, no matter how fast that pitch might be."

Jimmy walked slowly to the clubhouse, following the last of his players into the locker room.

Three days into spring training and everyone could see the potential in the team. They knew that Rome wasn't built in a day, but they also knew that it burned too. One thing was definitely going to be different though—Hank Rundle was finally coming to camp.

[7]

The Prodigal Son Returneth

BERNIE WAS EXCITED TO see what Hank Rundle could do. He was also concerned that Hank's prima donna attitude would come with him. His concerns were dead on. It was fifteen minutes into practice and still no sign of Rundle.

To say Johnny was irked would be an understatement. Bernie was close enough to see his coach glancing frequently toward the gate and knew his father well enough to recognize growing irritation.

It was half an hour into practice when Hank finally made his appearance. He had a big bat and a smooth glove to go with his 6'4" muscular frame. Everything about him said, Major League, except his attitude.

Coach Johnny, pen in his mouth, said, "Welcome to practice, Rundle. So glad you could join us."

Hank asked, "Who are you?"

Johnny took out the pen. He wanted to make sure Hank heard every word loud and clear. "Well Mr. Rundle I'm your new manager and for being thirty minutes late to practice today, you can give me five laps around the field."

Hank took a step towards Johnny. "Bullshit!"

Johnny was not intimidated. He'd dealt with guys like Hank before. "Make it ten." Now the entire team was watching.

Hank looked at his teammates. His tone was quiet. "I'm not doing ten laps for you or anyone else."

Johnny, pointing his finger at Hank with each word, said, "You know what, Rundle? You're right. Gentlemen, your teammate Mr. Rundle here has decided that he's too good to run laps. He'd appreciate it if all of you would do his ten laps for him! Drop whatever you are doing and take ten laps around the field to honor your teammate!"

Immediately the team began doing laps with the exception of Hank. As they passed him, each player had either a nasty look or rude gesture for Hank. Johnny hoped his point had been made. Apparently, it hadn't.

Hank was lackadaisical during infield drills, barely moving for ground balls and lobbing throws to first.

Johnny was not amused. "Mr. Rundle, are we boring you?"

Hank squinted into the morning sun. "Yeah, kind of."

Johnny pointed towards the dugout. "Well then Mr. Rundle, you just take the rest of the day off."

Pleased with himself Hank headed for the clubhouse after less than an hour of practice. Johnny cupped his hands around his mouth. "By the way, Mr. Rundle, I'm fining you $1,000 for your antics today."

Hank stopped and turned back towards the field. "Are you nuts?"

Johnny just grinned and said, "No, I'm your manager."

Hank threw his glove to the ground. "This, is complete bullshit!"

Johnny stayed cool. "Oh by the way, Mr. Rundle, if you're late tomorrow and don't show me any effort, I'm doubling your fine."

Hank picked up his glove and fired it down the corridor to the clubhouse as he stormed out of practice. Johnny shook his head.

After practice, Bernie was waiting for Johnny.

"Good day, huh?" Bernie asked his father, chuckling a little.

"Not bad except for Rundle."

"Yeah I saw that. What is that guy's problem?"

Johnny shook his head. "I don't know, but he'd better get his head out of his ass in a hurry or he's not going to see the field."

"He's probably your best player, you know." Bernie was playing the middle.

Johnny stopped walking. "That doesn't get him a pass. He plays by my rules, or he doesn't play."

Bernie and Johnny decided that it was a good idea for a meeting with Rundle after the next practice. Johnny had to get Hank on board. If he couldn't, they could lose the entire team.

Johnny decided to give the guys a little break and started practice an hour later. When he arrived, everyone was ready to go, except Hank Rundle. Johnny was pissed off big time. He spouted off to no one in particular.

"I give the guy an extra hour and he still can't get his ass here on time! That's the problem with these bonus baby players. They think they deserve everything without working for it. Well, I'm gonna knock him down a few pegs."

About fifteen minutes into warm ups, Hank popped his head out of the dugout.

Johnny pointed at his watch. "Mr. Rundle, practice began at ten o'clock. You're late. You owe me two grand."

Hank tightened the laces on his spikes. "I'll write you out a check for ten. That should cover me for a few days."

Hank had gone too far. A shouting match ensued.

"That's it, Rundle! You're suspended indefinitely! Get the hell off the field!"

Hank, arms extended, said, "You're suspending me?"

"Damn right I am!"

Hank took of his cap. "Fine! You'll find out the hard way how much you need me!"

"Yeah, you were a huge difference for this team last year!"

Hank pointed at Johnny. "I was the only good thing about this team last year and I still am!"

This did not endear Hank to his teammates as they all heard it.

Johnny gave a golf clap. "Nice job, Rundle. Way to throw your team under the bus. I'm sure you're very proud of yourself."

Johnny saw a flash of worry or maybe shame cross Hank's face as he turned to head back to the locker room.

Johnny wasn't quite finished with him. "Before you leave, Mr. Rundle, I want you in my office tomorrow morning at nine on the dot."

Johnny had players who wanted to play, wanted to learn, and desired to be successful. He had no time for Hank's crap today. He'd deal with it tomorrow.

The next day was an off day for the players, but not for Johnny. He was at the stadium by 8:30 in the morning, preparing for his meeting with Hank. Hank showed up five minutes early.

Johnny said, "On time. It's a start."

Hank sat down. "My checking account's running a little low until pay day."

Johnny got right to the point. "Hank, why are you being so difficult?"

Hank shrugged. "I guess I don't think I belong here."

Johnny took a sip of coffee, "So you think you've learned all and done all that you can at this level?"

Hank played with his fingers. "Yeah, I think so."

"Well, Mr. Rundle, until today I wasn't sure you could tell time."

Hank did not smile. He repositioned himself in the chair and Johnny had a brief insight: Rundle was ashamed of his behavior. Perhaps there's hope to turn this player around.

"Tell you what, get out there and show me that you've learned it all. If you really have, I'll let Jerry know."

Hank slouched in his seat. "You've suspended me indefinitely."

"I'll lift it in two days. Take that time and make sure you really don't have anything left to learn here."

Hank shrugged and got up. "See you in two days, bright and early. Shouldn't be with you for very long after that."

"Just make sure you're on time or I'll keep the other six grand from that check you gave me."

Hank may have thought he was the only guy worth anything on the team but not Johnny. Ricky was progressing well. Mark had settled in nicely at second while Miguel's transition to shortstop was going smoother than hoped. With all the good, not everything was rosy.

With Frank and Derek hitting the ball well and Hank's enormous potential, Johnny was working on a way to get them all into the lineup at once. He decided the best move was trying Derek into right field to see what he could do. Turning him into an outfielder wasn't going to be easy but it was the best move Johnny could make at that point.

Frank was another problem. He simply had no mobility. Johnny took him aside. "Frank, I like your bat a lot and I think your experience can be a big plus for the kids."

Frank frowned slightly and bowed his head. Johnny knew he sensed the talk wasn't going to be an all-out love fest.

Johnny asked, "How much do you weigh?"

"Two hundred ten, last I checked."

Johnny looked over the bridge of his glasses. "When was the last you checked?"

Almost in a whisper Frank answered, "About three years ago."

Johnny shook his head. "Frank, I'll bet you weigh at least two-forty if you weigh a pound. You need to drop thirty pounds by opening day. If you were two-ten once, you can be two-ten again."

"It's tough to get an old dog to change his habits, Coach, but I'll try. I'm going to miss my three-doughnut breakfast, though. I don't think two will fill me."

Johnny saw his work was cut out for him.

There was also a two-headed problem to deal with. Johnny needed to get Malcolm and Greg producing at the plate. Greg wasn't hitting the ball hard and Malcolm was struggling with his transition to hitting from the left side. Johnny thought that pairing them to work together might solve each one's issue.

Johnny said, "Greg, I want you to show Malcolm how to bunt and how to hit the ball on the ground. We need to get the most use out of his legs."

Coach Johnny hoped that watching Malcolm's aggressive swing might rub off on Greg too, just with more contact. Johnny yelled to Malcolm, "Let's see you drop a bunt for a hit!"

After missing badly on his first three attempts, Malcolm slammed his bat to the ground.

He looked at Johnny and threw up his arms. "I can't get this, Coach!"

Johnny yelled, "Greg, show him what to do!"

Greg stepped into the batter's box and dropped a perfect bunt that hugged the third base line. He next dragged a beautiful bunt between the pitcher and first baseman. Johnny asked Greg to step out then pulled him aside.

"All right, what's Malcolm doing wrong?"

Greg said, "He's sort of jabbing at the ball."

Johnny nodded. "Yeah, I thought so too."

Malcolm spoke up to defend himself, "Uh guys, I've only been batting as a lefty for a few days, remember?"

Greg said, "Shit, almost forgot that."

Johnny sent the two to an empty spot behind the cage and instructed them to work on bunting and nothing else for the rest of the day. He knew that if Malcolm learned how to bunt, he was going to be a very valuable player. Malcolm, on the other hand, wasn't so sure.

"This hitting from the left side, Coach. I can't see it working."

"Yeah well, if it doesn't you can go back to trying it from the right side for your new manager because my ass is getting fired."

With his chat over Johnny glanced down to the bullpen and wasn't sure what he saw. He wiped his glasses and a second glance confirmed it. Jake Williams was pitching with a neck brace! Johnny made a beeline for the bullpen.

"Hold up! Jake, what the hell is wrong with you? You can't pitch hurt!"

Coach Jimmy shed light on the subject.

"He's fine, Coach. I'm working on something."

Johnny pointed to his chest. "On what? Giving me a heart attack?"

Jimmy laughed. "I'm working on his focus."

"Just let me know the next time you're going to do something like this. I'll order some nitro pills."

Jake felt uncomfortable but threw a pitch with the neck brace on.

"Not too bad," Jimmy said.

"You try throwing with this thing around your neck."

"When you can keep your eyes on the target by yourself, you can take it off."

On Jake's next pitch his head began to turn but the brace kept it from happening. He threw a perfect strike.

"Son of a bitch, it's working", Jake said. He spoke softly, but Jimmy was close enough to hear and he smiled.

Jake continued throwing, getting more consistent with finding the strike zone. "Geez, maybe I'll keep this thing on permanently."

Jimmy was pleased and after a few more tosses, left the two of them to continue practicing.

Now, it was Charlie's turn. Jimmy called him over. "Charlie, did you learn anything from the other day?"

Charlie shrugged. "Not really."

Jimmy sighed. "Thankfully I did."

Charlie was confused.

"What do you mean?"

"Without a decent fastball, your curveball and changeup are a lot less effective. I have an idea. Are you ready to try something different?"

Charlie was clearly agitated but caved in. What choice did he have? "Just tell me what the hell you want me to do."

"First off, lose the shitty attitude." Coach Jimmy stared at Charlie until the player reluctantly met his eyes. His face clearly still showed displeasure, but grudgingly he nodded. "I'll work on it."

Jimmy noticed he neglected to add the 'coach' honorific but was satisfied to have even a cursory acknowledgement from the surly player.

"Next, I'm going to have you work with Bernie on throwing submarine style."

Charlie craned his neck forward. "The owner is going to teach me how to pitch?"

When Jimmy and Bernie were kids, Bernie was a decent baseball player. His knowledge of the game made up for his lack of physical makeup. He learned how to play every position on the field and developed tricks to help him get the most out of his abilities. It was his pitching trick that Jimmy hoped would work for Charlie.

Jimmy had explained his idea to Bernie, who was glad to help and was waiting for them in the bullpen. A skeptical Charlie asked Bernie to show him what he had.

Bernie wound up and coiled like a snake waiting to pounce. He dropped his arm to where his knuckles nearly scraped the ground and threw a perfect strike.

"Didn't think I could still do that," Bernie said, somewhat amazed and proud of himself.

"You don't expect me to throw like that, do you?"

Bernie put the ball in Charlie's glove. "It's what your coach wants."

"Well screw that! I'm not pitching like that!" He turned to walk away when Bernie said, "Then you won't be pitching much for this team."

Jimmy and Bernie saw the frustration in Charlie's face. Before he could boil over, Jimmy talked to him.

"Charlie, deception is going to be your best weapon. It'll make your fastball seem faster and your breaking pitches will be nasty. Right-handed hitters are going to hate facing you and if you learn how to do it right, it could mean a lot more chances to pitch."

After allowing this to sink in, Charlie asked Bernie to show him submarine style one more time. He was right on the money again.

Charlie was ready to give it a try. He mimicked Bernie's motion as best he could. His first pitch bounced eight feet short and ten inches wide of home plate. His next one was well over Ricky's head and rolled towards the dugout.

He turned to Jimmy. "I'm never going to get this shit."

"You've thrown two pitches. This is going to take a lot of work. You can either get frustrated or get to it—which is it going to be?"

Charlie didn't need long to decide. "Give me the damn ball!"

Bernie continued his instruction. He took the mound and said, "It's sort of like throwing a Frisbee. Watch."

Bernie hit the target again. For the next hour, the two men worked on Charlie's new motion. By the end, he'd shown some improvement from where he started.

Bernie said, "Not bad for your first day as a sidewinder."

"If you say so. I'll tell you one thing; my arm isn't sore."

Bernie patted Charlie on the back. "One of the benefits of throwing like that."

Coach Jimmy turned to his other problem child. Clark was stretching off to the side when Jimmy called him over. Clark, I want to try a new pitch with you today."

"A new pitch? What new pitch?"

Jimmy held up a baseball secured by the nails on his first two fingers. "A knuckleball."

Clark put his hands on his hips. "Are you shitting me? Why the hell should I learn a knuckler?"

"Like it or not, your fastball isn't what it used to be. I think you can get back your curve with work, but I can't see the velocity on the fastball coming back to anywhere near what it was. We may not be able to make the fastball faster, but we can make it look like it is."

Clark wasn't buying into it. "Screw that. No way am I learning to throw a gimmick pitch like that...no damn way."

"Fine. Have it your way, but if you go out there throwing the stuff you have now, and you get lit up, prepare to be no better than a mop up man for this team."

Clark pointed at Jimmy. "I don't mop up for anyone."

Jimmy pointed back. "Don't bet on it."

Defiantly, Clark stormed away and prepared to throw his way. Coach Jimmy let him go. Sometimes you have to let people prove the error of their thinking to themselves.

There was a radar gun set up behind the plate. Jimmy moved in to watch. Clark's fastball was only clocking in the upper 70s. Jimmy shook his head as he watched the defiant and desperate pitcher struggle to force his arm to perform to a no longer achievable standard. He hoped Clark would reconsider the knuckleball before it was too late.

[8]

Let's Play a Game

THE TEAM BOARDED THE bus for its first exhibition game of the season. "Mr. Rundle, you'll be sitting next to me today."

Hank wasn't amused. The coach was entirely too observant and knowing. It felt like every time Johnny looked at him, the coach saw right through him and didn't like what he saw. No, more like was disappointed for some reason.

He took his seat next to Johnny, put on his headphones, and turned up his music.

Once the bus took off and the players settled in, Johnny reached over and lifted the headphone from his ears. "Mr. Rundle, you and I need to talk. Your music can wait."

Hank turned off his music. "Fine. What do you want?"

"Mr. Rundle, you have all the talent in the world, but your attitude is piss poor. Son, you need to grow the Hell up if you want to be someone in this game."

Hank crossed his arms and turned his head away from Johnny.

"See, Mr. Rundle, that's the shit I'm talking about. Look at me when I'm talking to you, son."

Hank turned back. "Listen, I'm not your son so stop calling me that. I have no idea who my father is, but I know damn well it ain't you."

Hank saw a light go off in the coach's eyes and he was quiet for a moment.

"You're right, Hank, I'm not your dad. I'm your coach and as your coach I'm here to help you become the player I know you can be both on and off of the field."

Hank looked away again for a minute. He really wanted to be angry. "It's not fair that I'm stuck here with these pick up ball players. Every time I think about being stuck here, it just pisses me off more."

"Work with me here. You do have the stuff to make it in the bigs, and I can show you how to make it happen if you will let me." Johnny's voice was quiet, almost a whisper.

Hank heard the plea and more, he heard sincerity and a promise. For the first time he felt like someone cared about him as a person and not a commodity.

He looked back to his manager. It would be a lie to say all of his anger drained away, but something changed inside of him. It had been a long time since someone really believed in him and a sense of hope began to fight through the anger and frustration. "All right. We'll try it your way.

"Thanks." Johnny extended his arm and with that the two men shook hands.

Things were going to be better from here on out. The team star was finally on board.

It was a beautiful day in Florida and the Pride finally had a game to play. Johnny arrived at the field an hour before everyone else. It was only an exhibition game, but he was creating his first lineup as a professional manager and he wanted some time alone to let it sink in. Once everyone was dressed and ready to go, Johnny decided to address the team just as he had during his Pony League days.

"First game today, gentlemen. The final score doesn't matter but how you play does. You're being evaluated every day. The best twenty-five will come to Pennsylvania with us. I need you to give me the best you have every day, on and off the field. In the lineup or not, you all have something to do on every pitch. Watch the game. Pick up tendencies of the pitchers or hitters. Watch base runners and make sure they are touching the bags. Tell your coaches what you see. You may not be playing, but you are definitely in the game. What you see may help your team."

Most of the team had never heard anything like this and weren't sure how to react. Some clapped while the rest just sat silently. Johnny gave the lineup, which had Clark as his starting pitcher. Johnny was limiting him to thirty pitches for the game. Clark was the only player with any limit for today as everyone else was scheduled to play the entire game, something unheard of for spring training.

Clark's first pitch was a 77 mile per hour fastball called for a strike. He followed it with back-to-back curveballs for a strikeout. Johnny was still concerned. Clark struck out the next hitter as well, using curveballs and changeups. Feeling good, Clark started out the next hitter with a fastball. It had nothing on it and the batter slammed it high and deep into left field. The ball hooked foul at the last minute.

Bullet dodged.

Ricky called first for a changeup then a curve for Clark's next pitch. Clark shook off both signals. He thought it was a fluke that a kid hit his fastball and he was going to prove it. He threw another fastball, which came in at 79 miles per hour. The hitter crushed it into centerfield.

Greg broke hard towards the fence, arriving just in time to reach up and steal a home run. The inning was over, but Johnny wasn't exactly thrilled at what he'd seen.

It was the Pride's turn to get its first licks of the season. Much like he did during Pony League, Greg used his great batter's eye and drew a walk. Johnny managed the game like it counted and with Mark hitting, called for a hit and run. Greg took off and Mark stung a line drive up the middle. What normally would have been a single turned into an easy double play as the second baseman breaking to cover the bag made the catch and easy throw to first.

Now with two outs, Hank stepped and unloaded on a 2-0 room service fastball, landing it in the parking lot beyond the left field fence giving the Pride an early lead.

Frank followed with a ground ball deep into the hole at shortstop. For many, it would have been an infield hit but the slow-footed Frank was out by fifteen feet.

Clark gave up a single to start the second inning and followed by allowing a double into the right field corner. With runners on second and third and nobody out, the next batter laced a hanging curveball towards the shortstop hole. It looked like a sure two-run single, but Miguel had other plans. He dove with his glove extended. The ball smacked into the webbing of his glove and then, from his knees, Miguel threw to Hank at third catching the runner who had broken for the plate.

It was an incredible double play.

Clark had a chance to get out of the inning unscathed. He started the next hitter with a changeup for a called strike then threw another one. The second got rifled past Frank into right field. Derek was in right today, and his arm was going to get tested right away. His throw was on target but not quite as strong as he wanted. Ricky set up a roadblock for the runner that a S.W.A.T. team would be proud of. He caught the throw and made the tag to end the inning with the Pride leading, 1-0. Johnny stopped Clark at the top step of the dugout.

"That's enough for today."

Clark said, "I only threw eighteen pitches."

Johnny patted him on the back. "I know. Hit the showers."

Clark fired his glove to the ground in disgust and headed back to the clubhouse.

Miguel hit a two-out triple in the bottom of the second, giving Malcolm a chance to drive him home. It was the first time Malcolm was hitting left-handed in a game ever. Malcolm decided to bunt in hopes of getting a hit. The ball rolled towards third base, hugging the foul line almost the whole time. It looked like a hit but at the last second the ball rolled foul for strike one. Johnny called time out to speak with Malcolm.

"Nice effort there, but I don't want you bunting in a game just yet. Swing the bat."

Malcolm stepped back into the box puzzled. Why had he spent all that time bunting? He eventually struck out, looking awkward while doing it. Johnny gave him some words of encouragement.

"It's all right, Malcolm. We'll keep working at it."

Malcolm asked, "Can I hit from the right side for the rest of the game, Coach?"

"I don't think so. This is part of working at it."

So far, the day wasn't going according to Johnny's plan and it would get worse.

Frank allowed two balls to get by him that a more physically fit first baseman would have fielded easily. Ricky threw two balls into centerfield on steal attempts. Derek misjudged three balls and dropped another one in right field. At the plate, Greg failed to get a ball out of the infield in his last three at bats. Malcolm struck out three times without so much as fouling off a pitch after his bunt attempt. Hank was the only bright spot, adding a double to his home run.

In the end, Johnny's first game as a professional manager ended in an 8-1 loss.

He addressed the team in the clubhouse. "Gentlemen, today's performance proved that we've still got a lot of work to do. Put in the work and we'll get better."

Most of the players seemed to get it with two exceptions. Clark Gresham spent the entire time talking on his cell phone with an agent. Hank read text messages. Johnny wasn't pleased.

"Mr. Gresham and Mr. Rundle, kindly put down your phones... now!"

Clark and Hank both ignored Johnny's request. He grabbed Hank's phone from his hand.

Hank said, "What the hell are you doing?"

Johnny said, "Sit there and shut up."

Johnny took Clark's phone from his hand. He said to the agent, "He's busy getting his ass chewed out right now. He'll call you later."

Clark looked up at his manager. "What is your damned problem, Man?"

Johnny stood over his pitcher. "First off, I'm Coach, not Man. Second, you're my damned problem right now. Get your ass over with your teammates."

Reluctantly, Clark obliged.

Johnny said, "Mr. Gresham and Mr. Rundle, I'm fining each of you five hundred dollars for disrespecting me and your teammates at this meeting."

Hank said, "That's bullshit!"

Johnny said, "That's another five hundred."

Hank stared hard at Coach for a long 30 seconds, then backed down. "Yeah. OK. I guess I deserve the extra fine."

Johnny nodded and continued his talk. "Gentlemen, no one is forcing you to be here. If you want to leave and never come back, please do. You're of no use to this team. If you choose to stay, you play by my rules, got it? I'm the captain of this ship and I don't care how much money you make. When you're in here, you respect your coaches and teammates."

Johnny hoped that Hank may finally have come on board. Clark still hadn't come around. Johnny sent the team to the showers and asked Clark to come to his office.

When Clark arrived Johnny said, "Grab a seat."

Clark flopped into a chair.

"Clark, Jimmy tells me he asked you to do something and you wouldn't."

Clark looked around the office almost as if he was trying to find an emergency exit. "He wants me to throw a damn knuckleball."

"Did he tell you why?"

Now Clark looked at Johnny. "Yeah but I don't agree."

Johnny decided it was time to give Clark a reality check.

"Do you know why I took you out today after only eighteen pitches?"

Clark leaned forward nearly rising out of his chair and put his hands on Johnny's desk. "I have no damn idea."

Johnny took a sip of his soda. "Because I didn't want to see you get embarrassed out there."

Clark stood up. "Embarrassed? I pitched two innings, struck out two and didn't give up a damn run!"

"Clark sit down. You fooled the first two hitters. Both were kids who played Single-A ball last year, I might add. The next five guys hit you hard. If it weren't for your defense, you'd have given up at least three runs and maybe more."

Clark folded his arms like a pouting child. "It was my first game of the year. I'll be fine. I don't need to learn a damn gimmick pitch."

"You pitch again in four days. You'd better hope you're right."

Clark got out of the chair, It was obvious to Johnny that the pitcher felt like he'd just had his time wasted.

Bernie caught up with Johnny in the parking lot and they walked together.

"Don't worry about today, Dad. It was the first game. You've got guys who are adjusting to playing against this level of competition."

"I know, but I'm wondering if bringing them in was a mistake."

Bernie just put his hand on his dad's shoulder. "Give it time, Dad. It wasn't as bad as you think."

"Good, because from where I sat it looked pretty shitty. You want a ride back to the house? I don't see your car here."

"Nah. It's not far, I'd like to walk. Got some thinking to do. See you in the morning, Dad." Bernie thought best during his walks. He wondered if his dad may have been right and if bringing these guys in was going to work out. If it didn't, could he honestly fire his father and the coaches? What about the four guys who gave up their careers to give baseball one last try? Could Bernie really have them cut? Bernie hoped he wouldn't need to address these questions.

It was a tiring camp for Bernie thus far. *This owning a team thing isn't quite what I'd expected*, he thought.

It would not get easier any time soon.

On the morning after the team's first exhibition game, Johnny barked out his orders, "All right gentlemen I've got some notes here to help make you better ballplayers. Greg and Malcolm, I want you both in the batting cage. Greg, keep working on Malcolm's bunting. I want twenty-five bunts from each of you, and if at least fifteen aren't good, I want twenty-five more. When you're done with that, I want twenty-five swings from you each. Malcolm, watch the ball hit the bat. Greg I want you to try pulling the ball instead of chopping it or slapping at it."

Greg and Malcolm headed to the batting cages to start what had the potential for a long day. Johnny gave out his next assignment.

"Ricky, I want you working on your throws. Start off with ten to first base. Once you make ten catchable throws there, move on to second base and do the same thing. Once you make ten catchable throws there, finish up with ten to third base. Miss a throw at any base, and you restart that base until you get it right."

It felt more like boot camp than training camp.

Johnny continued, "Derek go into right field with Coach Jeffers. Once you catch twenty-five fly balls without missing one, you can have the rest of the day off. As soon as you miss one though, you start over. Coach, make him work a little, but make 'em catchable, all right?"

Coach Art nodded and went to work with Derek.

"Miguel, I want you to take twenty-five ground balls at shortstop from Coach Figlione. Each throw has to be catchable and on the bag. Miss a throw and you start from the beginning. Once you complete twenty-five in a row, you're done for the day. Got it?"

Coach Phil and Miguel prepared for their busy day. Frank grabbed his glove and headed to first base. Johnny stopped him.

"Uh Frank, I'm going to let Hank take the throws."

"How come?"

"I have other plans for you today. Prepare to work your ass off... literally."

Frank still didn't get it. Just then, a fit, young man approached Johnny. He made Greek gods look like Sumo wrestlers.

"Frank, this is Tony. He's a personal trainer. For the rest of this camp, Tony is your personal trainer."

Frank gulped hard. "Oh shit!" He began sweating without doing a second of exercise.

Johnny said, "Take him, Tony. He's all yours."

A grumbling Frank headed off with Tony looking like a man headed for the electric chair.

Before taking his position at first, Hank talked to Johnny.

"Coach, I've never played first base before. Why are you doing this to me?"

Johnny held up his fingers. "Three reasons. One, Frank's getting older and can't do it every day. Two, the more positions you can play, the better chance you have at a call up. Three, I'm the manager and I say so. Any more questions?"

Hank shrugged. "I guess not."

"Great. Now get over there and take the throws. Oh, and if you miss a good one, you owe me a lap."

Hank headed for first but Johnny stopped him again.

"Hank, you may want this."

Johnny tossed him a new, freshly broken in first baseman's mitt.

Hank managed to smile.

With practice underway, Johnny began his walk like a drill sergeant overseeing recruits. He talked with Bernie, who was watching Greg and Malcolm.

"How are they doing?"

Bernie leaned against the screen. "Greg's already done. He got down twenty-two good ones out of twenty-five. Malcolm is, sort of struggling."

"How much?"

"So far, he's seen eight pitches. He still hasn't gotten down a good one."

Clearly not what Johnny had hoped for.

Johnny said, "Greg, come here a minute!"

Greg headed to Johnny, who asked, "What seems to be Malcolm's problem?"

Greg mimicked Malcolm's stance. "He's still jabbing at the ball instead of letting it come to the bat."

Johnny nodded. "All right, let's solve the problem."

He entered the cage to talk with Malcolm.

"Greg tells me you're having some bunting issues."

Malcolm pouted like a child. "I'll never figure this left-handed hitting thing out, Coach."

Johnny put his hands on Malcolm's shoulders. "Just bunt one for me."

Malcolm stepped back into the batter's box. As the pitch approached the plate, he again jabbed at the baseball, poking the bunt foul towards third. Frustrated, he turned to Johnny. "See? I told you, Coach."

Johnny rolled his eyes. "Yeah you told me. Now quit bitching about hitting lefty and concentrate."

Malcolm made a face like he'd just gotten a whiff of cheese left out in the sun for six hours.

"What do you mean, Coach?"

"Malcolm, you've been saying you can't do this since I asked you to try it. Stop saying you can't. If you were hitting from the right side I wouldn't even have suggested this."

The reality and truth of what Johnny said struck Malcolm hard. Johnny was right. He had nothing to lose by trying.

Malcolm adjusted his batting helmet. "All right, Coach, let's get at this."

Johnny stood beside Malcolm and showed him how to cradle the ball to the bat instead of jabbing at it.

"Now, get in there and damn it, concentrate."

Malcolm stepped in and as the ball approached, he resisted the urge to reach out and get it. Instead he did as Johnny showed him and made an almost perfect bunt down the third base line.

"Not bad, Malcolm, not bad. Do it fourteen more times and you can take some full swings. Keep an eye on him, Greg."

Johnny went to watch Ricky working on his throws. Every throw to first was strong and on target.

Johnny said, "Hold up, Ricky."

Ricky took of his mask and turned. "Something wrong, Coach?"

"No. That's why I stopped you. Come here for a second. Ricky, what was going through your head yesterday with those two throws?"

Ricky looked at the dirt. "My two bad at-bats, Coach."

"And what are you thinking about today?"

Ricky shrugged. "Nothing. I'm just throwing."

Johnny looked to the sky and shook his head. "Dear God, you guys think too much out here." Johnny put his arm around Ricky's shoulder. "You've got to let a bad at bat or bad day at the plate go. If you can't do that, I can't use you. Understand?"

Ricky got quiet. "I just don't want you to think bringing me here was a mistake."

"No chance. Just do your best. I know what that is and it's all I ask."

Ricky nodded and got back to work.

Johnny felt practice was going well. He checked on Derek.

Johnny hollered, "How's he doing, Art?"

"He's...uh, doing okay." Johnny stopped the drill. "Fill me in, Art."

"He's fine for three or four, then he'll misjudge one like he doesn't even see it."

"Any type of ball in particular?"

"Pretty much anything that isn't right at him."

Johnny had Coach Art and Derek get back to work while he observed.

Art hit a ball that Derek barely had to move to catch. Derek wavered a bit but caught the ball. Art then hit one a little deeper and to Derek's right. Derek took a step in and recovered too late to make the catch. Derek hollered, "Wind got it!"

The flags above the stadium were still. Next Art hit one several feet short of where Derek was positioned. Derek looked unsteady again and the ball fell harmlessly in front of him. Johnny called Derek over.

Derek said, "Sorry, Coach. Wind is brutal today."

"Derek, there's no wind. What's going on out there?"

Derek shuffled his feet. "I'm not seeing the ball off of the bat."

"Yep, not seeing the ball can be a problem. Derek, I want you to see an eye doctor. Make an appointment for today and let me know how it goes. I think all you need are glasses."

Derek punched his fist into the glove and headed off to find a doctor.

Johnny had Miguel in his sights now. He was making the tough plays look easy. After making several less-than-routine plays, Coach Phil hit Miguel an easy two-hopper right at him. He fielded it cleanly and threw to first missing Hank by a good six feet. Miguel used some choice Spanish curse words.

Phil said to Johnny, "That's happened on every routine ball today."

It was time for another of Johnny's talks. He headed out to the field.

"Miguel how is it that you can make the throws on the tough plays but not the easy ones?"

Miguel removed his cap and scratched his head. "Maybe because I have too much time to think on the easy ones."

"Miguel, the next time you field an easy one think 'if I throw this one away, Coach is going to sit my ass next to him on the bench.' Can you do that?"

Miguel got Johnny's point. He took his position at shortstop and fielded the next two balls deep in the hole, making a great throw to Hank each time.

Johnny said, "Give him an easy one, Phil."

Phil hit as routine a ground ball as Miguel had ever fielded. Miguel made a perfect, chest-high throw to first. Both Miguel and Johnny were pleased.

Johnny yelled, "Just remember what I told you!"

Miguel raised his glove and yelled, "Si!"

Johnny said, "I think you'll finish pretty quickly now, Phil."

Johnny had one more question. "Hey, Phil, how's Hank doing over there?"

"It's like he's played there his whole life."

Johnny yelled, "Keep it up, Rundle! We'll make a ball player out of you yet!"

Hank tipped his hat. It seemed like he was finally getting it.

In the training room, Frank and Tony were starting their day.

"Okay, Frank, let's start with cardio. Hop on the elliptical machine. We'll ease you into it. Just give me thirty minutes."

"You consider thirty minutes easing into it? I was thinking more like three."

"Frank people a lot older than you can do thirty minutes on this machine with no trouble."

"Great. Let them do it."

Tony pointed to the elliptical. "Get on the damn machine, Frank. We've got a lot of work to do today."

Frank grumbled then started his thirty minutes. It took just five minutes before sweat was pouring out of him like water from a hose.

Tony clapped. "Keep it up, Frank. Only twenty-five minutes left!"

Between heavy breaths Frank found time to respond, "Up yours!"

The thirty minutes felt like twenty hours to Frank. He finished and looked like he'd just run through a car wash.

Tony handed him a towel. "Take five, Frank, and then we'll do the next exercise."

Frank was bent over with his hands on his knees. "There's more?"

Tony just smiled. "Frank, my man, we are just getting started."

Frank looked to the floor and could only say, "Shit."

Next was the inversion table where Frank would do sit ups.

"Okay Frank, I want fifty good ones."

Frank threw up his arms. "Fifty? Are you insane?"

"Drop the drama, Frank."

Three sit ups into the exercise, Frank was huffing and puffing like a chain smoker.

"This is stupid! It's damn stupid!"

"It's stupid that I have to deal with a whiny, fat ass that can't take care of himself for his job too, Frank!"

Frank found a sudden burst of energy from his building rage. He used that head of steam to plow through the rest of his sit ups.

"There. The whiny, fat ass is finished,"

"Maybe that task but you're not done with the workout yet. Take five minutes and we'll continue."

Frank used the time to change his shirt as the one he was wearing felt like it had gone through the washing machine with no spin out.

"I'll take it easy on you, Frank. This time I just want you to take a little walk on the treadmill."

Frank felt some relief until Tony gave him some details.

"You'll do forty-five minutes and I'll set the incline to ten percent."

Frank did a double take. "Wait, incline? What incline?"

"It's only ten percent, Frank. No big deal."

It didn't take long for Frank to feel the burn from his knees down. *This must be how they discipline prisoners*, he thought. The next 45 minutes were no easier than either of his first two tasks. Despite being sore from the knees down, Frank didn't complain. He wouldn't give Tony the satisfaction.

Tony gave Frank a fist pump. "Nice work, Frank. Didn't think you had it in you. Take lunch. I've already had something prepared for you. See you here in thirty minutes."

Frank was starving. He lifted the lid from his lunch and his smile quickly turned into a scowl. Underneath was one boiled chicken breast, a cup of steamed broccoli, and a cup of steamed white rice. Frank started talking to himself.

"How can they ask me to eat this shit? Where's the steak? What about a baked potato with butter? There's not even a damned dinner roll!"

While wondering what happened to the rest of his lunch, Frank noticed a note that read:

Frank,

Johnny and Bernie have given me total control of your diet. You'll have mandatory weigh-ins twice a week. Gain anything and they plan on fining you $1,000 for every pound. We are going to make you a lean, mean, first base machine.

Enjoy!

Tony

Frank was not amused. He didn't appreciate being treated like a child. Just as he was about to flip his tray, he heard someone behind him.

"How's your day going, Frank?" Johnny had stopped by to check on him.

"Uh, fine Coach."

Johnny peered over Frank's shoulder. "Great. Hey, that looks good. Better hurry up and eat though. Don't want you to be late for the second part of your session. Oh and Frank, I mean what Tony put in the note."

Frank muttered something under his breath then finished his rather unsatisfactory lunch.

Tony returned. "Okay Frank, you've fueled the machine. Let's do some weightlifting."

Frank got up from the table. "And by let's you mean me, right?"

Back at the workout room Tony stood between four different weight machines.

"Okay Frank, start with this overhead machine. I want you to do three sets of five at 150 pounds. When you finish that, hit the leg machine. Do three sets of five at 250 pounds. From there, hit the curls machine. Three sets of five at 50 pounds. Finally I want you to come to the bench press machine and do one set of ten at 200 pounds. I'll spot you. Got it?"

Frank's head was spinning and he wondered if his will was up-to-date. "You want me to do all this shit without dying first, right?"

Frank was using muscles he hadn't used in years and he felt it. He struggled through and finished, somehow managing to avoid shuffling off this mortal coil.

Tony said, "Not bad for the first day."

Frank was dripping from every pore in his body. "So I'm done now, right?"

"Not just yet. You've got one more thing to do."

Frank sighed another heavy sigh. "What is it?"

"Just a little bike ride."

Frank found just enough strength to look up at Tony. "How little?"

"Five miles on the stationery and your day with me is over."

Frank shook his head. "Only five miles, huh?"

Frank was certain that Johnny and Tony wanted to kill him. Every push of the pedal was a chore and every muscle in his body hurt when he was done.

"That's enough for today, Frank. Get some rest. Here is a list of meal options for you. We're limiting you to 1,800 calories per day until the end of camp."

"Only 1,800 calories? I usually have that by lunch time!"

"It's all you have, Frank, so get used to it. See you back here tomorrow morning at ten o'clock sharp."

"Tomorrow is an off day."

Tony tapped Frank on the shoulder. "Not for you."

Frank threw down his towel. "This is bullshit."

"It's your own fault, Frank. We'll do some different things. I don't want you getting bored."

Frank bent over to pick up the towel. "No we sure don't want that."

Frank showered and could barely lift his arms to wash his hair. He thought, *How am I ever going to survive this training camp?* Sometime between then and tomorrow, Frank hoped he'd figure it out.

While his teammates enjoyed some down time, Frank's second day of workouts began.

Frank asked Tony, "So, what tortures do you have in store for me today?"

Tony clapped his hands together. "We'll start with some step aerobics."

Frank did a double take. "Step what?"

"Aerobics. We're going to use these steps and some music to get in a cardio workout."

Tony turned on some loud, hard rock music.

"Frank, watch what I'm doing and try to keep up!"

It was difficult for Frank to go move-for-move with Tony. After thirty minutes, he was sweating profusely and was out of breath. He couldn't help but wonder what was next.

"What do you say to tossing the ball around, Frank?"

Frank's eyes lit up. *Finally some baseball, he thought.* "Just let me grab my glove."

"You won't need your glove."

"You want me to play catch without my mitt?"

Tony laughed. "Frank, we are going to toss around a medicine ball."

Frank's eyes opened wide then he slumped. "Oh shit."

Tony threw the medicine ball to Frank with enough force to throw him off balance. He gathered himself and gave Tony a chest pass.

Tony said, "Don't be afraid to throw it hard. I can take it."

"I did throw it hard."

After twenty minutes of tossing, they wrapped up and prepared for the last exercise of the day. Frank was glad his daily torture was almost done.

Tony asked, "Frank, do you have swim trunks with you?"

"Swim trunks?"

"Yeah. We're going to the pool."

Frank grinned. "No, I don't." He hoped it would get him out of swimming. It didn't.

"All right just put on your compression shorts and meet me at the pool."

"Shit, I mean fine. Just give me a minute to change."

Frank hated swimming.

A few minutes later Frank was at the pool.

"Just going to do a few laps today, Frank."

"How many is a few?"

Tony held up both hands. "Ten."

"Just ten? You make it sound like nothing."

Frank dove into the pool to begin his water torture. He stopped after finishing one lap, completely winded.

Tony yelled, "Come on, Frank! Only nine more!"

Frank stopped again after the second lap. Gasping for breath he asked, "Do you know CPR because I'm figuring on drowning sometime before I finish?"

"Just make sure you don't stop in the middle where it's deep, Frank."

Frank got through his laps without drowning. It took every last bit of strength he had to pull himself out of the pool. Tony was waiting.

"Good job, Frank. Rest tomorrow."

Frank dried his hair. "Great idea but we've got a game tomorrow."

Tony handed Frank another towel. "That should be a cake-walk compared to your last two days, right?"

Hank ran a towel over his chest. "Very funny."

Tony explained that Frank was going to work out with him every day that the Pride didn't have a game. Frank was in disbelief.

"So, I have to train with you and practice baseball?"

Tony nodded. "That's what Johnny and Bernie want."

Frank thought, *They are definitely trying to kill me.* He showered, headed to his room, and collapsed on his bed, praying for death to come and soon.

[9]

BACK TO THE GAME

THE START OF THE second exhibition game of the season
neared and Johnny had the team gathered in the locker room for
his usual pre-game talk. Johnny noticed something different about
Derek right away.

"Hey, nice specs!"

"Thanks, Coach. Guess you were right." The player grinned
and shrugged his shoulders, "But now I don't have any excuses for
screwing up out there."

Johnny nodded in agreement and moved on to read off the
lineup for the day. As the team moved out, he noticed Frank looking
uncomfortable.

"Frank, are you all right?"

Frank winced as he moved. "I'm fine. Just need to stretch a bit.
I can play." It was obvious to Johnny that his player was in need
of more than a stretch. After hearing the trainer's report, Frank
had to be feeling that workout plan in every muscle and ligament,
right down to his pinky finger. The coach waved him out to join his
teammates on the field.

In the bullpen, Jake began his warm up tosses. His first warmup pitch bounced short of Ricky and then careened off the backstop. The catcher brought the ball back instead of throwing it.

"What's up, Jake? You're all over the place."

"Yeah. I'm all nervous and anxious."

"Well, just remember what Coach taught you." Ricky slapped his teammate on the shoulder and gently pulled him around, heading for the field.

"Shit! Here we go."

"Time to play ball." Ricky smiled and jogged toward home plate.

After a short walk around the mound to gather himself, it was time for Jake's first hitter of the season. Jake started with two lively fastballs for strikes. Needing just one more strike, Jake decided it was time for a slider. He inconspicuously shifted to the left side of the pitching rubber, wound up and let fly. The pitch broke sharply and nestled itself into Ricky's mitt for a called strike three. Three pitches and one out recorded. Jake was pretty happy with himself.

"Nice start, Jake!" yelled Jimmy from the dugout.

He got the next two outs using just three more pitches. Not too shabby for a guy who was a basket case coming into training camp.

Malcolm batted first for the Pride. Still uncomfortable swinging from the left side, he dropped a bunt down the third base line. Richmond's rookie third baseman was playing deep and had no chance at throwing out Malcolm. It was his first base hit as a left-handed batter.

Miguel also took advantage of the rookie third baseman. He slashed a pitch by the kid, who had moved way in on the infield grass protecting against another bunt. The Pride had runners on second and third with nobody out.

With a chance to give the Pride the lead, Ricky popped up to the catcher, slamming his bat in disgust.

"Hey! Pick up that bat and get over here!" Johnny ordered.

Ricky looked like a little boy who just got yelled at by his father for forgetting to take out the garbage.

"Shake it off and get him next time. You're pressing. Don't."

Frank stepped up to the plate, barely able to move thanks to his workouts. He took three strikes right down the middle for the second out as he was too sore to even think about swinging the bat. Johnny called him over.

"Frank, what gives? Did he fool you that much?"

Frank still wasn't admitting the real reason he didn't swing. "Yeah Coach. He's throwing some nasty stuff today."

A promising inning now had its hopes pinned on Hank. He didn't disappoint, crushing a fastball over the left centerfield wall for a three-run home run. Derek, new glasses firmly in place, followed by smoking a curveball down the right field line for a double. Mark walked but after battling through a nine-pitch at-bat, Greg grounded out weakly to the pitcher ending the inning.

Jake stayed sharp and pitched three innings giving up just one hit and striking out five batters.

Charlie took over pitching duties in the fourth inning with the score still 3-0. Jimmy gestured for Charlie to throw submarine style. Charlie frowned and shook his head.

He threw three pitches using his old style and got ahead in the count, 1-2. On the fourth pitch, Charlie coiled like a snake and fired. It was a submarine-style fastball right across the hitter's knees for a called strike three.

The deception made the difference. Charlie gave Jimmy a wink. For the rest of the inning Charlie mixed in his new delivery with the old and got the next two hitters, one on a ground ball to Hank at third and the other on a pop up to Mark at second.

"You son of a bitch!" Jimmy yelled, a huge grin spread across his face.

"Thought you'd like that, Coach."

Charlie pitched another 1-2-3 inning in the fifth, getting help from Derek who made a beautiful running catch against the fence in foul territory to end the inning.

"Must be the new eyes!" Johnny yelled to Derek as he entered the dugout.

The Pride pushed another run across the plate in the bottom of the inning, but Johnny was concerned about Frank. After he hit a weak ground ball that turned into an inning-ending double play and was noticeably limping as he ran to first, Johnny called him over. "Frank, what the hell is wrong?"

Frank finally confessed.

"It's all that damn exercise, Coach. I feel like shit!"

Johnny burst into laughter. "Take a seat, Frank. As a matter of fact, go hit the whirlpool because you are not done with Tony by a long shot. Hank, grab your first baseman's mitt and take over for Frank."

Charlie pitched another great inning again getting a little help from his defense when Miguel fielded a ball deep in the hole at shortstop and made a fantastic throw to Hank who made a good stretch on his end.

Clark pitched the seventh inning. Johnny wanted to see how he'd do after his 18-pitch outing. Luck was again on his side as he allowed two hard line drives, one at Hank and one at Mark, for the first two outs. Malcolm caught a fly ball hit to the fence in centerfield with his back against the wall to end the inning. Johnny stared at Clark, saying nothing when he got back to the dugout. Clark's luck shifted in the eighth.

The leadoff hitter doubled on an 82 miles per hour fastball, advanced to third when Derek caught a deep fly ball in right field and scored on a sharp single back over the pitcher's mound. The single was followed by a double scorched passed third base putting runners on second and third with one out. Visibly flustered, Clark walked the next hitter on four pitches to load the bases.

"Jimmy, go have a chat with Mr. Wonderful, will you?" Johnny said.

When Jimmy arrived, Clark bellowed at him.

"What the hell do you want?"

"Checking to see how you feel."

Clark clutched the rosin bag. "I feel fine, all right? I'll take care of this."

Clark's next pitch was a fastball down the middle with little velocity behind it. The hitter rifled the ball down the first base line with base-clearing double written all over it. The base runners took off, but Hank made a stunning dive towards the line, coming up with a brilliant catch. He scrambled to his feet and stepped on first base to complete the double play and to get Clark out of the inning.

Johnny said, "Hell of a play, Hank! Hell of a play!"

Johnny gave Clark a stare. "You've got the ninth, too."

Clark hoped to finish the game off without issue. He wouldn't. After getting the leadoff batter to line out to Mark, Clark allowed consecutive doubles that made the score 4-2. The fourth hitter of the inning ripped a single into left field, putting runners on the corners with still just one out. Clark fell behind the next batter, 2-0, before allowing a three-run home run well over the centerfield fence making the score 5-4.

"Should I go out to talk to him again, Coach?" asked Jimmy.

"Nope. This is his mess. I'll talk to him when I think it's time."

Clark took a new ball from the umpire and paced the mound. He couldn't believe that anyone could hit a ball that far against him. Still fuming, Clark threw the next pitch as hard as he could. It plunked the hitter in the rib cage.

"What's that shit, old man?" the young batter yelled.

Clark pointed towards first. "Just take your damn base, punk ass!"

Ricky's previous work experience proved handy as he grabbed the young hitter and walked him towards first base whispering, "He isn't worth it. Just take your base."

With order restored, Clark started the next batter with a curve, which hung in the hitting zone. The left-handed hitter crushed it down the right field line and off of the foul pole giving Richmond a 7-4 lead. Johnny had seen enough and headed to the mound.

"You're done."

"Done for today or done?"

Johnny looked Clark in the eye. "We'll see."

The inning went further south as Richmond scored twice more. The final score was 9-4, Richmond.

Bernie met Johnny for their daily assessment.

"So, Coach, what did you think about today?"

"All right for eight innings."

"Yeah. Clark pretty much sucked, didn't he?"

"He's too stubborn to listen and I don't know if he'll ever change. If he won't listen, I have no use for him."

"Dad, give him one last chance. If he won't listen, I'll talk to Jerry about getting rid of him."

Johnny thought hard about it on the way to the car. "Okay. One more shot to listen but if he doesn't, he has to go."

Bernie agreed. On his trek back to the condo Bernie thought about how to tell Jerry a former all-star pitcher was going to be cut by a guy whose last experience as a manager involved kids who couldn't even drive to the games.

Jimmy was in the parking lot before practice with Clark's miserable outing still fresh in his mind. Clark pulled up in his pickup truck and was headed to the clubhouse.

"Hey Clark, can we talk?"

Clark brushed by Jimmy. "No. Not right now."

Jimmy grabbed Clark by the shoulder. "Let me rephrase that. We need to talk right now."

Clark dropped his equipment bag.

"What the hell would you like to talk about?"

"For starters, your shitty performance yesterday. Do you know what your fastball topped out at yesterday?"

"Probably around 91."

"Your best one clocked at 83."

"Yeah well, the gun's probably busted. I'll be fine once I get stretched out."

"You may not get a chance to stretch out."

Clark got into Jimmy's face. "What the hell does that mean?"

Jimmy pushed back. "It means one more shitty outing like that and you'll be out on your ass."

"Jerry won't let that happen."

"You don't think so? Do you really expect him to stop Bernie from cutting you? He doesn't want to see roster spots wasted on washed up, has-been, thick-headed pitchers like you!"

Clark's face got redder. "Washed up, has-been? What the hell have you ever accomplished? If your buddy wasn't the owner, you'd still be sitting at a desk playing with your shitty little calculator and looking at spreadsheets!"

All the wind came out of Jimmy's sails. Clark was right. Jimmy didn't earn this job. Bernie gave it to him because of a chance meeting at the gym. What had he done to earn this job?

Jimmy calmly said, "If I don't show what I can do, I'm out the door with you. The difference is, I have something else I can do. Baseball is all you've got so you can adapt, stay here and maybe get back to the Majors, or be a horse's ass, keep throwing the same shit and maybe if you're lucky, play in the Independent League as a circus sideshow act."

This was Clark's reality check. He wasn't the same pitcher. The surgery took care of that. Clark took a step back.

"I guess we both have some work to do."

Jimmy held up a baseball in his fingernails. "Are you ready to make a change now?"

Clark looked at his pitching hand.

"How long do I need to let my nails grow?"

Jimmy may have finally gotten respect from the one pitcher he really needed on his side.

It was time to get to work. Jimmy began his instruction. "All right, Clark, first grip the ball like this."

Jimmy showed Clark how to dig nails into the ball as his reinvention began. Clark duplicated the grip and Jimmy continued.

"Now when you release it, you push the ball out with those two fingers. Don't try to overthrow it or the ball will spin. That happens and all you've got is a really bad changeup."

Clark asked Jimmy to throw one for him. Jimmy took the mound and flipped a knuckleball to backup catcher, Alex Golden. It floated and danced its way to the plate finally fluttering across for a strike.

"Nice, but can you do it again?" asked a skeptical Clark.

Jimmy's next one had just as much movement on its path to the plate. Alex snatched at it like a kid snatching at a butterfly with a net, knocking it down just as it crossed the plate for another strike. Jimmy flipped Clark the ball.

"All right, Clark, your turn."

"Here goes nothin." He wound up and threw his first knuckleball, ever. It spun towards the plate and bounced five feet in front of Alex.

"Shit!"

"You didn't expect your first one to be perfect, did you?"

Clark took the throw from Alex. "I didn't expect it to suck."

"You aren't going to learn this pitch in one day."

"It better not take too long, or I'm screwed."

Clark took a deep breath and threw another knuckleball with a similar result. "Damn it all to hell!"

Jimmy tried calming his fledgling knuckle-baller. "You're throwing it like your fastball. Try taking something off the next one."

Clark threw the next one with less velocity. It had more tumble than spin, as it should, but still fell short of the target.

Jimmy said, "All right... better."

Clark glared at Jimmy. "My ass!"

"I told you this isn't going to be a quick thing. You have to work at it. When you figure it out, it's going to be a great addition to your arsenal. It's going to make your fastball look like it did when you were a rookie."

"If it doesn't, I might as well buy a ringmaster's hat."

Clark threw several more knuckleballs. None of them was quite right. Jimmy offered some words of wisdom.

"I know you're used to getting things right away, but it's not happening this time. The sooner you realize that, the sooner you'll be ready to use that thing in a game."

Clark kicked the pitching rubber. "It's so damn frustrating. Not just learning the pitch, but knowing that I have to if I want to have a chance to pitch in the bigs again."

"Clark, it's not how you get there, it's getting there that matters."

Jimmy was concerned that Clark wouldn't get it but at that point Clark's attitude was better and that was a step in the right direction. Jimmy just hoped the attitude adjustment wasn't temporary.

[10]

JERRY CHECKS IN

BERNIE AND HIS FAMILY were sleeping in with the team getting a needed off day. Sleeping in lasted until just past 7:30 when Bernie's phone rang. He fumbled his way out of bed to answer it.

"Hello," he said in a groggy whisper.

"Endino! Jerry Benjamin here! I didn't wake you, did I?" It had been about two weeks since Jerry left camp and headed back to Connecticut.

"Yeah you did, Jerry."

"Aw shit, and I waited an hour to call you, too."

Bernie walked to his coffee machine to make himself a cup. "Well, I'm up now. What's up?"

"How are things going at camp?"

"Fine, Jerry."

"Really? That's not what I'm hearing."

Bernie put cream and sugar into his mug then placed it under the brewing machine.

"Who are you hearing from?"

"Never mind who, Endino. Just tell me what's going on down there."

Bernie's voice volume was rising along with his blood pressure.

"Jerry, unless you tell me what you're hearing and who you are hearing it from, I'm not telling you a damn thing."

"Fine. It's Malcolm Jackson. He tells me you guys don't know what the hell you're doing."

Bernie was shocked. "Well he's wrong—dead wrong. We're making progress. Once the season starts, this team is going to be ready. Mr. Jackson is sorely mistaken."

"You haven't won a damn game yet."

Bernie took his fresh, hot cup of coffee from the machine. "It's freakin' spring training! Calm the hell down!"

Bernie's yelling woke Lizzie. Rachel calmed her and they both entered the kitchen. Rachel was not happy.

"Why are you yelling and who is that on the phone?"

Bernie covered the phone. "I'm sorry. It's Jerry."

Rachel held out her hand. "Give me the phone." She didn't demand often but when she did, Bernie heeded her request. In a voice so sweet it could take the bitter out of your coffee, Rachel addressed Jerry.

"Hello, Jerry. It's Rachel Endino. What is so important that you call us before eight in the morning on a Sunday?"

"Oh...uh, sorry Mrs. Endino. Didn't mean to wake everyone. Just wanted to check on the team."

"The team is fine. My husband and his father are doing a great job. They'll be ready when the season begins in two weeks. If you ever call us again before nine a.m., I will cut off your testicles, put them in a jar and will donate them to science. Got it?"

Jerry dealt with corporate big wigs on a regular basis. Bernie bet that he'd never had a conversation like this.

"Yes, ma'am. It won't happen again. You have my word as a gentleman. May I please speak with your husband again?"

Rachel handed Bernie the phone.

"Quite a lady you have there, Endino."

Bernie looked at his wife, containing his urge to laugh. "She's the best."

"Endino, I hope you aren't screwing with me about the progress of that team, especially my players."

Bernie sipped his coffee. "All the players are doing fine, Jerry."

"If you say so. I just don't want any more bad reports."

"I'll make sure you don't get any."

"Good. See you in a few weeks. I plan on being at your opener."

Bernie hung up the phone. He said to Rachel, "I don't understand how that man thinks."

Rachel gave Lizzie her bottle. "I don't think anyone does."

Bernie needed to call his father.

"What's up, Bern?"

"Enjoying your day off?"

"Yep. Just sitting outside having my coffee."

"Dad, I just got a call from Jerry."

"What did he want?"

"He said he got a call from one of the players that we weren't doing such a good job."

Johnny quickly took a sip of his coffee. "Who?"

It was like Johnny just asked Bernie who dented the car. "Malcolm."

"Damn it. I thought we were making progress with that kid."

"We just need to talk to him to find out what's going on. Let's meet with him before practice tomorrow."

"Probably a good idea."

Bernie heard the dejection in his father's voice. "Dad, don't let it get to you. Things are getting better."

Bernie hung up the phone and turned to get ready for a fun day with Rachel and the girls on the beach and boardwalk. He figured he'd need, it because he didn't expect his meeting with Johnny and Malcolm to be much fun at all.

Johnny said, "Come in and have a seat, Malcolm."

Malcolm still wasn't sure why Johnny brought him in early.

"What's up, Coach?"

"Malcolm, did you call Jerry Benjamin about the coaching staff?"

Malcolm looked up at the ceiling. "Yeah."

Johnny's fatherly side took over the conversation.

"If there's a problem why didn't you just come to me?"

"I didn't think you were listening to me."

"What do you mean by that?"

Malcolm sighed. "I've been telling you for weeks that I can't learn how to hit left-handed but you keep making me do it. You won't let me go back to what I know. All I have to show for it are a couple of bunt singles. I'm a joke up there, Coach, and it's your fault."

This didn't sit well with Johnny. He got out of his chair and leaned over the desk.

"My fault, Malcolm? Last year, from your strong side, you hit .203 and struck out 186 times."

Malcolm got defensive. "At least I hit .203. You aren't even giving me a chance up there with this lefty bullshit!"

Johnny gathered himself, sat down, and made a compromise.

"Malcolm, I'll tell you what. You can hit from the right side again but only when I say it's time. Until then, you're batting from the left side. I really want to get the most out of your speed."

Malcolm was reluctant.

"I want to hit from the right side all of the time. That's what I know, and that's where I'm comfortable."

Johnny got firm.

"You'll try this my way or you'll learn how to sit your ass on both the right and left sides of the bench."

Now Malcolm was pissed. Johnny didn't care. Not happy but not liking the prospects of spending time on the bench Malcolm said, "Fine. I guess I've got no choice, do I?"

"No, you don't, but I'll tell you what, show me you can hit from one side of the plate, any one, and we'll consider letting you bat full time on that side."

Malcolm thought for a second. He shook Johnny's hand. "All right, Coach. You have a deal."

"Good. Oh and Malcolm, no more calls to Jerry? If you have a problem, talk to me. I'm sure Jerry has other things to do."

Bernie thought things went as well as could be expected. Both men hoped that they wouldn't need many of these meetings. This team needed to come together quickly because in two weeks, it would be the real deal.

[11]

Time to Head Home

SPRING TRAINING WAS OVER. The Pride finished it with a 0-15 record. The games meant nothing, but Bernie was still a bit uneasy about not winning one.

Record aside, several good things came out of camp. Mark and Ricky were showing that they could still play, Hank was buying into Johnny's philosophy, and Frank had trained hard and was now, in his own words, "built like a brick shithouse." Also, Derek's new glasses were making a difference and he was becoming a serviceable right fielder. Miguel's transition to shortstop had gone fairly smoothly. Jake's control issues had become a distant memory. Charlie was comfortable with the down under pitching style, using it almost exclusively now. However, things weren't all peaches and cream.

Greg was hitting with all the authority of a Little Leaguer. He had to make better contact if he wanted a starting job with this team. Malcolm's plate issues lasted the entire training camp. He was now considered a switch-hitter but he wasn't doing much hitting from either side of the plate. Johnny's experiment may have done more harm than good. Clark was working hard with the knuckleball but hadn't been effective with it. If he didn't get things figured out, it might be the end of the road for him with the Pride, and possibly his playing days.

There was also a depth problem. Aside from Alex Golden the backup catcher, there weren't any bench players on the roster that gave Bernie or Johnny a great feeling. As for pitching, there was some raw talent but the Pride really needed one more reliable starting pitcher and so far, no one was emerging as a strong candidate.

The regular season was coming whether the Pride was ready for it or not. Somehow, this team had to make it work.

At least the stadium was ready. The parking lot was freshly paved. No more worries about turning an ankle on the gravel pit that was there before. The main entrance was open and bright. It didn't feel like entering the gas chamber any more. The dinginess was gone and a sleek, new exciting venue had taken its place. It was just how Bernie envisioned it.

The opener was almost fourteen hours from first pitch and Bernie was wide awake. He wanted a wonderful new era of baseball to begin. As he went to grab the morning paper from his front porch Bernie couldn't believe what he saw...snow flurries! April snow wasn't all that unusual in Pennsylvania but Bernie wondered why it had to happen today. Who would show up to watch baseball in weather like this? No sense in worrying about it. Bernie just hoped for the best. He decided to read the sports page. The headline read:

Endino Hoping to Bring Pride Back to Local Baseball

That's so cool! he thought. The local players, new uniforms, mascot and stadium renovations were all mentioned. Bernie liked everything right up to the last paragraph:

Bernie Endino hit the lottery. Some people buy yachts, mansions, luxury cars, or planes with that kind of money. Bernie decided his new toy would be a baseball team and so he brought in a bunch of his friends to play with it, as well. Thing is, sometimes you buy a toy that nobody knows how to use and before you know it, they break the thing before anyone figures out that you probably should have left it on the shelf. Maybe Bernie Endino should return this toy to the store while it's still in one piece, because I have a feeling that he and his buddies are going to smash it beyond repair.

Bernie was fuming! Rachel and Lizzie came down the stairs.

"Why are you up so early?" Rachel asked.

"Couldn't sleep. Big day today."

"Do you think they'll still play?"

"Not sure. Depends on how much more of this snow we get."

Bernie couldn't hold it in any longer. He vented to Rachel.

"I can't believe the article in this morning's paper."

Rachel sent Lizzie into the living room. Safely out of ear shot she said to Bernie, "What's the matter?"

He held up the article. "The damn writer ragged on me pretty good. Said I bought the team as a toy and I'll probably break it because I don't know how to play with it. Read the article when you get a chance."

Rachel read it and tried calming Bernie's nerves. She put her arms around Bernie's shoulders.

"Don't worry about the article. They're just trying to sell papers. Just show them you guys know what you're doing on the field."

Bernie knew Rachel was right. Win, and you can prove that those folks at the paper were dead wrong.

While the snow missed the area, it was still mind-numbingly cold as first pitch approached and the game wasn't getting postponed. The opening night opponent was Pride rival, Nantucket, and despite the cold Bernie was expecting a full house.

Bernie stopped by the clubhouse where Johnny was in his office working on the lineup.

"Hey, Dad. Mind if I come in?"

Johnny looked up from his lineup card. "It's your team."

Bernie spun a chair around and sat forward against the back of it. "So, have your lineup figured out for tonight?"

Johnny put the cap on his pen. "Pretty much. Still worried about Malcolm and Greg, though. I may start Freddie in place of one of them."

Freddie was Freddie Martinez. He was a 21-year-old, switch-hitting outfielder who had the rare combination of power and speed. He played with the Double-A team last season and had such an impressive spring training that he made the Pride. Johnny's first difficult decision of the season, and there hadn't been a pitch thrown.

"Well, I'll leave you to it. Going to take a walk around. Oh, had a message from Jerry. He's not going to make the game tonight. Something came up."

Johnny flashed a quick look at Bernie.

"Yeah, I know." Bernie smiled and stood to leave the office. "That was my first thought, too. With no Jerry, it should be a pleasant evening.

"I finished my lineup card." Johnny stood and joined Bernie at the door. I'll walk with you a ways until it's time for the first pre-game talk in the renovated stadium."

"Gather around!" Johnny stood in the locker room calling his players together. "Tonight, our journey starts. At the end of it, we hope to find a championship ring!"

The Coal Barons had only come close to winning a championship once fifteen years ago. They lost the deciding fifth game of the finals against Nantucket on a walk-off, three-run home run that season.

Johnny continued. "Practice what you learned in Florida. Think about the fundamentals. Remember, even if you aren't playing you can make a difference in a game, so watch."

Johnny read off the lineup. He'd gone through the first seven spots and Malcolm's name still hadn't been called.

Johnny looked towards Malcolm. "Martinez, you're hitting eight and will be in left field tonight."

Malcolm gave Johnny a cold stare. It was all he could do to keep from throwing his glove or spewing a string of profanities at his coach.

Johnny wrapped up the lineup telling Jake he was hitting ninth and pitching. His final words were, "All right men, hit the field for warm ups and try not to freeze to death."

Malcolm stayed back while his teammates headed up the tunnel. He stopped Johnny.

"Why, Coach?"

Johnny was direct and firm. "Because right now Freddie is better."

Malcolm could no longer contain himself.

"Yeah well, Greg sucked in Florida too, but he's not being benched!"

"Listen, for now Greg starts and if he can't cut it, I'll sit him. Don't worry. You'll get your chance."

Malcolm continued while saliva formed on the sides of his mouth from his anger.

"It's opening night, and you're benching me for a Double-A kid and some guy who was a damn gym teacher just a few months ago. I can't believe this shit."

Johnny pointed his pen at Malcolm. "Believe it and if you don't change your attitude, you may get your chance to start at Double-A. Now get your ass out there, loosen up, and be ready in case I need you!"

Malcolm angrily grabbed his glove and headed to the field. At that moment, he hated being part of the team.

Johnny knew Malcolm's actions were wrong, but his words made Johnny think. Was he favoring his old players?

He felt the temperature drop the instant he walked into the open air. It was getting colder as the thermometer on the outfield scoreboard read 36 degrees. Johnny hoped this temperature was the low point for the night.

It was tradition to have every player step onto the field and line up on the foul line for opening night. The PA booth was playing *Takin' Care of Business* over the speaker system. The players and the coaches were announced then finally the announcement everyone in the luxury suite was waiting to hear.

"And now your new Pride manager, Johnny Endino!"

Johnny stepped onto the field, shaking the hands of his coaches and players. Not even the argument with Malcolm could dampen his spirits. This was the moment he'd dreamt about for weeks. He took his spot on the foul line, and unable to contain his excitement, removed his cap, exposing his balding head, and waved it to the crowd then directly to the press box and then to his family in the luxury suite.

"Poppie!" yelled Anna.

Cold as it was, they had the windows open and Johnny heard his granddaughter call out. He didn't need to be there to know what his family would be saying.

"Yep, that's your Poppie."

"Look at him. He looks so happy."

"This is where he belongs."

Johnny turned back to his team and sent them from the lineup to their dugout with one last wave of his hat. It was finally time to start.

Jake's first pitch was a slider, followed by two fastballs. The last one was letter-high that the batter swung at and missed. A three-pitch strikeout to start the season! A pop fly to Mark and another strikeout later, the inning ended.

Greg was the first hitter of the regular season for the Pride. He stepped into the batter's box feeling tense and anxious. He'd never played in front of a crowd this big. His anxiousness got the best of him as he popped out to third base on the first pitch. Johnny noticed Malcolm in the corner of the dugout shaking his head.

Jake was brilliant through five innings, allowing just two hits while striking out seven batters. Nantucket's pitcher was equally brilliant, giving up just a seeing eye single by Miguel. Jake got the first two hitters of the sixth inning easily. With two outs and nobody on base it looked like another easy inning for Jake but he walked the Nantucket second hitter in the lineup after a great, ten-pitch battle.

"How many pitches is he at?" Johnny asked Jimmy.

Jimmy looked at his chart. "That last one makes it eighty-two."

"Have Charlie warm up. He's going in soon."

With his instructions given, Johnny headed out to talk with Jake and Ricky.

"Whadda ya think, Ricky?"

Ricky knew Jake was tiring, but as the new kid on the team, he was afraid to say so. Jake chimed in, "Still plenty left in the tank."

Johnny looked at Ricky, who remained quiet, then tapped Jake on the back. "All right go get this guy."

Jake wiped the sweat from his brow. How he was sweating on such a cold night was unfathomable. He took a sign from Ricky and threw a slider that bit too hard. It broke down and in to the batter, hitting him on the ankle putting runners on first and second with two outs.

Johnny said, "Think Charlie's ready yet, Jimmy?"

"Not yet, Coach. Probably needs a few more pitches, especially in this cold."

Johnny felt uneasy and the fact that Nantucket's cleanup hitter, Bryan Fowler, was batting didn't help matters. Fowler was Nantucket's best hitter and he was coming off of a monster season. Jake's first two pitches to him missed outside. Ricky called for a changeup but Jake shook him off. He also shook off Ricky's call for a slider. He wanted his fastball against Ricky's better judgment. Fowler's eyes got wide.

He swung and connected. The ball soared high and deep over the left field fence for a three-run home run, giving Nantucket the lead.

"Shit!" Jake yelled, taking a new ball from the umpire.

Johnny echoed the sentiment and headed to the mound. Taking the ball, Johnny said, "Good job, Jake. My bad. Should have gotten you out of here sooner."

While Charlie made his way in from the bullpen, Johnny asked Ricky, "Why didn't you tell me he was out of gas?"

Ricky looked to the ground and spit. "I didn't want to piss him off."

Johnny looked Ricky dead in the eyes. "Do you think allowing a three-run home run made him happy?"

Ricky hung his head.

Charlie's new side winding style managed to keep Nantucket in check for their next three innings. The game headed to the bottom of the ninth, the Pride still trailing 3-0.

Charlie was scheduled to bat first in the ninth. Malcolm was sure he'd be called on to pinch hit, so he picked up his helmet and bat.

"Joey, grab a bat! You're hitting for Charlie!" Johnny yelled. Joey was Joey Phillips, a backup infielder who made the team in spring training.

Malcolm dropped his bat and helmet hard. Johnny again ignored the mini tantrum.

Joey took the first pitch for a called strike, then swung and missed badly at the next two for the first out. Malcolm stared at Johnny from the corner of the dugout.

Greg hit a weak grounder to the pitcher for the second out. It was up to Miguel to keep the game alive. Miguel put up a great 13-pitch battle and worked a walk. Ricky followed and wasted no time, swinging at the first pitch and rapping it into the left centerfield gap for a double that scored Miguel from first base.

It was now 3-1 with Hank due up. Nantucket's pitcher wasn't letting the Pride's best hitter beat him. Hank walked on four pitches. Runners were on first and second and Frank came to bat as the potential winning run. He got a good pitch and crushed a line drive down the left field line. Ricky scored, cutting the lead to 3-2. Hank ended up on third while Frank strolled into second with a double. Now the winning run stood on second base. Johnny hollered, "Malcolm, run for Frank!"

Malcolm had mentally checked out of this game a while ago—hot about not starting and not being asked to pinch-hit. Startled, he grabbed his helmet and headed to second base, still focused on his sulking.

Derek took ball one. Malcolm led away from second, but he was not focused on the game. The next pitch to Derek was high for ball two. Now Malcolm was talking to himself while taking his lead.

How could he not start me? I could have done a better job pinch-hitting than that rookie. This is bullshit!

While Malcolm thought about how he'd been wronged, the Nantucket pitcher noticed how far Malcolm had strayed from second base. He wheeled and threw. Before Malcolm could react, he was tagged out to end the game.

A dejected Pride team left the field for the warmth of the clubhouse. Johnny was the last one to get there.

"All right gentlemen, not the start we wanted, but good effort. You guys didn't quit and we had a chance to win. Season's just starting. Shower, warm up and we'll get 'em tomorrow. Malcolm, in my office after you're showered and dressed."

Several minutes later, Malcolm showed up at Johnny's office door.

"Malcolm, sit down and close the door please."

Malcolm slumped into the chair across from Johnny.

"Malcolm, sit up. I've had enough of your pouty bullshit."

Malcolm was getting a lecture, like it or not.

"Malcolm, if you don't wise up, you can bet you won't see the field again for a long time."

Malcolm stood up, pushing his chair back hard.

"You started your guy instead of me. You used the Double-A call up to pinch-hit instead of me. Looks like I don't stand a chance at playing much, anyway."

Johnny then got up, both hands on his desk. "Is that what you think, Malcolm? Do you think I'm playing favorites or have something against you?"

Malcolm crossed his arms. "Sure looks that way."

Johnny picked up a piece of paper. "You didn't start tonight because Nantucket started a tough right-hander, one you were 1-21 against with 11 strike outs in your career. Know why I didn't call on you to pinch-hit? Because Joey is left-handed and he put the ball in play a lot more than you did this spring...a lot more. Is that enough for you?"

Malcolm stared at the paper in Johnny's hand and could only muster, "Whatever."

Johnny felt like he was talking to a 10-year-old.

"Smarten up, Malcolm. I've got enough to deal with here without your attitude problem."

"Can I go now?"

"Yeah, go. Get out of here. Think about what I said. You might want to put more work into your game than your pouting, as well."

Johnny locked his office and headed out to his car where Bernie was waiting.

Bernie said, "Almost had 'em."

"Yep, almost. Hey, where is everyone else?"

Bernie blew on his hands. "They left. Everyone was cold and tired but they were all proud of you."

"I still haven't managed to win a game yet. What's there to be proud of?"

"Stop it, Dad. Just stop it."

"When I win a game, I'll stop it."

Bernie was cold and tired too. He wasn't up for a fight. "I learned long ago not to challenge you when you're being this stubborn."

"Good. Glad you've learned something. Let's go home and get out of this cold. I've got to do this again tomorrow and it had better be warmer."

Bernie looked back at the stadium. "Guess I should have had Jerry put a dome over this place. See you tomorrow night, Dad."

Despite the loss, the night was successful. Johnny had some things to work out and Bernie was going to give him plenty of time to do it.

A tough opening night loss was followed by two more losses to Nantucket by scores of 8-1 and 6-2. Johnny's talk with Malcolm didn't seem to take as he continued sulking and not working. Jerry was finally going to see his first Pride game of the season. While Johnny worked on his lineup, Bernie stopped in. Johnny had a question for him.

"Hey, Bern, let me ask you something. Do you think I'm favoring my old players?"

Bernie countered with a question of his own. "Do you think you have better guys sitting on the bench?"

Johnny thought about it, pointed his pen at Bernie and winked.

"Thanks, Bern."

Bernie arrived at the luxury suite to find Rachel and the girls as well as a guest.

"Hey, Endino! It's about time you showed up!" Jerry was on the floor playing with the kids.

"Hi, Jerry. Good seeing you."

Jerry put down the blocks he was playing with. "So, think they'll do something different and win for a change?" Bernie was not amused by Jerry's tone but with his kids there, he was holding his tongue.

In the clubhouse, Johnny was giving his pre-game talk.

"Okay, gentlemen, over here please! New day. Let's put the last three behind us and stay focused. The wins will come..."

Johnny noticed Malcolm wearing ear buds underneath his cap. He said nothing but took the lineup card in his left hand then took the cap off the pen in his right hand. Staring at Malcolm, Johnny drew a line on the lineup card and quickly wrote on it. He mixed up the lineup for the game, hoping for a change. As he got to the eighth spot in the lineup, Johnny focused on Malcolm and read, "Greg, you're in center today."

Malcolm ripped out his ear buds and put his phone back in his locker. He knew he'd blown another chance but still felt no responsibility. It was clear that, in Malcolm's mind, Johnny was playing favorites again.

Clark finished his warm up tosses without throwing a knuckleball. He started Nantucket's leadoff hitter with a curveball for strike one and followed it with a changeup for the second strike. Jimmy was expecting a knuckleball from his pitcher, but Clark threw his curveball instead. It hung in the strike zone and the Nantucket hitter turned it into a leadoff double. Jimmy just shook his head. Clark's first pitch to the next batter was an 84 mile per hour fastball that got tagged off of the centerfield wall for another double. Four pitches into the game, it was already 1-0, Nantucket.

In Bernie's suite, Jerry remarked, "Geez, Gresham's got nothing out there."

Clark took a signal from Alex Golden, who was catching to give Ricky a rest. He called for a knuckleball, but Clark shook him off in favor of his changeup. It just sat in the strike zone as if on a tee. The ball left a vapor trail, landing over the left field wall for a home run and a 3-0 Nantucket lead.

Jerry quipped, "Three runs and five pitches. Well, at least he's efficient in his ineffectiveness."

Jimmy strolled to the mound to talk with his pitcher.
"What are you doing out here?"
Clark kicked some dirt around the mound. "What are you talking about?"
"Why won't you throw the knuckleball?"
Clark stared at Jimmy. "Jimmy I'll look like a joke if I start throwing that thing for real."
"Would you rather come out here and get your ass handed to you for a few innings every time you pitch? Listen, if you want a chance at getting back to the big leagues, this, is your best chance. It's either use the knuckleball or be done playing baseball."
Deep down Clark knew Jimmy was right. "All right, I'll start using the knuckleball."
Fowler stepped in to face Clark. Taking Jimmy's advice, Clark started him with a knuckleball and it was a beauty. It danced to the plate and dove away from Fowler as he swung and missed. Fowler looked towards the mound almost in disbelief. Jimmy's next knuckleball approached the plate and looked like it would hit Fowler before it floated across the inside corner of the plate for strike two. Fowler gripped the bat tightly and readied himself for the next

pitch. Jimmy stayed with the knuckler. It was tantalizing to Fowler as it approached belt high, right in his power zone. Fowler swung, expecting to launch the baseball into orbit. At the last second the ball dipped near his ankles for the third strike. Jimmy stood in the dugout pleased.

His confidence building, Clark started the next hitter with a fastball. He swung well after Alex caught it. Clark threw another fastball, catching the hitter off guard for strike two. In his entire life, Clark never thought it would be his fastball catching hitters off guard. Down 0-2 in the count, the batter believed the next pitch must be the knuckleball. Clark instead stayed with his fastball. Despite it being clocked at only 83 miles per hour, it was fast enough to get by a hitter looking for a 60 miles per hour knuckleball. Clark was in a groove. A first pitch knuckleball to the next batter was popped up to Miguel. After allowing three runs on five pitches, Clark was out of the inning seven pitches later.

Jerry's face actually brightened. "Well I'll be damn...uh darned. The old man learned a new trick."

With one out in the bottom of the second, Frank stepped in to bat. Jerry asked, "Who's that?"

Bernie said, "Frank Carlson."

"Carlson? That can't be Carlson. Carlson's...well, fat."

"He was fat, Jerry. We had him on a training program in Florida."

"Holy shit...Shitake mushrooms!" Jerry caught himself, remembering young ears were present. "He looks like a real athlete!"

Almost as soon as Jerry got the words out of his mouth, Frank hit a majestic home run over the left field fence to cut the Nantucket lead to 3-1.

Jerry nodded. "Not bad. Not bad at all."

Finding new life by embracing the knuckleball as part of his repertoire, Clark pitched six more scoreless innings, allowing just two hits. Unfortunately, the Pride couldn't put together any offense either and they trailed 3-1 as the game moved to the bottom of the eighth. With his spot in the batting order due up, Clark knew his day was done. He just wished he hadn't been so stubborn when the night began.

Greg popped up a bunt to the pitcher to start the inning. In his first 16 at-bats of the season he had collected just one hit. Johnny called on Joey to pinch-hit for Clark with no reaction from Malcolm. At this point he figured his only chance at playing would be if the entire team pulled a hamstring. Joey managed to draw a walk however Freddie struck out. It was Mark's job to keep the inning alive and for a moment it looked like he would. He hit a line drive towards the left centerfield gap. If it fell, Joey would score easily from first. Nantucket's centerfielder, however, had other plans. He got a great jump and made a diving catch, saving a run and ending the inning.

"Shit!" yelled Jerry from the suite.
"Hey! There are kids here!" Rachel yelled back.
Instinctively protecting his crotch, Jerry apologized.
"Sorry, ma'am. Lost my head there for a minute."

Johnny called upon team newcomer, Christian Perez to pitch the ninth. The left-hander stood 6'6" tall and threw hard. Christian's biggest problem was that he didn't have a solid pitch to complement the fastball. He struck out the first two hitters of the inning, dominating with the fastball. He fell behind the third hitter 3-1. Not wanting to issue the walk, he took something off of his fastball and threw a strike that got far too much plate. It got deposited over the centerfield fence for a home run and put the Pride behind 4-1 heading into the last of the ninth.

After Derek grounded out to second base starting the inning, Hank stepped in and drove a frozen rope over the fence in left centerfield. The Nantucket lead was now just 4-2.

"Rundle's looking great," said Jerry.

"Ever since my dad sat him down and set him straight, he's been fantastic." Bernie said.

Now rattled, the Nantucket pitcher walked Frank, bringing the tying run to the plate. The Nantucket manager decided it was time to bring in his hard-throwing closer, Sam Bowers.

Miguel was the first to face Bowers. The first pitch soared over the catcher's head and Frank took second. Miguel caught the Nantucket third baseman napping, dropping down a perfect bunt for a base hit and moving Frank to third.

Johnny's managerial wheels were turning. "Ricky, grab a bat! You're hitting for Alex!"

Ricky stepped to the plate as the potential winning run. He was looking for a fastball and got one. With a mighty swing Ricky slammed the ball into deep centerfield. It had 'game-winning home run' written all over it but again, the Nantucket centerfielder made a great play, reaching over the fence to make the catch. Miguel scrambled back to first base barely beating the throw. Frank had alertly tagged up and scored to cut the Nantucket lead to 4-3 but the Pride was down to its final out.

"Son of a...!" began Jerry before catching himself and avoiding Rachel's wrath.

The hopes of keeping the game alive rested on Greg's shoulders. He quickly fell behind in the count 0-2, looking bad in the process.

"Geez, this guy sucks!" Jerry said.

"Jerry, you're language!" Bernie yelled.

"I said sucks. That's not a curse!"

At that point, a miracle might be the only chance for keeping the game alive. The miracle came on the next pitch as Bowers threw a slider that bit a bit too hard and hit Greg on his right foot. Greg crumbled to the ground as Johnny and the trainer rushed to check on him.

"I'm fine, really," Greg said.

The trainer did a quick exam of Greg's ankle. "Looks like just a bruise."

"Sure you are all right?" Johnny asked

Greg got to his feet. "Fine. Don't worry about it. I can run."

With two on, two out and down a run, Johnny needed a pinch-hitter for Christian. His choices were light-hitting utility man, Mike Dillon or Malcolm.

Johnny looked to the end of the bench. "Malcolm, are you ready to hit?"

Malcolm somewhat surprised, grabbed his bat and a helmet. "Always."

"All right. Bowers is a right-hander, so I want you hitting from the left side."

Malcolm dropped his shoulders. "The left side?"

"I need that extra step for when you put the ball in play. Hit from the left."

Malcolm wasn't happy. Neither was Jerry.

"What the Hell is he doing?"

Rachel, in a very calm voice, said, "Mr. Benjamin, I've heard enough of your swearing today in front of my kids. Either cut it out or get out." This was Jerry's stadium. He could say and do anything he wanted. "Sorry again, ma'am. Tough habit to break."

Malcolm took a fastball for strike. He stepped out of the box, still pissed off that he was hitting from the left side. The next pitch was a slider and again Malcolm took it for a strike.

Johnny yelled some encouragement from the dugout.

"Protect the plate, Malcolm! Big hitter here!"

Malcolm thought, *All right, if you want to play you're going to have to do it Johnny's way. Focus!*

Malcolm managed to foul off a slider to stay alive. Bowers stretched and both Miguel and Greg broke from their bases. It was a double steal! Bowers bounced a fastball in front of the catcher and both runners advanced safely. It was now a 1-2 count on Malcolm, with the tying and winning runs in scoring position.

Bowers quickly grabbed the rosin bag then tossed it away slightly frustrated. His next pitch was a fastball over the outside corner of the plate. Malcolm hit a high chopper towards third. Greg crossed the plate as the third baseman fielded the ball and threw to first. Malcolm appeared to arrive at the bag just ahead of the throw. The umpire yelled, "Out!"

Malcolm turned to argue but Johnny was already in the umpire's face.

"What the hell kind of call is that? Did you even see the play? How the hell can you call him out? This is bullshit, complete and total bullshit! No way he's out! No damn way!"

Johnny continued his rant to no avail. Instead of a tie game with runners on the corners, the game was over and the Pride was 0-4 to start the season.

Johnny put his arm around Malcolm and walked off the field telling him, "You beat it. You were safe." Johnny next got loud enough for the umpire to hear. "You were robbed and that umpire is the damn thief!"

"You're gone, Endino!" yelled the umpire.

Johnny turned around. "The game is over, genius."

Malcolm suppressed a laugh.

In the clubhouse, Malcolm thanked Johnny for defending him.

Johnny said, "That's my job. Are you ready to start doing yours?"

Malcolm nodded then said. "Yeah, I'm ready."

In Bernie's suite, Jerry headed out the door but before leaving he turned. "Tough one today, Endino. I think we got screw...uh robbed."

Bernie shrugged. "Things happen. One of these may go in our favor down the road."

Jerry buttoned his coat. "I'm heading out, Endino. I'll give you a call soon. I like what I'm seeing here. Tell your dad to keep doing what he's doing...well, he can win one once in a while."

After his family left, Bernie chatted with Johnny in his office.

"Hey, Dad, rough one today."

Johnny said, "We got screwed."

"Yeah I think Malcolm was safe too."

Johnny sat back in his chair.

"Are we ever going to win a game?"

"Yes, you'll win a game. Heck, you could easily have two wins already."

"At least we're done with Nantucket for a little while. Maybe we can turn it around against Utica."

Bernie knew that once the team broke into the win column, things would keep getting better.

[12]

HAVE TO WIN SOMETIME

JOHNNY HAD MANAGED NINETEEN games as a professional and his team was still winless. He wanted that to change; he needed that to change.

While he was working on his lineup for the night's game, Greg came to Johnny's office door on crutches.

"Hey, Coach. Looks like I'll be out of commission for a few days. The foot swelled up like a balloon last night. Nothing serious but the doctor wants me to ice and rest it for about a week."

Johnny raised his eyes to the ceiling for a second. "We'll have to make due without you. Just do what the doctor told you."

Johnny didn't need this right now. The team was struggling and now he'd be a man short for at least a week. What other shit can happen?

Game time approached and Johnny gathered the team. Reading off the lineup, Johnny got to the eighth spot.

"Greg's going to be out for about a week. Malcolm, you'll be in centerfield tonight. Just bat from whatever side makes you feel more comfortable tonight, all right?"

These were the words Malcolm had wanted to hear for months.

It was Jake's turn in the rotation and he was off to a good start, throwing a slider for a strike. He'd come a long way since spring training. If not for one bad pitch in the opening game, he may already have a win under his belt. He was sharp early, putting down Utica down in order. He continued to mow down Utica batters and was perfect through the first three innings.

Finally, with one out in the fourth Jake had a little trouble when he allowed a double just beyond Frank's dive and down the first base line. A bit rattled, he walked the next batter, putting runners on first and second base with only one out. His first pitch to the next Utica hitter was a slider that didn't break like he wanted it to. Utica's batter smashed the ball by Jake.

It looked like a certain single into centerfield but Mark wasn't about to let that happen. Shading slightly towards the second base bag, Mark dove for the ball. In one brilliant move, he fielded it in the webbing of his glove and flipped it to Miguel covering second base. Miguel caught the ball in his bare hand and, while doing a pirouette that would have awed Baryshnikov, he fired a strike to Frank, completing a remarkable double play to end the threat and the inning.

It was the spark the team needed. Freddie led off the bottom of the fourth inning with a sharp single to centerfield. After Miguel bunted him to second, Ricky ripped a 2-0 pitch by the diving Utica third baseman for a run-scoring single. Hank followed with a single putting two on and one out for Frank. After falling behind in the count, 2-0, the Utica pitcher grooved one right over the heart of the plate. Frank launched it deep into the night for a three-run home run and the Pride's lead had swelled to 4-0.

Over the next four innings, Jake was dominant allowing no runs and just one hit. The Pride headed to the ninth inning with the 4-0 lead intact.

Johnny let Jake start the ninth inning, but just in case, Charlie was warming up in the bullpen. Jake caught a break when the leadoff hitter hit a hard, one-hopper right to Frank for the first out. After walking the next batter, Jake paced around the mound. His first pitch to the next hitter was a fastball but his velocity had fallen off since the game began. The hitter drove the ball into the right field corner for a run-scoring triple. The lead was now 4-1 with a runner on third and one out.

Charlie still wasn't ready. Johnny hoped Jake had enough to battle through for at least one more hitter. Knowing that his fastball had lost velocity, Jake started the next hitter with his slider. It had no break and the batter crushed a towering drive to deep centerfield. Malcolm turned tail and ran full tilt towards the wall. As he hit the warning track, he glanced aside to see how close he was to the wall, then planted his right foot into the padding and jumped as high as he could. The ball descended into the pocket of his glove. It was an amazing catch! The runner scored from third base but now there were two outs and the Pride still lead, 4-2. Johnny went to the mound.

"How are you doing, Jake?"

Jake knew he had nothing left yet still wanted to finish.

"Feeling great. I can get this last out."

Johnny turned to Ricky. "What do you think?"

Ricky glanced at Jake. "He's done for today."

Johnny took the ball from Jake and called for Charlie. Walking off of the mound, Jake snapped at Ricky, "Thanks, Pal."

Jake didn't go into the clubhouse. He sat in the dugout stewing over being taken from the game.

Charlie started with two sidearm fastballs. The batter wasn't fooled by either one, but hit both just foul passed Hank at third. He hadn't been great, but Charlie was only a strike away from finishing off the Pride's first win of the year. Charlie chose a changeup for his 0-2 pitch. It proved to be the right choice as the batter popped it up into centerfield. Malcolm camped under it making the catch for the final out and clinching not just the Pride's first win of the season, but Johnny's first win as a professional manager. As a jubilant team of Pride players left the field, Malcolm came over to Johnny and handed him the ball.

"This belongs to you, Coach." Johnny gave Malcolm a pat on the back on their way back to the clubhouse.

Johnny's post-game address had a tone different from any of his previous blistering recaps.

"Gentlemen, nice job today. I told you if you just stuck with what you knew, the wins would come. Hopefully, this is just the start. Let's keep working and getting better. Shower up, head home, and get some rest. We've got to do it all over again tomorrow night."

The clubhouse had a happy feel to it, happier than it had been since spring training. Amidst the happiness however, Johnny noticed that Jake was still sulking.

"Jake, come into my office for a minute."

Jake's got up from the stool in front of his locker and sulked his way into the office.

"What's wrong?" Johnny asked.

Jake hollered, "Ricky sold me out!"

"Calm down, Jake. How do you figure he sold you out?"

"I could have finished that game and he told you I was done!"

"Jake, he was saving your ass, not selling you out. You had nothing left. You know it, and I know it. Did you want to risk losing that game?"

Jake looked up at the ceiling then down at the floor. He realized now how stupid he just sounded.

Johnny imparted some wisdom.

"You might want to go and thank your catcher for making sure you got out of there with your first win of the season."

As Jake began to leave he looked to Johnny. "You might want to thank him, too."

Right after Jake left, Bernie came into the office beaming. "Finally got that off of your shoulders."

"Yeah, whadda ya know? The old man gets a win."

"The first of many, Dad."

Johnny held up a finger. "One at a time, Bern. One at a time."

Everyone was gone, but Johnny decided to stick around for a little longer. He sat back in his chair holding the game ball, commemorating the win. He was holding tightly just like he planned on doing with the memories of the night. A tear formed in the corner of his eye as he thought to himself, *Holy shit! I really did it!*

The good feeling of getting that first win was short-lived. April saw some bright spots, but they were spread out and not coming often enough. After taking a weekday afternoon 8-3 loss in Raleigh, the Pride carried a 10-17 record into May. The team was already eight games out of first place and dead last in the Northern Division.

With May 1st being an off day, the team stayed in a little town named Holly Springs the night before traveling to Athens, Georgia for their next series. Johnny and his coaching team, Phil, Art, and Jimmy, grabbed some dinner in town and headed back to the hotel. Along the way they spotted a baseball game.

"It's early. Let's watch for a bit," Johnny said.

The four men grabbed a seat on the metal bleachers. It was a local adult baseball league, something Johnny and his coaches hadn't seen in quite a while. It was the third inning and the score was 3-0 in favor of the Bats whose opponent for the day was the Dirt Devils.

The Bats' pitcher took the mound. He stood 6'5" and was a tower of muscle. The batter stepped in and the pitcher rocked and fired.

It was a fastball that hit the catcher's mitt before the batter could even think about swinging. He threw a second fastball that got a swing from the batter, who was nowhere close to actually making contact. Ahead 0-2 in the count, this big muscle of a pitcher dropped a curveball over the outside corner for strike three. Johnny looked at his coaches with a raised eyebrow. They all wanted to see more.

Geared up for a fastball, the next batter was well into his swing when he realized that a changeup was heading his way. To say he looked foolish was an understatement.

"Shit, this kid can pitch!" Jimmy said.

Johnny had an idea.

"Jimmy, do you have a camera on your phone?"

Jimmy pulled out his phone. "Yeah."

"Film this kid, will ya?"

The four coaches stayed for the rest of the game as the kid continued mowing down the Dirt Devils. He pitched all nine innings, striking out fifteen batters and tossing a perfect game. As icing on the cake, he also collected two hits on the night including a double in the Bats' 7-0 win.

Johnny said, "I have to talk to this kid. Jimmy, can you send that video to Bernie?"

Jimmy sent Bernie a text with the video. It read:

Bernie,
Your dad wants you to see this. What do you think of the kid?
Jimmy

Within a few minutes, Bernie texted back:

Get him!

Johnny walked to the Bats dugout and found the team manager.

"Coach, my name is Johnny Endino. I manage a Triple-A team in Pennsylvania. What's the name of the kid who pitched tonight?"

"Pleased to meet you, Mr. Endino. That's Luke Simms. Best player in this league. He's already pitched two no-hitters this season. Tonight's was better, though. Last game he walked a guy."

"Would you mind sending him over here?"

The Bats' coach yelled out, "Luke! Guy over here wants to talk to you!"

Luke strolled over to his manager and Johnny.

"Luke, this here is Mr. Endino. Says he's a manager for a team up North."

Johnny stuck out his hand. "Son, it's a pleasure to meet you. You're a heck of a pitcher."

Luke shook Johnny's hand with a strong, firm grip. "Thank you, sir."

Johnny started his line of questions.

"Son, how old are you?"

"I'm twenty-two, sir."

"And where did you go to college?"

"Didn't go to college. Went to work with my dad right after high school. He runs a repair shop in town. We fix stoves, refrigerators. Stuff like that."

"Son, why aren't you pitching for a pro team?"

Luke wiped his sweaty brow. "Mr. Endino, my dad was forty when I was born. He's run a shop in this town for thirty-five years. He works sixteen hour days, five days a week and another eight on Saturdays. Heck, if someone really needs him, he'll work Sundays, too. My mom passed away four years ago. That business and me are all he's got. I can't leave him to play baseball."

Johnny heard the words but also heard regret in Luke's voice.

"Luke, do you mind if I talk to your father? I think you have a future in baseball and I'd hate to see you miss out on a great chance."

"He'll be by in a few minutes to pick me up. I suppose you can talk to him then."

It wasn't long before Paul, Luke's father, pulled up in his store van. Luke knocked on the driver side window.

"Dad, there's a man here from a professional baseball team. He wants to talk to you about me."

Paul said, "Baseball? You're a repair man, not a baseball player."

"Dad, please just talk to him, all right? He thinks I can play pro ball."

Reluctantly, Paul shut off the car and got out.

"Nice to meet you, Mr. Simms. I'm Johnny Endino. I think your son here can pitch for us."

Paul shook Johnny's hand. "My son repairs appliances, Mr. Endino. I don't mind him playing baseball around here after work, but he's going to take over the business someday, and he can't learn the business if he's off chasing some long-shot dream of playing professional baseball."

Johnny saw the disappointment in Luke's face. He persisted.

"Mr. Simms, no disrespect to you but Luke's a grown man. Why don't you let him make the decision?"

Paul furrowed his brow. "My boy is a repair man and he's going to stay here and learn my business."

Johnny nodded. "I understand. It's just a shame that Luke won't get to share his talents with anyone outside of Holly Springs."

Paul said nothing. Johnny gave up. He shook Luke's hand again. "It was nice to meet you. Good luck to you, son. You really do have one hell of an arm."

Johnny reconvened with his coaches.

"Let's go."

"What's the story with the kid?" asked Coach Phil.

"No story. He's not interested. His dad says he's a repair man, not a baseball player."

Before Luke and Paul left the parking lot, Luke stopped his dad.

"Dad, I don't want to see you kill yourself in that shop and I don't know if I want to take it over."

The revelation stunned his father.

"You have to take over when it's time. I've run the business for thirty-five years. This town needs us."

"Dad, this town will do just fine without us. Let me try baseball. If I'm as good as these guys say, you won't have to worry about money ever again. I can take care of you."

Paul finally saw how much this chance meant to Luke. "Go. Chase your dream. If it doesn't work out, I'm always here for you."

Luke's eyes glistened. "Thanks, Dad. I'm going to make you proud of me."

The two men hugged.

Paul said, "You'd better tell them. Hurry!"

Luke ran through the parking lot where he saw the coaches in the distance. "Mr. Endino! Mr. Endino, wait! I've changed my mind! I want to play!"

Johnny and his coaches stopped in their tracks. Luke caught up to them and Johnny said, "Good to have you along, son. Our bus leaves tomorrow morning at ten. Meet us in the hotel lobby by 9:30. We have to take care of some paperwork and things before you can play, but you should be pitching for us by next week."

Luke beamed. "I'll be there by nine, Mr. Endino and don't worry. Whenever you want me to pitch, I'm ready."

In Pennsylvania, Bernie had some work to do, even though it was 10:30 at night. He dialed Jerry. After five rings, a groggy voice on the other end of the phone said, "Hello? Who is this?"

Bernie was amused that he'd woken Jerry up for a change.

"Jerry, it's Bernie. Listen, I have a kid that you need to sign."

"Sign? What kid? Why am I signing him? What the hell are you babbling about, Endino?"

Bernie explained what his dad and the other coaches had watched.

"So what? The kid can get guys out in a pickup league full of has-beens and never-will-bes. Why the hell should I spend any money on him?"

"Jerry, I have video. I'm sending it to you right now. Fire up your computer and watch it."

"Don't tell me what to do, Endino."

"Jerry, please just watch."

"Fine. I'll watch it later."

"No, you have to watch it now. The kid will be on a bus to Athens with the team tomorrow."

Jerry was now fully awake. "Hold on a minute. Why is he already riding with the team?"

"Because I told my father to bring him."

"Oh you did? Endino, you may own that team but I still own the Major League one you know, the one that pays the player salaries."

"Jerry, once you see the video, I'm sure you'll want the kid."

"All right, I'll watch it now but God help you if I don't like what I see."

Bernie sent the video and waited anxiously on the phone. After several minutes, Jerry said, "All right, I watched. Give the kid a contract through the season, but I'm only paying him the league minimum for now, got it?"

"You won't regret this, Jerry."

"Endino, right now the only regret I have is selling you that team. Good night."

With his pitcher in place, Bernie called Johnny with the good news.

"Bern, if this kid can throw for us like he did for his pick up league team, we may have just solved our pitching rotation problem. He can potentially be our ace."

"Get some rest, Dad. Four game set against Athens coming up."

"I will. I have to call your mother in the morning anyway. Wish she were here to celebrate. Kiss the kids for me too. I miss them."

To be honest, Bernie hadn't thought about this part of the job. As the owner, he could choose if and when he traveled. Johnny couldn't. It prompted Bernie to ask one last question before hanging up.

"Dad, you aren't sorry you took this job are you?"

"Sorry? No, Bern, I'm not sorry at all. It's something I'd always wanted to do. It's just an adjustment. Really, I'm fine. Talk to you tomorrow."

In his hotel room, Johnny sat alone, still holding his phone. He wasn't bullshitting when he told Bernie that he was glad he took the job and that it was something he'd wanted to do. It's just that sometimes he wished that he could share every minute of this fantastic journey with his family.

[13]

THE FRIENDLY CONFINES

JOHNNY AND THE PRIDE had spent nine days on the road and now were flying home. Catherine, Bernie, Rachel, and the kids were all waiting at the airport to greet Johnny and the team. As soon as Johnny came through the jet way, Anna ran to him.

"Poppie! Where did you go? Was it fun? Did you bring me somthin'?"

"Anna Banana! Yes, I did bring you something." Johnny pulled a stuffed dog from his luggage and handed it to her. Anna gave it a big hug then did the same to her Poppie.

"I love her, Poppie. I'm gonna call her Ally." Catherine gave her husband a warm hug and a kiss.

"Welcome home." It was all she needed to say.

"How was the trip?' Bernie asked.

Johnny picked up his bags. "Long and frustrating."

"Well, you're home now. Maybe things will change for the better."

Just then Anna tugged at her Poppie's shorts. "Poppie, did you bring somthin' for Lizzie too?"

Johnny put his bags down and picked her up. "Do you think I'd forget Lizzie?"

Johnny took a tiny t-shirt out of a bag. It read, 'Poppie's Punkin.'

On the way to the cars, Bernie asked, "Dad, think Luke can be ready to start tomorrow?"

"He's rested, but do we want to throw him into the mix already? Jimmy hasn't really had time to work with him yet."

"I know, but I'd like to see what he can do as soon as possible. No sense on waiting, right?"

"Are you telling me to start him?"

"No, I'm just asking if you think he can start tomorrow. You're the manager, but I'd really like to see what Luke can do."

"Let me sleep on it, okay Bern? We'll talk about it in the morning."

Rachel said to Bernie, "Let your father do his job."

"Rachel, you can't give me a new toy and expect me not to play with it."

She laughed lightly. "No but you can at least let your father check it out so you know what to do with it before you break it."

Bernie got it. "Fair enough. I'll back off but..."

"No 'but,' Bernie. Just let him handle it."

Bernie still hoped Johnny would let Luke make his first minor league start. He wasn't afraid that his new toy might break.

It was four hours before game time and Johnny was already working on the lineup. He called Luke into the office.

"Grab a seat, Luke. How do you feel?"

"I'm good, Coach. I'm happy to be here. I mean, I miss my dad a little bit but I promise I'm not homesick. Once I'm pitching, I'll be fine."

"Think you're ready to start pitching tonight?"

Luke sat up in his chair. "Tonight? Heck, Coach, I've been ready to pitch since we got on that bus to Athens last week!"

"All right, you're starting tonight. Just go out there and do your best. We aren't expecting you to be perfect."

Luke left the office, excited to get his chance.

Johnny called Jimmy in.

"Jimmy, Luke's starting tonight. Take him out to the bullpen and check his mechanics. See if you have any tips for him."

Down in the bullpen, Jimmy said, "Just take some nice, easy tosses to loosen up, Luke."

It only took a few minutes before Luke was ready to throw from the mound. It was the first time he'd ever set foot on a professional mound, and he didn't want to wait any longer.

Jimmy said, "No curveballs or changeups until I ask for them."

Luke nodded then delivered his first pitch.

"Shit!" exclaimed Alex as the ball popped into his mitt.

Jimmy said, "Luke, I said take it easy."

"Coach, I did take it easy."

Jimmy shook his head in disbelief. "All right. Throw another one."

Luke's motion was fluid and as easy as a lazy river.

As the next pitch popped his glove Alex said, "Damn it to hell! Cut that shit out!"

"Sorry," Luke said, although he didn't know what he'd done wrong.

Alex shook the sting out of his hand. "Jimmy if this kid can't check himself, I'm outta here!"

"Don't be such a baby, Alex. All right Luke, let's give him a break. Throw a curveball."

Luke snapped off a curveball. It had a crisp, downward break on it; so crisp that Alex missed the ball and got hit on the knee portion of his shin guard.

"Son of a bitch!" Alex threw down his glove, hopping in pain.

"Are you okay?" Jimmy asked.

"No, Jimmy, I am not okay. My damn knee is killing me. You catch him, Jimmy. I'm done."

"Walk away and I'm having you fined."

"My checkbook's in my locker. Just tell me what I owe you." Alex limped back to the clubhouse.

Jimmy didn't need to see any more. Luke's mechanics were impeccable. Johnny called Jimmy into his office.

"How'd he look? I heard Alex cursing when he got back here so I'm a little worried."

"Coach, he was," Jimmy had to pause. "...just fantastic. Alex is pissed because he got his hand and knee hurt." Jimmy chuckled.

Johnny smiled and got back to work on his lineup. One player in particular was creating a dilemma for him.

"Greg, come into my office for a minute."

Greg was still in shorts and a t-shirt.

"What's up, Coach?"

"Greg, I'm glad you're part of this team. I think you've been a help with Malcolm and you can definitely play defense."

Greg knew all this praise was leading to a 'but.' After a pause, Johnny said, "Greg, I have to sit you for now. You just aren't hitting enough. Freddie's looked pretty good, so I'll be starting him."

Greg understood. His batting average was only .204 and still hadn't had an extra base hit.

"Whatever's best for the team."

Johnny finished with some damage control.

"Don't give up on me, Greg. Keep working in the cages."

Greg nodded with a determined look in his eyes and left. Johnny went out to address the team.

"All right, gentlemen, everyone over here! We're home, where everything is familiar and comfortable. Don't get too comfortable. The key to success is owning your own house. We haven't done that very well yet. Let's change that starting tonight. Give our fans a great effort but don't put out the welcome mat for Fort Wayne, all right?"

Johnny read off the lineup. He closed with, "Luke, you're on the mound tonight. Gentlemen, give your new teammate all the support you can!"

As the team pre-game meeting broke up, Alex, limping and with ice wrapped around his catching hand and knee went to Ricky. "God bless you."

Crowds had been sluggish since the first week of the season. This night was different. Using social media, Bernie leaked information about a new, young pitching phenom who was starting.

With a warm, welcome home ovation, the Pride took the field. In the bullpen, Luke grabbed the rosin bag and looked around the full stadium. He was so overwhelmed that he almost forgot how to breathe. His first warm up pitch bounced about twenty feet in front of Ricky.

"Take it easy, Luke. Just like you did with Alex," Jimmy said.

Luke's next pitch skipped off of the dirt and by Ricky's outstretched mitt.

Two warm up pitches into his first scheduled start and Jimmy needed to talk with Luke.

"Luke, what the hell is wrong?"

Luke panned the stadium. "I've never pitched in front of so many people before. It's kind of scary."

This wasn't what Jimmy needed to hear fifteen minutes before first pitch.

"Luke, have you ever been in a tough spot before?"

"Yeah, sure. A bunch of times."

"How'd you work through it?"

Luke looked around as if he hadn't heard the question. "Coach, you'll laugh at me when I tell you."

"Just tell me."

"When I was a kid I used to watch this thing on TV called, 'Schoolhouse Rock.' Have you ever heard of it?"

Jimmy wasn't sure where the conversation was heading.

"Sure. I watched it too."

"Well there was this one that I really liked. It was kind of soothing, you know?"

"Which one?"

Luke, a little embarrassed, quietly started singing, "Three. It's a magic number..."

Jimmy tried but couldn't suppress a laugh.

"I knew you'd laugh."

"I'm sorry, really. If that calms you down then use it. Hum it to yourself if you have to."

"I'll feel stupid if I start humming."

"If it helps you pitch the way we know you can, then trust me, you won't sound stupid. Hell, I'll have every player on this team learn that song if it helps."

Luke retook the mound, still feeling nervous. He began humming to himself, "Three. It's a magic number..." Ricky didn't need to move his glove an inch as the blazing fastball smacked his mitt.

"Shit, that stings!" Ricky yelled.

Jimmy grinned. He yelled, "Better get some extra padding for that mitt, Ricky!"

Luke continued humming and firing strike after strike. He was feeling much more at ease and that spelled problems for Fort Wayne.

"How'd it go?" Johnny asked Jimmy.

The pitching coach grinned and shook his head, saying, "He was really humming out there."

Fort Wayne's leadoff hitter stepped into the batter's box. Luke started him with a knee-high fastball for strike one. The small sponge Ricky's put in his mitt did very little to take the sting out.

Luke's first real professional pitch was clocked at 98 miles per hour. He threw another fastball that the batter swung through for strike two. That one registered at 99 miles per hour.

The Fort Wayne hitter geared up for another fastball. Just like he did in Holly Springs, Luke dropped a curveball over the outside corner that froze the hitter for strike three. Three pitches into his first pro game, and Luke already had a strikeout. Luke also struck out the next two hitters. The crowd roared as Luke came off of the mound.

Johnny yelled, "Great inning, Luke! Three strikeouts!"

"It's a magic number, Coach."

The Pride offense fed off of the stadium's energy. They scored three runs in the bottom of the first, keyed by a home run courtesy of Ricky.

Luke continued firing his fastball while mixing in a sharp-breaking curveball and devastating changeups. He ran his string of strikeouts to six through two innings. The crowd seemed to roar louder as the Pride came off of the field.

Luke prepared for his first professional at-bat in the bottom of the second with Miguel standing on second base. He got a fastball and smashed it by the surprised Fort Wayne third baseman. Miguel scored easily and Luke had himself a double. The Pride lead was now 4-0 and there wasn't a person in the stadium not impressed by this young man from Holly Springs.

Luke continued putting away Fort Wayne hitters with incredible ease. Through five innings, he hadn't allowed a base runner and had struck out twelve Fort Wayne hitters. Meanwhile, his teammates were giving him all the offense he needed, tacking on two more runs to push the lead to 6-0.

Before he took the mound to start the sixth inning, Johnny stopped Luke.

"How do you feel?"

"Tank's not even close to empty, Coach."

Luke backed up his word, setting Fort Wayne down in order yet again in the sixth. The roar of the crowd had settled into a buzz now. Luke started the seventh inning by missing badly with his first two pitches. His next pitch was a changeup. The Fort Wayne batter ripped it towards the third base line. Hank dove and made an incredible play for the first out of the inning.

Johnny said, "Jimmy, something doesn't look right with Luke. Go talk to him, okay?"

Jimmy met Ricky and Luke at the mound. "Coach sent me out to check on you. Is everything okay?"

Look looked around the stadium. "Why is everyone so quiet now? It's making me nervous."

"Wait, first you were nervous because there were so many people, and now you're nervous because they got quiet?"

Luke pounded the ball into his mitt. "Yeah...kinda."

Jimmy shook his head. "Just make your own noise in your head. You know..." Jimmy began humming, 'Three. It's a magic number.'

Ricky gave Jimmy a strange look. Jimmy smiled. "Don't worry about it, Ricky. It's just a thing to calm him down. Get your ass back behind the plate and let's get these next two outs."

Refocused, Luke struck out the next two hitters. Seven perfect innings were now in the books.

Luke lead off the bottom of the seventh inning. The first pitch buzzed up and in, just missing Luke's head as he hit the deck. Luke calmly picked up his bat, dusted himself off and prepared to hit. Jimmy and Johnny didn't react as calmly.

"What's that shit?" Jimmy yelled to the Fort Wayne pitcher.

"Garbage move, Pitch! Garbage!" screamed Johnny.

Luke calmed his coaches. "It's all right, guys. No worries."

Luke took a strong cut at the next fastball and sent it towering over the left field fence for a home run and a 7-0 Pride lead. When Luke got to the dugout he said, "See? I told you. No worries."

Luke started the eighth inning just six outs from a perfect game. He hummed his song and induced a pop up to Frank for the first out. Two batters and two strikeouts later, eight perfect innings were in the books. With a 7-0 lead and three outs from perfection, Luke started the ninth inning. Adrenaline pumping hard through him, Luke failed to throw a strike on his first three pitches. His perfect game in danger, Luke stepped off of the mound. He grabbed the rosin bag, closed his eyes and again began humming, 'Three. It's a magic number.'

Taking the pitching rubber, he delivered a fastball for strike one. With the batter now locked in and looking for another fastball, Luke fooled him with a changeup for strike two. The count was full. Luke reared back and fired a fastball. The swing was well late and Luke had another strikeout, his 18th of the game.

Two outs to go.

The next batter was child's play for Luke, striking out on three pitches. Twenty-six batters up and all retired. Just one out left. Luke wiped the sweat from his brow and prepared to face what everyone hoped was his final hitter of the night. His first pitch was a fastball at the knees, taken for strike one.

No sense to change now, Luke thought, throwing another fastball that the batter swung through for strike two. *Now I've got him.*

His next pitch was a beautiful change up. The batter swung and just got the tip of the bat on the baseball. As the ball rolled seemingly harmlessly foul down the third base line, Hank waited for it. While the ball spun sideways, it hit a pebble-sized clump of dirt. The combination of the funky spin and clump of dirt kicked the ball fair. By then it was too late. The runner was safely on first base with a hit, a lucky one, but a hit. Hank retrieved the ball and walked over to Luke.

"Man, I'm sorry. I just cost you a perfect game."

"Don't worry about it. I wouldn't have had the chance in the first place if not for you."

Luke was referring to Hank's fantastic play in the seventh inning that temporarily preserved the perfect game.

He calmly worked out of the stretch position for the first time all day. He finished off the game on three more pitches, all fastballs and all clocked at 99 milesperhour. Luke had his first win in his first game as a professional pitcher. His teammates all shook his hand, gave him high fives and rubbed his closely cut hair. As Luke got to the dugout, Johnny smiled and said, "Not bad, rookie."

"I guess. Could have been better."

Johnny laughed. He didn't know how much better Luke could get, but he was excited thinking about the possibilities.

[14]

MORE CHANGES

ART AND GREG MET at a local doughnut shop to talk about Greg's struggles. "Dad, I'm not so sure this was a good idea."

"Greg, Coach Endino knows what you can do. That's why he asked you to be a part of this team. Why do you think this isn't a good idea?"

"I was good when I was a kid but these guys are pros. They've been doing this constantly for a while. I've been out of the game and I'm not sure I can come back."

"Greg, just stick with it. We know you can play the game. It's just going to take a little work."

Greg took a sip of coffee. "Dad, what if it doesn't come back?"

Art put his hand on Greg's shoulder. "Well if it doesn't come back, you gave it your best shot and got a chance that not a lot of people get in a lifetime."

Greg smiled and took another sip of coffee. If he was going out, he was going out fighting.

With Luke bolstering the pitching staff and the lineup slowly improving, the Pride showed signs of life. After a 5-2 win to start their series in Fayetteville, the Pride finished May with sixteen wins and pushed their overall record to 26-30. Despite the improvement, the team could only pull itself into fourth place and was a full ten games behind division-leader Nantucket in the standings. Still, Johnny and Bernie were optimistic, and so were the fans now filling the seats. Things were looking up until Bernie got a phone call.

"Endino! Jerry Benjamin here! How's life treatin' ya these days? That team of yours is starting to look damn good!"

"Hey, Jerry. Yeah things are coming together. Still, a long way to go though. Thanks for checking in. I'll let my dad know you called."

Jerry wasn't finished.

"Hey, gotta tell you something. I'm bringing two of your guys to Connecticut."

Bernie didn't want to hear it but knew it was part of minor league baseball. "Who am I losing?"

Hank's numbers were fantastic. He was hitting .327 and already had nineteen home runs. Bernie was sure Hank was going to the big league team. What Jerry said next came as a shock.

"Our regular first baseman pulled his hamstring. He's going to be out at least two weeks. I'm giving Carlson his chance."

Frank wasn't doing badly, hitting .261 with six home runs and twenty-seven runs batted in, but they weren't numbers that normally get a player his shot to play in the big leagues. This was simply a matter of need and Hank just hadn't worked much at first base since spring training.

"Okay. Who else am I losing?"

"Charlie. We need bullpen help and I like what he's done so far. That funky motion of his might just work."

It was a great opportunity for Charlie, but now the Pride was left without a closer.

"Fine, Jerry. So, who are we getting to fill the gaps?"

"We've got a kid at AA named Pete Robinski. Big kid. Hits the ball far when he hits it."

"When he hits it?" Bernie closed his eyes and rubbed his temples.

"He tends to strike out a bit, but I'm sure you guys can fix him."

"And how about the pitcher?"

"I'm sending you a guy with big league experience. You can expect Wil Robinson to report for tomorrow's game."

Bernie hoped he'd heard wrong. "Wil Robinson as in, 'Danger' Wil Robinson?"

Jerry swallowed. "Uh, yeah."

Wil Robinson was a 26-year-old relief pitcher who had bounced back and forth between the big leagues and the minors for the past three seasons. He got his nickname, 'Danger,' from an old TV show and his uncanny knack for getting himself into trouble on the pitching mound just by setting foot on it.

"Jerry, Robinson isn't help. He's a project."

"I have faith that you guys can straighten him out. The kid just needs some coaching. He'll be fine."

He sounded like a used car salesman trying to move a lemon off of his lot. Bernie just shook his head knowing that he had no choice but to hope his Dad could work these guy into the team.

"All right, Endino, gotta run. Got business to take care of. Say hello to that family of yours and tell your manager...umm, your father... well whatever you want to call him, about the changes. Oh, and tell Hank and Charlie they're coming to the big leagues as soon as you can. Don't want your dad putting them in his lineup tonight."

As soon as the call ended, Bernie broke the news to Johnny.

"Hey Dad. How's Fayetteville?"

"Really warm. Whadda ya need, Bern?"

"I just got off the phone with Jerry. I need you to take care of something before tonight's game. Tell Frank and Charlie that they are going to Connecticut tomorrow to join the Mantids."

He expected disappointment from his father's but got quite the opposite.

"Hey, that's great! They'll be thrilled! I'll let them know right away."

"You aren't upset?"

"Bern, our job is to get these guys ready to play in the Majors. These are my first two guys to graduate from here, I think it's fantastic!"

Bernie was so surprised that he nearly forgot about the replacements.

"Jerry's sending you reinforcements." He had to pause before going on. "You're getting a Double-A first baseman named Pete Robinski and he's giving you a pitcher with Major League experience."

"As long as he isn't pushing 'Danger' Wil Robinson on me."

Bernie let out a nervous laugh. "Funny you should mention him."

"Aw shit, he's sending me Robinson, isn't he?"

Now it was Bernie's turn to go into used car salesman mode.

"Maybe Jimmy could help him just like he helped Charlie. There's something there he can work with, I think."

Johnny had just gotten through two projects and now Jerry was sending him two more. Johnny laughed to himself, *This is what you always wanted to do, right Johnny? You wanted to teach guys how to be good at the game of baseball and wanted to do it at the pro level. What the hell were you thinking?*

Johnny had some good news to distribute. He started at Charlie's room.

"Who is it?" Charlie asked hearing the knock at his door.

"It's Coach, Charlie. Can I come in?"

"Uh wait a second, Coach! I'll be right there!"

Johnny was growing impatient as he waited outside. He heard another voice with Charlie but couldn't make out who it was. Johnny yelled, "Charlie, open up! It's important!"

"I...I'm coming, Coach!"

Charlie finally opened the door but not the chain. "What's up, Coach?"

"Can I come in?"

"Uh...well...um..."

Through the crack, Johnny noticed why Charlie was hesitant. Inside his room was a beautiful brunette wearing nothing more than one of Charlie's t-shirts.

"Charlie, what you do is your business but I've got big news for you, so I suggest you have your visitor get dressed and get out of here. I'll come back in a few minutes, all right?"

"Yeah, Coach. Thanks."

Johnny walked away muttering to himself, "Kids."

He arrived at Frank's door hoping this meeting was less awkward.

"Hey, Coach, what are you doing here?"

"Can I come in? I've got something to tell you."

"Sure, Coach, let's talk."

Johnny sat at one of the chairs by a small desk in Frank's room. "Frank, I got a call from Jerry Benjamin a little while ago."

Frank let out a sigh. "I'm outta here, right?"

"Yeah Frank, you're no longer part of this team."

"Shit. Guess this is the end of the road then. Now what?"

Johnny had his fun. He let Frank off the hook.

"Frank, you're no longer part of this team because you're going to Connecticut to join the Mantids."

Frank instinctively hit his manager on the shoulder. "You son of a bitch! Are you shitting me? Are you shitting me?"

"Nope. You're heading back to the Bigs."

Frank sat down and gathered himself. "I can't believe it. It's been a long time. I spent ten years in the Independent League after I got cut from Boston. Ten years. Never thought I'd see a Major League game from the dugout again."

"Take advantage of this, Frank. Enjoy the time, because you don't know how long it will last. You'll get fifteen days to prove that you should stay. Do whatever it takes so I don't have to see you again, all right?"

Frank shook Johnny's hand. "I'll do my best, Coach. Thanks for your help. Couldn't have made it back without you." Johnny saw tears in Frank's eyes before he turned away.

"Pack up. I've got a kid coming to take your place tomorrow and I need the room."

Frank packed then tracked down his teammates to say goodbye. Much as he liked them, the only time he hoped to see them again, was as Major League teammates.

Johnny returned to Charlie's room.

"I'm back, Charlie. Can I come in now?"

"Sorry about before, Coach. I..."

"I don't want to know. Charlie, Jerry Benjamin called today. He wants you to report to Connecticut as soon as possible."

Charlie's eyes got wide. "The big leagues want me?"

"Jerry wants to see what you can do at the next level."

Charlie had been having a solid season. His earned run average was 2.12 and he had saved ten games.

"This is great, Coach. Really great. Wow, the Bigs!"

"They're sending a car to take you to the airport in two hours. You might want to call your friend and let her know, too."

Charlie quickly packed and dressed. He also said goodbye to his teammates. His final stop was Jimmy's room.

"Hey Jimmy, it's me, Charlie. Got a second?"

"What's with the suitcase? We've got a game tonight."

"I'm not going to the stadium with you guys. Coach just let me know. I'm going to Connecticut to join the Mantids."

Jimmy shook Charlie's hand. "Wow, big time huh? Congratulations."

"Yeah, it's great. Jimmy, I just wanted to thank you for helping me out. Not sure I'd get invited to Connecticut otherwise."

Jimmy had one more piece of advice. "You'd better get going. Missing the plane to Connecticut is not the way to start your big league career."

Charlie left. Jimmy thought, *Son of a bitch. I'm actually making a difference.*

The Pride played short-handed that night and even though they managed to win 3-1 behind Luke's complete game three-hitter, it wasn't the win that felt most satisfying. Seeing two of his players moving on to the next level gave Johnny the most satisfaction, and he was going to follow their big league stories too.

Johnny's hotel room phone rang.

"Mr. Endino, it's Maurice at the front desk. There are two gentlemen here to see you telling me they play for you. Would you like me to send them up?"

"Thank you, but just tell them I'll meet them in the lobby in a few minutes."

Johnny quickly headed downstairs to meet his newest Pride members.

"Coach Endino, I'm Pete Robinski. Looking forward to playing for you." Pete was a mountainous kid, about 6'6" and 250 pounds of muscle.

"Glad to have you, Pete. I hear you can hit the ball a long way."

"Yes sir, but I have a little problem with hitting it sometimes."

The meeting with Johnny's other new player wasn't as cordial.

"Guessing you're Wil."

"Yeah," said Robinson, stone-faced and miserable.

"I'd like you to be our closer."

Wil wasn't exactly paying attention to his coach. "Whatever."

Johnny was not thrilled with the attitude of his new pitcher. "We play tonight at seven. The bus leaves for the stadium at 4:30. Pete, be ready to start tonight at first. Wil, if the opportunity is there, you'll get to close tonight."

Wil blew a bubble with his gum. "Can't go tonight. Pitched an inning two days ago."

Johnny knew full well that the inning Wil pitched two days ago was the only inning he'd pitched in the last five days. There was zero reason that if called upon he couldn't pitch.

"Fine, Wil. Meet me in my office at five so we can discuss a few things. You guys settle into your rooms and I'll see you down here later."

"Yes sir!" said Pete. Wil said nothing. He would be a tough nut to crack.

When 4:30 came everyone was on the bus and ready to head to the stadium except for Robinson. It was another five minutes before he arrived.

Johnny pointed to his own wrist. "Robinson, you might want to fix your watch. It seems to be running a little slow." Wil just looked at his new coach and grabbed an open seat.

It was five o'clock and Johnny was waiting in his office with no sign of Wil. Ten minutes passed, and still Wil hadn't made it to the office. Johnny headed to the lockers.

"Robinson, my office please!"

Wil slowly took out his earbuds. "I'm not dressed yet."

Johnny's face was red like a fire engine. "I don't give a shit! Get your ass into my office...NOW!"

Wil sat and Johnny calmly read him the riot act.

"Robinson I don't know what type of bug is up your ass, but I'm not putting up with your shit. I don't have a hell of a lot of rules but the ones I have, I expect to be followed, got it?"

Wil snapped his gum. "Whatever."

That set Johnny off.

"That's it. I just met you, and already I want to beat the living shit out of you. What is your problem, son? What makes you so special, huh? Why shouldn't you have to follow the team rules? Come on, Robinson, tell me why? Tell me why you think you're so damn special!"

Wil pounded Johnny's desk. "I'm a damn Major League pitcher! I don't belong here with you and your misfits! I'm better than riding on buses and eating at shitty diners! Your rules don't matter to me! I make my own damn rules!"

At this point you could fry an egg on Johnny's head. Refraining from another tirade, Johnny began speaking calmly.

"Robinson, if you belonged in the Majors, do you think Jerry would have sent you here? I've seen your numbers, and to be honest, I'm surprised you weren't sent down a long time ago. You may think your hot shit, but let me tell you something, if you decide to play by your own rules, you aren't going to be playing in any of my games and I can almost guarantee you won't be pitching again in the Majors. You might want to think about that, or get used to riding on buses and eating in shitty diners."

Johnny stood up and walked to the door of his office, holding it open wide, "Now, get your ass out of my office, finish putting on the uniform, and get out to the bullpen. Oh, and Robinson, if I do decide I need you to pitch tonight you damn well had better warm up and be ready to go."

Wil got up and quietly followed Johnny's orders. He still wasn't thrilled to be there, but he sure as hell didn't want to spend the rest of his career playing AAA baseball. He'd reluctantly abide by Johnny's rules as long as it meant he'd have a chance to go back to the Majors.

Johnny closed the door with more firmness than usual and took a few minutes to settle himself down before rounding up the team for his usual pre-game address.

"All right gentlemen, let's get together! We have two new faces tonight. Two of your teammates are now in Connecticut."

Johnny paused as the team cheered and hollered for Frank and Charlie. He continued, "Keep working hard gentlemen, and it can happen for you too."

Johnny next introduced Pete and Wil to the team and read off the lineup. Jake pitched a solid game but got little help from his offense. In particular his new teammate, Pete, and an unlikely candidate, Hank gave him all the support of a hammock tied to one tree. Pete went 0-4 with three strikeouts. Hank not only went 0-4, but committed two errors. Despite it all, the Pride carried a 4-3 lead into the bottom of the ninth inning. Johnny called on Wil to close out the game.

Wil went into his elaborate windup and threw his first pitch. It promptly clipped the hitter's elbow. After a sacrifice bunt to move the tying run to second, Johnny asked Jimmy, "Is it me or did Robinson's velocity go way down to that last hitter?"

"I was thinking the same thing. Could've just been his changeup."

"Maybe, but why make it easier for the hitter to get down the bunt?"

Wil's first pitch to the next hitter was crushed to deep centerfield. Malcolm took off and made an outstanding catch to rob the batter of at least a double. The runner from second base however, tagged up and advanced to third. The Pride was somehow just one out away from stealing a win.

Wil went into his elaborate lineup and threw a fastball. It bounced well short of Ricky and rolled all the way to the backstop, allowing the runner from third to scamper across the plate with the tying run.

"Shit!" Johnny and Jimmy yelled almost in unison. Wil's next pitch was a curveball that didn't break. As the ball spun towards the plate, Wil knew he'd blown it. The hitter's bat made a sound that no pitcher likes to hear. Without turning around, Wil walked towards the dugout with no doubt in his mind that he'd just given up a game-winning home run. 'Danger' Wil Robinson had struck again.

In the hotel lobby, Johnny caught up with his pitching coach. "Jimmy, can we talk before you hit the sack?

"Sure. What's on your mind, Skip?"

"Wil is on my mind. I talked to Ricky, and those pitches Wil threw that we thought were changeups were actually fastballs."

"Really?"

"Yep. I didn't believe it either. Talk to him tomorrow, okay? Do something with that windup. I don't know how he can consistently throw strikes with all this going on." Johnny mimicked Wil's motion.

It had been a rough few days. After Johnny left for his room, Jimmy decided to stop in hotel bar to grab a beer and relax a little. As he sat down he noticed Wil at the other end of the bar. Jimmy got his beer and went to sit by his project. "Okay if I sit here?"

Wil took a sip of his Jack and Coke. "Free country."

Jimmy took a swig from his bottle of beer. "You know, Robinson, you could be a decent pitcher someday."

Wil took another drink from his glass. "You don't say? Well thanks for that vote of confidence, Coach. Coming from you that means very little."

"You know, Robinson, you're a real asshole. We're trying to help you and you insist on giving us your shitty attitude. What's your problem?"

Wil put down his glass. "I am a decent pitcher. I'm better than decent. I don't belong down here with this circus act and I sure as Hell can't learn anything from you."

"You know what, Robinson, you're right. You can't learn shit from me. Know why? Because that skull of yours is so thick nothing can penetrate it. Better get used to this circus, pal, because you're gonna be in the center ring for a while."

With that Jimmy went back to the other end of the bar. So much for his relaxation.

As he left Jimmy, Johnny's thoughts shifted to helping Pete. Although it was late, he stopped by Pete's room. "Pete, it's Coach. You still up?"

Pete opened his door.

Johnny entered, noticing Pete's interesting sleepwear. "Marty the Moon Man pajamas, huh?"

"Uh yeah. They were a gift."

"It's okay. I like cartoons too."

Pete changed the topic. "Sorry about tonight, Coach. Guess I just had some jitters."

"I understand that, but you struck out a lot in AA too. I'd like you to come with me to the park a little early tomorrow. Let's see if we can figure out your problem and maybe get it fixed."

"Sure. I'm willing to try anything."

Johnny left fully exhausted. He got to his room where Catherine was fast asleep. He was glad she made the trip. It made being away from home much easier and put things into perspective. Family was always the most important thing. As long as he remembered that, he could handle anything—even a pitcher with attitude issues and a first baseman with *Marty the Moon Man* pajamas.

[15]

THE NEW PROJECTS

THE NEXT MORNING, PETE and Johnny were in the batting cages early. Pete made solid contact pitch after pitch without a miss. After about ten minutes, Johnny had Pete stop.

"Geez Pete, I didn't notice anything wrong. You hit every pitch out of that machine hard."

"Yeah, I never have trouble in the cage, Coach. It's out on the field where things get messed up."

"All right, let's hit the field. I'll throw you a few pitches and we'll see what happens."

Johnny didn't exactly have a live arm anymore, but he could still throw a few different pitches at Pete to at least see how he reacted. He started with a fastball, which was more like a straight changeup coming from Johnny's arm. Pete crushed it into the left field seats. Pete did the same with Johnny's next straight pitch. Mixing things up, Johnny flipped a mediocre curveball to Pete. He swung and missed badly.

Interesting, thought Johnny.

He went back to a straight pitch and again Pete crushed it.

Now Johnny thought, *Maybe he just can't hit curveballs.*

Johnny tested his theory and threw another breaking pitch. This time, Pete ripped it into left field. Johnny was baffled. Making sure it wasn't just a fluke, Johnny threw another curveball. This time Pete missed badly then pounded the top of his helmet.

It was something Johnny noticed Pete doing in the game. "Pete, why do you pound your helmet every time you miss a pitch?"

"I do that when I guess wrong, Coach."

Johnny finally got Pete's problem. He was a guess-hitter. Pete's brain was getting in the way of his hitting.

"Pete, why are you guessing? Don't you ever watch a pitcher during a game?"

"Not really, Coach. I don't really pay a lot of attention unless it's my turn to bat."

"Do you ever watch tapes or videos of pitchers on your down time?"

"No. When I'm not playing I watch cartoons, movies, shit like that."

Johnny puts his hands on Pete's shoulders and looked him square in the eyes. "Pete, you can hit. I can help you but you'll have to start watching games and studying pitchers. You can still watch your cartoons, but Marty the Moon Man isn't getting you to the big leagues."

Pete adjusted his batting helmet. "All right. I'll pay attention and watch video of the pitchers."

Johnny pointed to his own temple. "Smart man. You can start right now. There's a laptop in my office. Let's turn it on and see if we can find some footage of Gunderson."

Gunderson was Todd Gunderson, the kid who was starting for Fayetteville in the next game. Johnny and Pete found video and watched for the next two hours.

Pete said, "See that, Coach? When he gets ahead, he likes throwing his changeup out of the strike zone."

Johnny was impressed. He asked, "See anything else?"

"Yeah, he throws a lot of fastballs early in the game then he'll mix in that slider more and more as he gets through the lineup for the second time."

Johnny saw that Pete was getting it and hoped it would translate into the game. He had some more instructions for Pete.

"Take what you learned into the batter's box with you but don't over think it. Bottom line here is simple. Just watch the ball hit the bat." It was Johnny's standard of effective hitting advice.

The team was filing into the clubhouse. Johnny approached Wil. "Soon as you're dressed I want you, Jimmy and Alex to head down to the bullpen."

"What for?"

"Just do it and don't give Jimmy a hard time."

With a little attitude, Wil answered. "Fine."

"Fine. That's just what I'm doing for your attitude problem. I'm fining you $500. You're going to learn if it bankrupts you."

Wil said nothing and headed to the bullpen.

Jimmy said, "Okay, Wil...just start with a few from the windup. Let's see what you've got."

Wil took his elaborate windup and fired. The pitch had plenty of velocity but flew over Alex's head.

"Shake it off and throw another one."

Wil's second pitch one-hopped Alex and hit him just above the knee.

Alex said, "Son of a bitch, Jimmy, not another one!"

Jimmy waved down to Alex. "Relax, Alex. Wil, give me one from the stretch."

Wil took the stretch position and threw his first strike. It didn't have the velocity of the first two pitches but at least it was accurate. Jimmy took him aside.

"What's the deal with that big windup?"

"Just something I started doing a few years ago. It's deceptive."

Jimmy flattened his hand and raised it above his cap. "Not deceptive enough to get guys to swing at shit over their heads."

Wil pointed at Jimmy with his glove. "Screw you, Jimmy."

Jimmy took that open hand and held all five fingers up in Wil's face. "That'll cost you another $500."

Wil rolled his eyes as Jimmy continued.

"I want you to simplify the wind up. Cut out all the bullshit and just pitch. Give me your glove for a second."

Jimmy took Wil's glove and toed the pitching rubber. He'd almost forgotten how good it felt. He wound up, his hands almost still, and threw a perfect knee-high strike.

"Nice velocity, Coach," Alex called out.

Jimmy flipped Wil a ball and his glove. "Your turn."

Wil mimicked Jimmy's wind up, resulting in a strike over the corner of the plate with very good velocity and movement.

Jimmy said, "Nice. Do it again."

Wil gave Jimmy another eye roll, pitched, and threw another strike.

"That's the idea. Keep doing that."

Wil threw a mix of pitches at Jimmy's request. His control and even pitch movement showed improvement. Jimmy had him stop and began a new line of questions.

"Wil, I notice when you go into the stretch you take a lot off of your fastball. What gives?"

Wil opened up to Jimmy.

"I've got guys on base and I don't want to mess up so I take something off to make sure I don't throw the ball away."

"How's that working out for you?"

Wil shook his head. "Not so good."

"Wil, don't be afraid to throw the ball. Just keep things simple, like with the windup. Focus on the target and let it rip. If you make a mistake once in a while, so what? Ricky and Alex know how to keep your mistakes in front of them. If they can't, shake it off, and get ready to throw your next pitch. You can't dwell on it."

Wil was buying into Jimmy's instruction and was ready to give it a try. He relaxed and just pitched from the stretch, throwing a perfect strike without compromising his velocity. After throwing a few more successful pitches out of the stretch, Jimmy stopped Wil.

"Save some for the game. We might need you later...that is, if your arm isn't too exhausted to throw two days in a row."

"Screw you, Jimmy." This time Wil said it without the animosity.

The Pride's two new projects seemed headed in the right direction.

Johnny's starting pitcher for the game was Jorge Santiago, a kid from Sacramento, California, who had a decent fastball to go with a very good sinker.

Jorge pitched well, allowing just four hits in eight innings of work. His lone mistake was a sinker that didn't sink, which turned into a solo home run. Unfortunately for the second consecutive game, the Pride bats struggled. They managed only two hits and four walks through eight and two thirds innings and trailed 1-0 with only one out left. Mark stepped into the batter's box. Out of the corner of his eye he noticed the Fayetteville third baseman playing deep. The pitcher delivered and Mark dropped a perfect bunt down the third base line. It came to rest on the third base foul line as Mark reached first base. Pete had a chance to keep the inning going. He stepped into the batter's box 0-2, with a walk for the game. He'd hit the ball hard twice, but right at the shortstop both times. As he settled into the box, Pete remembered the videos of Gunderson and his pitching pattern on the night thus far. In Pete's first at bats, Gunderson attacked with fastballs. The walk in his last at bat was intentional. Gunderson started Pete with two fastballs. Pete hit both hard, but just foul. He was down in the count, 0-2, but he had a good idea what was coming next. Sure enough, Gunderson threw a changeup. In the past, Pete would have swung and missed but thanks to his study session he took the pitch for ball one. Gunderson got the ball from his catcher, frustrated that Pete didn't bite on the changeup. As his next pitch approached the plate, Pete immediately recognized it as a slider, the exact pitch he expected. He swung and hit a high, arching fly ball towards right centerfield. It carried over the fence for a two-run home run and a Pride lead. Pete got back to the dugout where Johnny was the first person to meet him.

"Just like the videos," he said to Johnny while his teammates mobbed him.

The Pride carried a 2-1 lead into the bottom half of the ninth inning. Jorge struck out the first batter and got the second to fly out to Malcolm on the centerfield warning track. It looked like Wil wouldn't be needed for this one, but Jorge walked the next hitter then allowed a double to right field. Fayetteville now had the tying run on third and the winning run on second. Johnny brought in Wil.

Wil prepared to face his first hitter using his new, more compact windup. He started with a fastball for strike one. Already he felt more in control. Wil went to his curveball on the next pitch and the batter hit a routine ground ball to Hank. It looked like a Pride win but Hank threw it well over Pete's head. By the time Pete retrieved it, the runners from third and second had scored and the Pride ended their road trip with another heartbreaking loss. Johnny walked up to Wil, "Good job. Not your fault."

Johnny was at a loss. What was wrong with Hank? Another 0-4 night that included three strikeouts and a tapper to the mound plus his third error in two days. Johnny could only hope he'd pull out of this slump soon, because he certainly didn't need another project.

Travel schedules in the minor leagues can be head scratching. The Pride caught a flight home from Fayetteville so they could play two home games against Ithaca. After those two games, they headed back on the road for two games in Ithaca. It was just enough time to say hello to family and friends and get some laundry done.

Johnny wanted to use the travel as an excuse for what became a six-game losing streak but he knew it wasn't the real reason. Normally, losing streaks are linked to several factors but taking a good look at this one, most of it was due to an unlikely source: Hank. In his last six games, Hank was 0-24 with sixteen strikeouts at the plate. In the field he'd committed five errors. On the bus ride home, Johnny had Hank sit with him.

"Rough few games, huh?"

Hank just stared at the bus floor. "I guess so."

"Not like you, Hank. Something on your mind, kid?"

Hank pounded the arm of his bus seat.

"It should have been me in Connecticut, not Frank."

It was hard to argue with Hank. Johnny did his best to explain.

"This was a matter of need. The Mantids needed a fill-in at first base for a few weeks while their first baseman healed from a hamstring injury. You just don't have enough experience over there."

Hank gritted his teeth. "I can do it, Coach. I know it."

Johnny tapped his own chest with both hands. "I'll take some of the blame on this one. I should've played you in a few games at first. Sometimes, I forget the real purpose of this team is to get you guys ready for the next level, not to win."

Hank sighed. "It's all right, Coach. I guess I should have come to you instead of letting it eat at me and hurting the team."

"You'll get your chance. Jerry would be crazy not to give it to you."

"Thanks, Coach. I'll be ready to go tomorrow night. You can count on it."

Johnny hit Hank with his hat. "You'd better be, or your ass will be right next to mine on the bench. Go sit with Malcolm. He might get lonely."

Johnny believed that his main job was preparing his players for the Major Leagues. He also didn't take losing games lightly and there was no reason he couldn't accomplish both. Johnny still had a few old tricks up his sleeve, and now was the perfect time to start using them.

The bus pulled into the parking lot during the wee hours of the morning. Johnny arrived home tired but couldn't sleep. His mind was already working on the wrinkles he'd be adding for the Pride's game in less than sixteen hours. He stayed up until five a.m. writing down strategy.

It was going to be a good day. Johnny felt it. He was finally ready to sleep yet he was already excited to share his ideas with Bernie.

Bernie's phone rang.

"Hello."

"Bern, it's Dad! Hey, can you meet me at the stadium in half an hour? I've got some stuff to show you."

Johnny sounded as excited as a kid who just got a new baseball glove.

"I was just headed out to do a few things."

"Oh, all right. I guess it can wait."

Now Bernie was curious. "What's up?"

"I just have a few plays to show you. I'm pulling some stuff out of the archives and I want to know what you think."

Bernie said, "Dad, I'm sure whatever you are doing is going to be great. That's why I hired you. I'll just be surprised tonight with everyone else."

It was still several hours before first pitch when Bernie got to the stadium. Bernie entered his suite to, "Endino! Where the hell have you been? I've been here for over an hour!"

Jerry was there as an unexpected guest.

"Hey, Jerry. What brings you here?"

"I had some time, so I figured I'd come check on you. Things haven't been going so good, have they?"

Bernie grabbed a flavored water from the mini fridge. "Team's in a little slump. It happens. I'm not worried." Bernie was bullshitting at this point. He was damn worried.

Jerry grabbed a cigar from his pocket. "Let's hope your right. Hey by the way, that pitcher of yours is doing all right for us. He's got some good stuff; just what we need in the bullpen. Didn't think he'd ever develop."

Bernie seized the opportunity to praise his father.

"My dad noticed his problem in spring training. Once he saw the issue, the fix wasn't too hard."

Jerry gave Bernie some news.

"I'll be getting rid of Frank soon. I think his best days are behind him. He's only two for fifteen since we brought him up. Tony Willis is just about ready to come back, so we won't need Frank."

"What are we going to do about Pete?" Pete had been stinging the ball since his call up. Bernie really didn't want to lose him to the Double-A team.

"Pete's not going anywhere. I'm releasing Frank."

Bernie had a sick feeling in his stomach. Frank had worked so hard. Bernie didn't want to discuss it and changed the subject.

"Should be an exciting game, Jerry. My dad tells me he's got a few tricks up his sleeve."

"He'd better be a damn Vegas headliner magician."

As the Pride took the field, Bernie noticed a few of Johnny's wrinkles already in place. So did Jerry.

"What the hell is Rundle doing at first and why the hell does he have Robinski at third? Robinski hasn't played third since high school!"

Bernie made a motion up and down his arm and said, "Sleeve, Jerry. Sleeve."

It was Jorge Santiago's turn to pitch and started with a scoreless first inning against Albany. Johnny's next wrinkle was in the batting order. Mark lead off for the first time all season. Mark was hitting well as of late, and he was one of the faster players on the team. On the second pitch of his at bat, Mark singled to centerfield. Freddie bunted him to second with Hank drawing a walk. Two on and one out now for Pete.

"Let's see just how much better Robinski is," Jerry said.

It didn't take long for Jerry to find out. Pete had become voracious at studying opposing pitchers. He jumped all over Albany pitcher, Jim Albers', first pitch fastball and drilled it over the centerfield wall for a three-run home run.

Jerry said, "Guess he is learning something from you guys."

The three-run lead held up into the fourth inning when Jorge ran into some trouble. After getting the first two outs of the inning, Jorge gave up a home run followed by a single and a walk. With two on and two out, Albany's dangerous slugging right fielder, Pablo Ramirez, stepped to the plate. Johnny yelled, "Heads up, gentlemen!"

Jorge looked in for a sign then went into the stretch. As he looked over his shoulder at the runner on first base, Malcolm inched towards the second base from centerfield.

Jerry yelled, "What the hell is Jackson doing? This guy can crush a ball over his head!"

The runner on second extended his lead, thinking Jorge had forgotten about him. Jorge peered in at Ricky for another signal. Ricky dropped a single finger, his middle finger to be exact. Jorge wheeled towards second, and fired the ball towards Malcolm, who was now in a dead sprint towards second base. Malcolm caught the perfect throw and before the base runner knew what was happening, Malcolm tagged him to end the fourth inning and the threat.

"Holy shit! Never saw that one before!" screamed Jerry.

Bernie just looked at him, rubbing up and down his arm again. "Sleeve."

The next offensive threat by either team didn't happen until the top of the eighth inning. With one out, Jorge allowed a double. Johnny quickly got left-handed reliever, Christian Perez, up in the bullpen. Jorge walked the next batter putting two runners on with one out. That was enough for Johnny. He took out Jorge and brought Christian into the game. Christian got to the mound and Jorge headed for the dugout as expected, but so did Derek and Pete.

Jerry was again perplexed.

"Now what the blue hell is going on?"

Bernie scratched his temple. "I'm really not sure."

While Christian warmed up, Hank shifted to third base, Freddie went to right field, and Derek exchanged his outfield glove for his first baseman's mitt.

Bernie said, "Defensive switch, Jerry. Just tightening things up. Probably going to send Greg to the outfield."

Sounded logical but Jerry noticed something odd.

"Oh yeah, then where the hell is Santiago going?"

Sure enough, Jorge had an outfielder's glove and was heading to left field. Bernie figured out Johnny's strategy. He hadn't seen him use it since Pony League days.

"Watch this, Jerry. If it works, you're gonna love it."

Christian faced the left-handed hitter and struck him out on three pitches. As the right-handed pinch hitter was announced, Johnny headed to the mound.

Jerry said, "He strikes a guy out on three pitches and there's nobody warming up in the bullpen! No offense, Endino, but your father is losing it!"

Bernie turned. "Pay attention, Jerry."

Johnny took the ball from Christian. As he left the field, Greg came out of the dugout to play centerfield while Malcolm went to left. However, Jorge wasn't walking off of the field. He was coming back to the pitcher's mound. Bernie explained it to Jerry.

"Since Jorge was never taken out of the game, he can go back to pitch to the right-handed hitter and we don't need to go through three pitchers."

Jerry took a bite on his cigar. "And this is legal?"

Bernie nodded. "Yep. Let's see if it works."

On a 1-2 pitch, the batter popped a ball into shallow left field. Miguel clearly couldn't get to it from shortstop. As the ball descended, Greg charged hard. The runner from second had already crossed the plate. Greg dove with his glove fully extended. The ball landed in it for the third out, disallowing the run and the Pride still ahead, 3-1.

Jerry said, "Your father got lucky."

Bernie just shrugged. "Looks like solid managing to me."

The Pride needed just three outs to finish off a win. Christian started the ninth inning. The inning got off to a bad start as he allowed a home run to the first batter, cutting the Pride lead to 3-2. Johnny called on Robinson to close out the game.

"He's got Robinson closing, huh?" asked Jerry.

"Well, you took Charlie from us, so someone had to take the job."

Robinson's ninth inning also got off to a rocky start as he gave up a double and a four-pitch walk. Two on, and nobody out now for Albany.

"Aw shit, here we go. 'Danger' is at it again," Jerry said.

Jimmy had a talk with Wil and Ricky.

"Focus and keep it simple out here. Ricky, give him a good target. Wil, maybe you should try humming out here."

Wil started the next batter with a slider. He hit a two–hop ground ball to Miguel who flipped the ball to Mark covering second. Mark next wheeled and fired to first base to complete the double play. Now there were two outs and a runner on third.

"Not bad, huh, Jerry?"

Jerry, still the skeptic, just looked at the field. "He's not out of the woods yet."

Wil's confidence grew from that double play ground ball. He started the next hitter with a fastball, 95 miles per hour right at the knees.

Jerry noticed something else.

"Hey, what happened to that wild wind up?"

"Jimmy fixed it. The new one works better, huh?"

"We'll see."

Wil stuck with the fastball. The batter swung under it for strike two. Now in full command, Wil took the sign and delivered his next pitch, a changeup. The batter stood like a statue and watched as the umpire bellowed, "Strike three!"

The Pride had held on for a hard-fought 3-2 win, their first in a week. Bernie asked Jerry, "So, what did you think?"

"I don't know how well this is gonna work but that was some fun shit to watch."

"It's supposed to be fun, Jerry. It's baseball."

Jerry took out another cigar as he headed for the door. "Yeah well it's still a business, Endino. Try not to forget that while everyone's having fun."

It had been a good day. Maybe this was the spark the team needed to start winning. Bernie headed to the clubhouse to see his father.

"Hey, Coach, mind if I come in?"

"Hey, Bern, come on in and sit down! So, what'd you think?"

Bernie flipped around a chair. "It was great, Dad. Even Jerry was impressed."

Johnny's eyes opened wide. "Jerry was here?"

"Yeah. He decided to drop in and check on things. Nice timing for your tricks. I recognized a few of those from the Pony League days."

Johnny winked. "I've still got a few more."

Bernie was looking forward to what Johnny tried next. He had a feeling that things were really going to be exciting from here on out.

The series opening win over Albany renewed a fire in the Pride players. They swept four games from their neighbors to the north, a perfect way to head into a day off before traveling to Quakertown. As a reward, Johnny canceled practice. Johnny and Bernie took the opportunity to play golf.

Bernie was lining up his tee shot and said, "Team's on a good little run, huh?"

Johnny said, "Yeah, they actually look like a baseball team."

"What do you think is going to happen with Frank? Jerry said he's going to cut him."

"He's not cut yet, Bern. He still has a chance to prove himself up there."

After a day of golf, Bernie turned on the Mantids game. Frank was in the lineup but his statistics just weren't good. He had just three hits in twenty-seven at bats. Bernie called Jerry.

"Jerry, Bernie Endino here. Hey, I know you're busy right now, but I've got something to ask you."

"We're in the middle of a game here, Endino. This had better be important."

"Jerry, if you decide to release Frank, would you have him call me?"

"As soon as I give him the news Saturday, I'll ask him to give you a call. Doubt he'll feel like talking though."

"Just tell him I have an offer for him, okay?"

"You won't have a spot for him on the team, remember?"

"I know. Please just give him the message."

"All right. Gotta run...we've got the bases loaded and two outs...aw shit! Pop up to second!"

Bernie hoped Frank would call. He had plans for him. For now, Bernie had to pack for Quakertown.

The bus to Quakertown was barely out of the parking lot when Bernie started talking to his dad about the team.

"Looks like Malcolm is finally coming around with the switch-hitting," Bernie said.

"He's been working a lot with Greg. It seems to have helped. Wish I could say the same about Greg."

Bernie understood. Greg had lost his starting job and when he was getting a chance to play, he wasn't producing. His defense was fine, often stellar, but he was only hitting .201. Bernie asked, "What do you think we should do?"

Johnny sat back in his seat, putting his hands behind his head. "We might have to let him go. I don't know how to tell him and shit, I wonder how Art will take it."

Bernie took a sip from his sparkling water bottle. "Let's see how this weekend goes. If we don't see an improvement, we can talk with Greg and Art together, okay?"

Bernie changed topics.

"Clark has really embraced the knuckleball."

"Yeah, he's working hard. He and Jimmy have bonded too."

Clark had become one of the team's strengths. In his fourteen starts, he'd won eight games while losing just four.

Bernie segued into his next idea.

"Hey, Dad, looks like Jerry is going to release Frank."

"I noticed he wasn't doing too well."

"I told Jerry to have Frank call me. I think we can use him."

Johnny turned to Bernie with a puzzled look on his face. "Where? Pete's been killing the ball."

"I was thinking he could be your hitting coach so you could concentrate on managing."

Johnny sat back and thought for a second. "It's a good idea. Do you think he'll go for it?"

Bernie tilted his head. "I don't know, but I've got to try."

The bus arrived in Quakertown. As soon as he settled into his hotel room, Bernie called Rachel. The kids had a restless day but nothing Rachel couldn't handle. Bernie still felt guilty about coming on this trip, despite Rachel's assurance that everything was fine. It gave him a sense of how Johnny must feel. It was only going to be a few days, and Bernie already missed his family.

A few hours later, the team bus left for the stadium. Bernie had a seat near the Pride dugout for the game. Luke was pitching and he'd been nothing less than brilliant since Johnny found him. In four starts, he was 3-0 and had only allowed two earned runs.

Luke continued his mastery on the mound. He pitched a brilliant two-hit shutout while Hank, Pete and Ricky all hit home runs in a 6-0 Pride win.

"You're on a roll, Coach," Bernie said, entering Johnny's office in the visiting clubhouse.

"Yep."

He wasn't as happy about the win. Bernie wanted to find out why.

"What's up, Dad?"

"Greg was zero for four again tonight. I'm not sure I can wait until we get home to talk to him."

"Dad, just sit him for now. Really, it'll be better if you wait until we get home. Enjoy the winning streak, okay?"

"I guess I should. Might be my only chance."

Bernie stood. "Shower up and let's get on the bus. I'll treat you to a beer at the hotel bar when we get back."

Bernie saw how Greg's struggles were affecting his father. In the end, it was a business and like it or not, Greg might need to be released. Bernie and Johnny just needed to figure out how to break the news to him.

The Pride was rolling. They'd already won the first three games of the trip, with the latest being a 5-3 victory behind a good outing from Jake, a four-hit night from Freddie that included a three-run double, and a perfect ninth inning from Robinson for the save. They'd won seven straight after the six-game losing streak. One game left in Quakertown before hitting the road back home.

Johnny felt differently about the team now. He didn't think there was ever a game they couldn't win. "This is what I hoped for," he thought.

Bernie arrived in his room, noticing the message light on his phone was lit.

"Bernie, it's Frank Carlson. Sorry I missed you. Give me a call tomorrow, okay?"

He was glad Frank called, even though it meant he'd been released by the Mantids. Bernie hoped Frank would accept his offer to be the hitting coach. For now, he just wanted some sleep. Tomorrow was an afternoon game and he still wasn't packed to head home. In between, he had a call to make that could net him a new hitting coach.

Morning came early. Bernie grabbed a quick bite then hastily packed. Folding was not an option. Finished, he made his call.

"Hey Frank, it's Bernie Endino. Sorry I wasn't here to get your call yesterday."

"No problem. Jerry said you wanted to talk to me. What's up?"

Bernie looked around the room to make sure he hadn't left anything behind. "I know things didn't work out with the Mantids, but I have an offer I'd like you to consider."

"What kind of offer?"

"I'd like you to join us as a hitting coach. I think you'd be great."

There was a long silence on the other end. "I appreciate it, Bernie, but I don't know. It's less than twenty-four hours since I got released. I'm not sure what I want to do right now."

"I understand, but would you at least take a week to think about it?"

"All right, Bernie. I'll think about it but no promises."

"Thanks and whatever you choose, good luck."

Bernie was nearly late for the team bus. He ran down six flights of stairs just to make it. He was drenched in sweat when he took the seat by his father.

"A little wet there, Bern."

A sweat-stained Bernie said, "I'll shower at the stadium. I'll just wear one of the spare jerseys or something."

Clean and wearing a Pride jersey, Bernie took his seat in the stands. Winning eight in a row wouldn't be easy. It was a nip and tuck game from the start. Quakertown jumped out to a 2-0 lead after one inning but the Pride quickly tied the game in the second. Quakertown retook the lead in the bottom of the fifth with a run but Pride again respond with a run in the sixth. The score remained tied at three after eight innings. Bernie wouldn't admit it to anyone but at this point, he was just hoping for no extra innings. He wanted to get home to his family. He had no such luck as the game stayed tied after nine. He texted Rachel:

Game's going into extra innings. Hope it doesn't last too long. Cross your fingers.

Rachel texted back:

Will do. I had Anna cross hers, too.

Neither team put up a scoring threat in the 10th or 11th innings. The game duration was nearing four hours. In the top of the 12th, it looked like the Pride would take the lead when Derek hit a deep fly ball down the right field line but it was caught by the right fielder with his back against the wall.

The game headed to the bottom of the 12th, still tied. Johnny had to use a young pitcher named Tim Mathis and hoped he could get through the inning. Tim wasn't having a great season, leading Johnny to use him more in mop up duty and never in a tight game. Sure enough it only took one pitch to see why Johnny rarely used Tim. His first pitch fastball got turned into a monstrous home run over the left field fence, ending the Pride winning streak. Bernie wanted to be upset about it but he wasn't. He was just happy he'd be home in a few hours. In the meantime, he talked to his father about the game.

"Tough one, Dad. Winning streak couldn't go on forever though."

"I feel bad for Tim. He's been working hard with Jimmy but he's just not getting it."

"Dad, why don't you call Tim in. I'll talk to him."

A few minutes later, Tim arrived.

"Have a seat," Bernie said.

Tim knew this wasn't going to be a good meeting.

"Tim, I don't think you're quite ready to be here. Coach and I feel you'd be better off back in Double A until you get some more experience."

Tim looked at the floor and shook his head. "I figured that's why you brought me in here. Man, this sucks."

Johnny gave Tim some encouragement.

"You're young. This isn't the end. Go back and keep working at it."

Tim left knowing his next stop was Bristol, Connecticut, home of the Mantids Double A team.

"Now we need another pitcher," Johnny said.

"I'll call Jerry. I hope he's got someone for us."

Johnny reminded Bernie, "Don't forget to tell him we'll need another outfielder too."

"Oh yeah. Greg. I almost forgot."

Bernie had been dreading this for a while. His father said, "It'll be all right. This is just part of the game."

"I know, but doesn't make it any easier."

On the ride to the hotel, Johnny said to Bernie, "It's too bad about Tim. Jimmy was really working hard with him. Funny thing is, Jimmy actually looked better than Tim."

Bernie sat back in his seat. Right then he thought he had the solution to his pitching problem.

"Dad, hold off on talking to Greg until we get back. Tell Tim he's staying with us for a few more days too, okay?"

"Why?"

"Please just do it. I have an idea, but I have to run it by Jerry first."

"Do you want to tell me what this idea is?"

Bernie tapped his dad's knee. "Not yet, okay?"

Johnny shook his head. "All right. I'll hold off and hope whatever your planning works."

Bernie just thought, *Yeah, me too.*

[16]

THE WINDS OF CHANGE KEEP BLOWING

BERNIE HAD PUT THE tough Quakertown loss behind him. He was home now and anxious to share his idea with Jerry.

"Hey, Endino. Surprised to hear from you."

Bernie got right to the point. "Jerry, I need something from you."

"Now what?"

"We're cutting Greg Jeffers in a few days so I'll need an outfielder."

"Sorry to hear that, Endino. I know your dad's fond of him. I'll get you an outfielder. Got a guy that I wanted to move up anyway. Is that it?"

"Now that you mention it, we'd like to send Mathis back to Double A for a while. He isn't ready."

"You can send him back, but Bristol's already short on pitching so I don't know what you'll do."

"That's the good part, I already have an idea for his replacement."

Bernie could actually hear Jerry bite hard on his cigar. "Endino, what kind of scheme are you running now?"

"No scheme. I just have a guy that I think will be a good fit."

Jerry was tired of the waiting. "All right...who?"

201

"Jimmy McConnell."

"Shit, Endino, I just about fell out of my chair! McConnell? Your pitching coach? Are you nuts?"

Bernie had worked this out in his mind. "When Greg gets cut, that opens up a roster spot for a player of my choice per our agreement. Jimmy's done some work on the side and my dad tells me he looks good. When we were in high school, Jimmy was the best pitcher in our league, hands down. If he doesn't take a line drive off of his head, I think he'd become a hell of a pitcher. I still believe he can. I want him to get a chance."

"Nice story, Endino, really, but what makes you think McConnell will even want to pitch again?"

The question had never crossed Bernie's mind.

"I just need to talk to him, Jerry. I'll get him to do it."

Jerry had gotten used to the lunacy surrounding the team. "All right, if you can talk him into pitching, he can have the roster spot."

"Thanks, Jerry."

"You're a crazy son of a bitch, you know that, Endino?"

"Maybe, but admit it...you're enjoying this, aren't you?"

"Not sure how much I'm enjoying it, but life's been different since I met you. Let me know how your talk goes."

Bernie hung up the phone thinking, *Maybe Jerry's right. Maybe I am nuts...but then again, maybe I'm just crazy smart.*

Bernie was finally ready to sit down with a cup of coffee and the morning paper. There was an article on the team in the sports section and it was much different than the one he'd read on that snowy opening day. This one used words like 'resilient,' 'fun to watch,' 'up and coming,' and 'poised to make a run.' Someone else was noticing.

With his coffee finished, Bernie called Johnny who was still agonizing about talking to Greg. Cutting a guy was tough enough and even worse when you've been friends for what seems like forever.

Bernie let Johnny know that he'd have a replacement for Greg soon. It didn't make Johnny feel any better. Bernie hoped he could improve his father's mood.

"I do have some potentially good news, Dad."

"I can use some of that. Give it to me."

"I think I have your replacement for Tim and he's available right away."

"Who is it? Is it that Cuban kid from the Double A team? I think he'd be fantastic."

"No, not him. I'm thinking of someone with a little more experience...like Jimmy."

Bernie heard nothing on the other end for a while. "Dad, are you still there?"

"Yeah, I'm here. Just getting my head around this. Jimmy, huh? He was great when you guys were in school, Bern, but he hasn't thrown in a game for over a decade."

Bernie decided he needed a second cup of coffee and began to prepare it. "You said he looks good."

"I said he looks better than Tim. That's a little different."

"Okay so better than Tim, but that's still better."

Bernie heard Johnny began tapping his pen on the table. "I don't know about this, Bern. It sounds crazy."

Bernie put cream and sugar into his freshly brewed cup of coffee. "No crazier than a guy with no professional managing experience running a team full of guys that played for him when they were teenagers."

Johnny laughed. "Okay Bern, we'll see what Jimmy can do. I have nothing to lose, right?"

"Exactly. He can't be worse than Tim was anyway."

Bernie's morning on the phone spilled over into early afternoon as he called Jimmy.

"What can I do for you, Boss?"

"Jimmy, you're doing a great job for us as pitching coach."

Jimmy interrupted. "And what's the but?"

"The but?"

"Yeah, the but...it always comes after a compliment like that. You know, 'you are a pretty girl with a nice smile 'but', I have to dump you'. The but."

"I guess there is a but Jimmy, but this is a good one."

"A good one?"

"Yeah. My father says you're looking good on the mound. He saw it when you were working with Tim."

"I just showed him a few things. I don't know what your dad saw."

Bernie and Jimmy played a lot of poker together in high school. Jimmy was using one of his old poker moves and Bernie decided to call him on it. "I figured. I mean, what can you be throwing? Maybe 80-83 tops on your fastball?"

Jimmy got hot. "I'm touching 90-92, asshole!"

Bernie smiled. "Hey, I'm your boss...and how do you know you're touching 90-92?"

"Sorry. Okay so I've been throwing a bit on the side. I had one of the scouts clock me."

"It's okay, I'm glad. Jimmy, I want you to take Tim's place in the bullpen."

Bernie heard Jimmy's phone hit the floor. A few seconds later Jimmy said, "You want me to what?"

"I want you to be part of our bullpen."

"I can't, Bernie. No way."

"Yes you can. Anyway, it's not like we'll be using you in close games or anything. We just need a guy who can pick up some innings in blowouts."

"Geez, when you put it like that, how can I not say yes?"

"I didn't mean for it to sound that way, Jimmy. You'll fill a need and it'll help us out if you give it a shot."

"Bernie, throwing on the side and throwing in a game are way different."

"Good, then your arm should be well rested. Seriously, Jimmy, will you do it? If it doesn't work out we'll bring Tim back from Double A. Either way, you're my pitching coach."

Jimmy again pulled the phone away from his ear for a second. "Wait, you want me to be a pitcher and a coach?"

"You can do it. Plus, who better to know if you have your stuff out there or not?"

Jimmy laughed. "All right, you talked me into it. I'll give it a try. Just promise me your dad won't put me in unless he absolutely has to."

"I'll talk to him. Thanks again, Jimmy."

Bernie was thrilled that Jimmy was joining the bullpen but remembered Johnny's upcoming lunch with Coach Art and his son Greg. He thought, *Maybe this is as good as today is gonna get.*

Johnny was again sitting in the diner where Art agreed to be his coach. This meeting promised to be less pleasant than the first.

Art and Greg arrived together and took a seat at Johnny's table.

"Thanks for coming today, guys. I want to talk to you before we hit the road tomorrow. Greg, I can't tell you how thankful I am that you came out for this team, and Art, working with you again feels like the old days. That's why this is so tough for me. Greg, as much as I like having you, I have to cut you. The numbers just aren't there."

Greg dropped his eyes to the table.

Art said, "Whoa, Johnny! You can't cut Greg. If he's gone, I'm going too."

It was the reaction Johnny feared.

"Art, I have to think of the team and Greg just isn't helping enough right now. I'd still like you to stay."

Art slammed his coffee cup to the table, spilling a little.

"Come on, Greg. We're done here."

Greg put his hand on Art's shoulder. "Wait, Dad. Coach is right. I haven't done my job. He carried me as long as he could."

Greg looked at Johnny. "Sorry I let you down, Coach."

"Greg, you didn't let me down. You busted your ass out there every day and you've been a big help with Malcolm. I'd like to keep you on as one of my coaches if you'll do it."

Art asked Greg, "You're okay with this?"

Greg had a slight smile. "Fine, Dad. Not too many guys get a chance like I did."

Art put his hands on the table. "Johnny, if the kid is all right with it, then I guess I can't be mad, can I? Looks like the Jeffers boys will be coaching together."

The meeting had gone better than Johnny expected. He not only retained Art, but also got Greg to stay on with the coaching staff.

As for the Pride's last game before the new outfielder arrived, they won and pulled within one game of .500. Malcolm collected three hits, including a squeeze bunt single that brought home the game-winning run. Greg was the first man out of the dugout to congratulate him.

As the team was checking into its hotel in Utica, a short, thin, young Asian man wearing glasses approached Johnny.

"Hello, sir. My name is Yoshinori Ito. Would you happen to know if this is the Pride baseball team?"

"Yes it is. If you want autographs would you please wait just a few minutes until after they check in?"

"Oh no sir. I do not want autographs. I am looking for the manager."

"I'm the manager. Are you my new player?"

"No sir. I am the interpreter for your new player. He is coming in now."

The second Asian man was only about 5'9", but he looked like an athlete with a sleek and muscular frame. His name was Hideki Mariyama, a 22-year-old outfielder from Japan.

Johnny put out his hand. "Welcome to the team."

Yoshinori translated Johnny's words. Hideki smiled and responded through his interpreter.

"Hideki says that he looks forward to playing for you and he hopes that he can help the team to win."

"Please tell him I'm sure he'll do just fine." Yoshinori passed this along to Hideki who nodded to his new manager.

"So, Yoshinori, do you mind if I call you Yosh? It will just be easier for me. You can just call me Johnny, okay?"

Yoshinori nodded politely. "Yes, that will be fine."

Johnny had just one more question.

"Yosh, does Hideki speak any English?"

Yoshinori moved his head a bit from side to side. "He knows a few words, but right now he still is not comfortable with the language."

A few hours later, Johnny made his way to the lobby for the bus to the stadium. He was usually the first man there but not this time as Hideki and Yosh were already there waiting.

"You two are early. I like that."

Yosh responded, "We did not want to miss the bus."

"Yosh, please tell Hideki that I'd like him to get his uniform on as quickly as possible then meet me on the field. I want to see what he can do."

At the stadium Johnny instructed Hideki through Yosh to take his position in centerfield. Johnny started by hitting him a few routine fly balls. Hideki fielded each of them flawlessly. It was time to ramp up the workout. Johnny hit a line drive towards right centerfield. Hideki got a great read on the ball off of the bat and on a dead run, made the catch. Johnny continued hitting balls to both right and left centerfield. Each time Hideki made the difficult catches look easy. Coach Phil had been watching for several minutes.

"Shit, Johnny, is there anything this kid can't catch?"

"Not so far, Phil. Let's see how he does going back and coming in on the baseball."

Johnny hit one over Hideki's head and towards the centerfield wall. With his back to Johnny, Hideki sprinted towards the spot where he expected the ball to fall. At the last minute, he looked up and made the catch.

Johnny had one more test. He tossed the ball into the air and hit a shallow pop fly. It was much shallower than Johnny wanted as the ball descended just behind second base. Hideki went into a dead sprint towards second base and at the last second, dove and caught the ball.

"Well I'll be damned. I hope he can hit," said Phil.

Johnny said, "Let's find out."

Johnny had Hideki take a few swings. Hideki stepped into the left-handed batter's box to face Coach Art. He hit the first pitch into the protective fence in front of the coach. Hideki did the same with the next two pitches prompting Art to yell, "Johnny I think I quit!"

Johnny laughed and said, "Throw him something inside!"

Coach Art took Johnny's advice. Hideki adjusted and hit a line drive into right field.

"All right Art, throw him one on the outside half now!"

Art obliged and Hideki promptly slapped the pitch into left field.

Johnny was satisfied with what he saw. "Yosh, please tell Hideki to come in and that he's starting tonight."

Game time approached and Johnny began his talk. "Gather around, gentlemen!"

The team formed the circle that had become ritual for them.

"First, I want you to know that Greg has retired, but he's staying on as a special consultant to help you guys with your bunting, base running, and outfield defense."

Greg appreciated that Johnny said he retired and not that he was cut.

"Taking Greg's spot will be Hideki Mariyama, our new outfielder, and his interpreter, Yosh Ito!"

After greeting their new teammate, the team headed out to the field. Every player was aware that a win tonight meant a .500 record.

The game was tied through three innings, with the Pride's only hit being a single to centerfield by Hideki. Utica finally broke the deadlock in the fourth when Clark hung a knuckleball that got hit over the left field fence.

After Ricky and Derek were retired easily to start the fifth inning, Mark dribbled a curveball down the third base line. After traveling no more than 30 feet, it came to rest on the chalk with Mark reaching first base.

Hideki stepped in for his second at-bat with the Pride. Along with a good swing, he also had an excellent batter's eye and worked the count to 3-1.

Johnny had an idea. He signaled to Phil coaching third who relayed the signals to Mark standing on first base. As the pitch approached the plate, Mark took off for second base. Hideki served a line drive just over the head of the shortstop into the left centerfield gap. Mark scored easily from first base and Hideki rolled into second with a game-tying double. With two outs and Clark stepping to the plate, another run was a near impossibility. Clark only had one hit in the entire season, and that was in April on a slow ground ball to the shortstop. The first pitch to Clark was a fastball. Somehow he managed to hit it hard but just foul by first base. He did the same with the second fastball.

"He's on this guy," Johnny said to Phil.

Coach Phil said, "Yeah, but if this next pitch is anything but a fastball, he's screwed."

At second base, Hideki noticed the pitcher wasn't paying much attention to him. He increased his lead off second base and as the pitcher delivered the two-strike pitch, Hideki broke for third base.

The pitch was a sharp-breaking slider that Clark took a horrible swing at for strike three. Because of its sharp break, however, the ball skipped by the Utica catcher and an alert Clark took off for first base.

The catcher chased the ball to the backstop and came up firing to his first baseman. Clark and the ball arrived at virtually the same time.

The umpire gave the 'safe' signal as Clark crossed the bag. A livid Utica first baseman spun around to vehemently argue the call with the umpire.

Meanwhile Hideki had rounded third base and was heading home. The catcher yelled frantically at his first baseman but by the time he heard the call, it was too late. Hideki crossed home and the Pride now led, 2-1.

Johnny clapped hard. "Son of a bitch!"

Hideki got to the dugout and was greeted with back slaps and handshakes from his teammates.

"Hell of a play, Hideki! Hell of a play!" Johnny screamed while Yosh interpreted.

It was still 2-1 as Utica came to bat in the bottom of the ninth. Wil came in to pitch and hopefully to close out the win. The first two outs came easily. Wil delivered his first pitch to the next hitter. The batter hit what looked like a routine ground ball towards first base.

That should do it, thought Johnny. Unfortunately, in baseball sometimes what looks routine can turn into the unusual. As the ball approached Pete, it struck first base and skipped by him into right field. What looked destined to be the final out of the game had turned into a two-out double.

"Aw, shit!" Johnny yelled.

Coach Phil said, "We're still in good shape."

"Yeah but Jones is up."

Jones was Tony Jones, Utica's third baseman. He was a power hitter that already had twenty-two home runs on the season.

Johnny decided to talk with Wil to discuss strategy. He got to the mound and a visibly upset Wil said, "Can you believe that shit, Coach? This game should be over! Hit the damn bag! That's a bullshit hit!"

Johnny put his hands on Wil's shoulders. "All right, just calm your ass down. It's part of the game. I think we should walk this guy."

Wil took a deep breath. "Let me go after him."

Johnny looked Wil dead in the eyes. He saw a fire that no one could put out.

"All right Wil...he's yours."

Wil got Jones to swing and miss at a first pitch changeup. He followed with a slider that Jones again flailed at and missed. He wasn't going to fool around. Wil threw a high fastball. It was where he wanted it to be but Jones swung and made contact. Very good contact. The ball sailed into deep centerfield. It seemed like the best anyone could hope for was that the ball stay in the park and the game would just be tied.

Hideki turned his back to the infield and took off towards the fence just as he'd done during his pre-game workout. As he got to the wall, Hideki looked up to see that the ball was clearly headed out of the park. He planted his right foot into the padding of the centerfield wall and launched himself straight up. With his glove fully extended, the ball hit the webbing of his glove. He closed the glove tightly around the ball, then covered it with his bare hand as he landed on the warning track, going into a roll. When he finally stopped rolling, Hideki held the ball high into the air. He saved the game, and the Pride was finally at .500!

"Holy sweet mother of God!" Wil yelled.

"Son of a friggin' bitch!" screamed Johnny.

"Well I'll be damned," Coach Phil whispered.

Tony just stood near second base in disbelief for a second. Then he took off his helmet and fired it towards his own dugout.

As Hideki came in from centerfield, Derek and Freddie grabbed him and lifted him into the air. A huge smile came to his face and stayed there all the way into the clubhouse.

As the celebration continued, Johnny stood in the center of the clubhouse shouting.

"Gentlemen, hell of a win tonight! A hell of a win! Great job by everyone, but I think you guys will agree that tonight's game ball should go to our newest team member, Hideki Maryiama!"

The team cheered wildly then took the hero of the evening and promptly put him into the shower wearing his full uniform. Yosh didn't understand the ritual.

Johnny said, "It's okay, Yosh. It means they like him."

After all the merriment dissipated, Johnny sat in the manager's office. He thought about the discussion he had with Bernie and how he'd said a .500 record is all he wanted out of the season. He also remembered Bernie saying that there's no way a .500 record would be enough. As it turned out, Bernie was right. Now that the team was at .500, Johnny felt they could do more. There were seventy regular season games left, and Johnny wanted there to be a few more after that.

The next morning, Bernie sat with his coffee reading the paper. The sound of his phone broke the serenity of the morning.

"Hey Bern, it's Dad. I didn't wake you, did I?"

"No, Dad."

"Great. Hey, is there anything you forgot to tell me about our new outfielder?"

Bernie thought for a minute, "Nothing comes to mind."

"So the fact that he's Japanese and speaks very little English didn't seem important to you?"

Bernie thought, *Oh shit! That's what I missed when my phone was cutting out!*

"Dad, I didn't know. The connection on my phone wasn't so great when Jerry called."

Johnny laughed. "It's all right, Bern. Jerry sent an interpreter with him."

Bernie took a sip of his coffee. "Glad to hear it. Hey, congrats on getting to .500."

"Yeah, but let's hope we can stay there."

"Dad, I haven't finished my coffee yet and I'm in no mood to start with you. Just be happy about it."

"I know but..."

Bernie interrupted. "I'm hanging up now, Dad."

Bernie wondered why Johnny couldn't be happy with accomplishing something but then again, he also understood. If Johnny settled with just getting to .500, he was afraid he and the team would lose focus and he wasn't about to let that happen.

[17]

Another Day, Another Debut

WITH LUKE SCHEDULED TO pitch, Johnny liked his chances at moving over .500. Luke had been brilliant since Johnny found him pitching in that amateur league. After the Pride went down without a whimper in the top of the first inning, Luke took the mound. He got through the first inning but it took a leaping catch by Miguel on a line drive and a fantastic running grab of a deep fly ball by Hideki to keep Luke out of trouble. He wasn't so lucky in the bottom of the second inning. Utica's batters strung together two singles, a double and then a home run to take a 4-0 lead.

"Luke looks off his game tonight," Johnny said to Jimmy.

As a precaution, Johnny had Christian begin loosening up in the bullpen.

Luke started the third inning by walking the first batter on four pitches. The next batter hit a ball to the left field fence, but Malcolm ran it down for the first out. The following batter crushed a ball into the gap between Hideki and Derek for a run-scoring double. It was now 5-0 in Utica's favor.

Coach Jimmy took a slow walk to the mound.

"What's up, Luke?"

"I don't know, Coach. Just don't have my game tonight."

215

"Hang tough for a little longer. We're getting Christian ready."

Luke still couldn't get things going. Two pitches into the next batter, he allowed a two-run home run giving Utica a 7-0 lead. As Luke's night ended, Johnny took the ball from him and said, "It's all right, kid. Learn from it and we'll get 'em next time."

Christian ran into some trouble as he gave up a single then walked a batter.

"Should I go talk to him, Skip?" Jimmy asked.

Johnny was chewing on a toothpick. "No. I want you to loosen up. You're going in next inning."

"I'm what?"

"We're already down 7-0, Perez's spot is up third next inning, and you're the only fresh arm we have right now. Get loose. I'll take the pitching coach duties for a while."

All the color drained from Jimmy's face as he grabbed his glove and headed for the bullpen.

Meanwhile, Christian gave up a run. With the score now 8-0, the Pride seemed lifeless. After six innings, the Pride had sent up eighteen batters and all eighteen had been retired.

Johnny brought Jimmy into the game. In a million years, Jimmy would never have believed he'd be in this position. He hadn't pitched competitively in over ten years and here he was, not just back on the mound, but in a professional game. To say he was nervous would be an understatement.

Ricky came to the mound, handing Jimmy the baseball. "No worries, Coach. Just you and me playing catch."

Jimmy smiled. "Yep. Just you and me playing catch...in front of 6,000 people."

Ricky laughed and headed behind the plate. Jimmy wound up and delivered his first professional pitch. It sailed high over Ricky's head and to the backstop. Jimmy paced the mound to calm himself and delivered his next pitch. It was a strike right down the middle, which the batter hit off of the left field fence for a double.

Jimmy thought, *Oh shit. I'm in trouble.*

With his fastball not fooling anyone, Jimmy went to the curveball. It hung and the batter drilled a line drive towards the first base line. Pete dove towards the line and fielded the ball on one hop. Jimmy ran over to cover the bag, getting there just in time to record the out while the runner from second advanced to third.

Jimmy walked back to the mound shaking his head.

Please just let me survive this, he prayed.

He went back to his fastball, delivering another strike that was right down the middle and that was crushed by the batter.

The line drive made its way to Hideki in centerfield and it was sinking in a hurry. Hideki's great speed helped him to catch the ball off of his shoe tops for the second out.

The runner from third broke for the plate.

"Home!" Ricky yelled.

Hideki came up throwing and fired a laser beam to a waiting Ricky. The ball arrived well ahead of the runner. Ricky applied the tag to complete the double play and ended the inning. Jimmy had thrown four pitches, allowed three hard-hit balls, and hadn't allowed a run.

As he came off the field, Johnny grinned. "Good work, Jimmy. I need just one more from you."

"Good work? Coach, I was awful out there. Awful."

"Hey, nobody scored. That's all I ask. I don't care how it looked."

Three more Pride batters, and three more outs. As Jimmy took the mound to start his second inning, Ricky gave him another pep talk.

"Just keep throwing strikes, Coach. You've got a great defense behind you. Let them do their jobs."

Jimmy heard Ricky's advice but had a different plan. He was throwing strikes. Maybe he needed to show a little wildness. The first batter of the inning dug into the batter's box. Jimmy looked in for the sign then fired. His first pitch was high and tight, knocking the hitter backwards. Jimmy looked in, shrugged at the batter, and called time to talk to Ricky.

Ricky arrived and took off his mask. "What's going on, Coach?"

Jimmy rubbed up the baseball. "I did that on purpose. I need you to talk it up behind the plate. Make these guys think I'm a loose cannon out here. Do that, all right?"

Ricky grinned behind his glove. "You got it, Coach."

Ricky settled back in behind the plate and began talking to the batter.

"Poor guy. He's a wreck out there. Says he can't get a good feel for the ball. I'd hate to be you."

Jimmy threw a curveball that started towards the batter's head. As he bailed out of the batter's box, the ball broke over the inside corner of the plate. At the last second, Utica's batter swung and hit a slow roller back to Jimmy who flipped it to Pete for the first out.

Jimmy started the next hitter with a fastball on the outside part of the plate for strike one.

Ricky continued with the psychological game. "Wow! That was supposed to be inside! Can't wait to see where the next one ends up."

Jimmy's next fastball was purposely up and in, forcing the batter to jack knife out of the way.

Ricky pounded his mitt. "Nice job. I wouldn't step in against this guy." His banter was getting to the batter who said, "Shut the hell up!"

Jimmy threw a slider over the outside corner for strike two. He noticed the batter flinch when the ball left his hand. Jimmy knew he had him. He threw another slider slightly further inside. The batter jumped backwards but the ball broke sharply over the inside corner for a called strike three. Two down and one to go.

The next batter stepped in. Ricky said, "Boy, has he been lucky out there. I thought he was going to kill one of you guys."

The batter said, "Sit your ass behind the plate and be quiet!"

Jimmy was going to have some more fun. He wound up and threw a fastball high off of the backstop. Despite never really being in danger of getting hit, the batter ended up sprawled out on the ground. He got up and took two steps towards the mound.

Ricky said, "Settle down, big guy. He's not doing it on purpose." Ricky began to chuckle.

The batter reluctantly took his spot back in the box. Jimmy went back to the slider, which the batter swung at awkwardly for strike one. Jimmy's next pitch was a high fastball. The batter swung almost defensively, and missed for strike two. Jimmy was confident now. He finished off the Utica batter with a curveball taken for strike three. Jimmy had gotten through two innings without allowing a run. Johnny couldn't be happier.

"Great work, Jimmy! You really bailed us out."

"Thanks, Coach. I'm done now, right?"

"Yeah. Have Casey get loose."

Casey was Casey Francis, a 27-year-old right-handed reliever who got most of his work in games where the decision seemed well in hand.

"Good. Thanks." He then walked through the tunnel to the clubhouse and promptly threw up.

All Johnny wanted from his team now was a hit. Pete was the first batter of the eighth inning. He swung at the first pitch and drove it deep into centerfield. Not deep enough however, as it was caught on the warning track for the first out. Ricky became the Pride's first base runner of the night, drawing a walk.

Al Dixon, Utica's pitcher, wasn't happy with the umpire's calls and angrily paced the mound. He became more agitated when Derek rolled a ball just passed Utica's second baseman for the team's first hit of the night.

"Look at this guy. He's losing it out there," Johnny said to no one in particular.

Mark then surprised everyone by dropping a bunt down the third base line.

With the bases all of a sudden loaded, Utica's manager came out to talk with his pitcher.

Dixon said, "Can you believe this shit? A bullshit seeing eye grounder and a friggin' bunt down 8-0! This is garbage!"

His manager said, "Calm down. It's still 8-0. Reel it in and finish off this inning."

The words fell upon deaf ears. With his temper reaching a boil, Dixon hit Malcolm in the thigh. It was 8-1 with the bases still loaded and just one out.

"We're getting to him. This one may not be over." Johnny said, watching closely from the side. Johnny told Freddie to grab a bat because he was hitting for Jimmy. He then called the bullpen.

Jimmy, who had just finished worshiping the porcelain altar, answered the bullpen phone. "What's up, Skip?"

"Get Casey up and ask Wil how he feels."

"Wil?"

"Yeah. Just in case."

Freddie stepped in to hit. Just a few minutes earlier Dixon was working on a perfect game, and now he was just trying to keep it together. As the first pitch came in, Freddie faked a bunt and the pitch sailed high for ball one.

Dixon's focus was shot. He thought, *Shit-head faking a bunt down 8-1. What are these assholes doing?*

Freddie squared again as if he was going to bunt. This time Dixon threw one up and in on purpose, sending Freddie to the ground.

The umpire pulled off his mask. "Do it again, Dixon, and you're done tonight!"

Dixon took a step towards the plate. "Do what?"

"You know what I mean. Just pitch."

The unraveling continued as Freddie drove the next pitch into the right centerfield gap.

Derek and Mark scored as Malcolm rolled into third and Freddie cruised into second with a double. It was 8-3 and the Pride was threatening to score more.

As Dixon's next curveball tumbled towards the plate, Hideki noticed the first baseman playing in and away from the bag. He slapped the ball hard past first. It rolled into the right field corner and brought home Malcolm and Freddie. By the time the Utica right fielder retrieved it, Hideki was standing on third with a two-run triple. Suddenly it was 8-5.

Miguel's at bat started with two well-struck balls that both went foul.

Dixon didn't mess around and he threw a fastball on the inside corner. Miguel got just enough of the bat on it to roll the ball towards first. The first baseman tagged Miguel for the second out as Hideki scored, cutting the lead to 8-6.

Johnny called the bullpen.

"Jimmy, get Wil up. Now!"

Hank took his turn at bat. He'd had a rough night thus far, striking out in all three of his at bats. Johnny took him to the side.

"Forget the first three, Hank. We've got him now."

Hank rubbed some more pine tar on his bat handle and stepped to the plate.

Dixon knew he was one out away from ending the miserable inning, and also that Hank hadn't been able to touch him. Dixon's slider had been Hank's kryptonite and Dixon stuck with it.

As the ball approached the plate, Hank did something that no one would expect. He dropped down a bunt! It was a beauty too. It got by Dixon and rolled to a stop just in front of the third base bag.

Hank was on first and Pete stepped to the plate as the tying run.

Dixon was ready to turn in his jersey for a straitjacket. *A bunt! A son-of-a-bitching bunt from their best friggin' hitter! What a bunch of friggin' assholes!* Focus now completely gone, Dixon hit Pete on the shin with his first pitch.

The umpire yelled, "That's it, Dixon! You're done!"

Dixon threw up his hands. "It was a friggin' accident!"

"I warned you, Dixon! Get off the field!"

Utica's manager dragged Dixon off of the field and brought in his closer, Carl Pearce, for a rare four-out save attempt.

Pearce's weapons were a high-powered fastball and a nasty curve. As Ricky watched Pearce warm up, Johnny gave some advice.

"He likes to throw that curve to start off hitters, then he'll go to the hard stuff. If he starts the curveball over the plate, lay off. If you see it coming at you, stay in there and rip it because that one's going to drop into the strike zone. He'll use that curve as his finisher if he gets two strikes on you but if you recognize it, you can hit it."

Ricky listened intently to his manager's instruction. Sure enough, Pearce began with a curve. It started off dead center of the plate. Ricky wasn't fooled and he watched as the ball twirled its way out of the strike zone for ball one. Pearce was done fooling around. He threw his fastball next for strike one then another for strike two. Ricky remembered what Johnny said. Pearce delivered his next pitch, a curveball that began at Ricky's head. Ricky resisted the urge to back out and held his ground. As the ball broke over the plate,

Ricky swung and hit a towering fly ball towards left centerfield. It continued rising and finally fell well beyond the fence for a three-run home run! Somehow the Pride had gone from down eight runs and having no hits to leading 9-8!

"Holy shit! Holy shit! Holy shit!" Coach Art yelled.

"I don't freakin' believe it!" Coach Phil chimed in.

Johnny tried to restore order, although on the inside he was as much in disbelief about what had transpired as anyone.

He also had a decision to make: Bring in Casey, or go with Wil for two innings. He chose Wil. Robinson, like Pearce, wasn't used to pitching more than one inning at a time. This would be a real test.

Wil pitched his first inning as if it was the last. He got two strikeouts and a pop fly. The ninth wasn't as simple. He gave up a base hit, followed by a walk to the first two batters of the inning.

Two on and nobody out and making matters worse, Tony Jones was up next. Wil was apprehensive about the match up. Ricky gave him a pep talk.

"You got him yesterday. You can get him today."

Wil said, "Yesterday he hit a ball that was over the damn fence. I didn't exactly fool him, did I?"

Wil had an idea. He'd been working on a circle change up with Jimmy. Maybe now was a good time to debut it. Ricky put down the signal for a fastball. Wil nodded, but his mind was made up. He was throwing the changeup. Jones, who was guessing fastball, swung hard.

Despite being fooled, he still hit the ball hard down the third base line. Hank, who was protecting the line, fielded the ball right at the bag. He stepped on third for the first out then fired to Mark at second for out number two. Jones' swing had thrown him off-balance and he struggled to get out of the batter's box. Mark seized the opportunity and threw on to first base. Pete stretched as far as he could while the ball and Jones arrived at the bag almost at the same time. Almost. The ball got there just a bit sooner.

The Pride ended the game with a triple play!

"Un-freaking-believable!" Johnny screamed.

"Holy shit!" Coach Phil added.

On the mound, Wil pumped his fist. Ricky came out, arms raised, and said, "What the hell was that? It sure as hell wasn't your fastball."

Wil said, "Changeup. Been working on it with Jimmy."

"Nice pitch. Maybe next time you want to fill me in, huh?"

Johnny addressed his troops. "Not much I can say, gentlemen. You didn't quit out there. Most incredible thing I've been a part of this year. Special thanks to Jimmy for giving us two innings today and for getting his first professional win. Shower up and let's go home!"

Jimmy hadn't realized that he was, in fact, the winning pitcher. It was his very first game and he got the win. *Heck, I didn't even pitch well*, he thought. *What did I do to deserve that?* His next thought was that he hoped to get to do it again.

[18]

A BUMP IN THE ROAD

THE PRIDE HEADED INTO July playing well. They'd won seven of their last ten games and began the month with a 45-40 record. While things had improved, the team was still in third place behind Nantucket and Quakertown. With fifty-nine games left to be played, there was still plenty of time to make a playoff run. Amidst all the positives, however, Johnny was concerned about a player, and it was a concern he hadn't expected.

Luke had dominated up to his start against Utica. At first Johnny shrugged it off as a bad day. Even the very best professional pitchers run into this, but it hadn't been just the one time. Luke had been hit hard in his two starts since Utica. Johnny decided it was time for a sit down with his young pitcher.

He met Luke for breakfast at a diner near their hotel in Nantucket. It was known for great coffee and an amazing Western omelet. Johnny had the omelet. Luke chose the Fisherman's plate, which included six strips of bacon, four scrambled eggs, two slices of wheat toast and hash browns.

Johnny said, "Geez Luke, hungry?"

Luke said, "Not really, Coach. Haven't had much of an appetite lately."

Johnny shook his head. "Luke, is everything all right? You seem to be a bit off lately."

Luke reached into his pocket and pulled out a letter. Johnny saw the sadness in Luke's face as he handed it over.

"Read it."

Johnny took the paper from Luke's hand.

Luke,

I've been following you in the papers. It looks like your coach was right. Baseball might be your calling. I'm closing the shop. There just isn't enough business coming in and I can't afford to keep it open. I'm not sure what I'll do now but I'm sure something will come up. I wish you were here but you have a dream to chase. I hope you catch it. I'll write you again soon. I love you.

Dad

Johnny handed the letter back to Luke. "When did you get this?"

Luke played with his napkin. "A couple of weeks ago. I didn't want to tell anyone. It's my problem, anyway."

Johnny took the napkin away from Luke. "Luke, we're your friends. If you have a problem, you can talk to us about it. We want to help."

The waitress arrived with their breakfast. Luke poked at his but didn't really eat. He was frustrated and angry. "How can you help? Can you find customers for my Dad? Can you find a job for him so he can pay his bills?"

Johnny knew Luke's anger wasn't aimed at him. He calmly said, "Luke just know we are here for you."

Luke stared at his plate. "I know, Coach, and I'm sorry for taking it out on you. I know you just want to help. I just wish you could."

"Yeah, me too. Let's at least try to enjoy breakfast. It's my treat. Also, I hate wasting food that I'm paying for."

Once Luke started eating, he put away the huge breakfast without much trouble.

For a guy without an appetite, he did some damage to that, Johnny thought.

As the two left, Johnny got an idea. "Hang in there, kid. This is going to work out. I know it. Concentrate on your job, all right? You don't pitch again for five days."

Back at his hotel room, Johnny put his plan into action then turned his attention to running the team and figuring out how to beat Nantucket. In five meetings with Nantucket thus far, the Pride had only beaten them once. In fairness, most teams had trouble beating Nantucket. They carried a 58-27 record into the first game of July and lead the division by eight games over Quakertown. The Pride sat thirteen games out of first place. If they couldn't beat Nantucket, making the playoffs was going to be tough.

Unfortunately, the Pride's fortunes against Nantucket didn't turn around as July began. Nantucket scored early and often, and there was no nine-run inning for the Pride. Things got so bad that Johnny had Mike Dillion, his utility player, pitch the eighth inning.

The lone bright spot was another good outing from Jimmy, who pitched two more innings without allowing a run. It was a 15-1 massacre pushing the Pride fourteen games out of first place. The next two games were more competitive but still, both ended in Pride losses. The hot streak they closed June with was now nothing but a memory.

They'd started July with three straight losses to Nantucket, and four in a row counting the last day of June. The team headed home seven games behind Quakertown for the wild card spot and sixteen games behind Nantucket for first place. At least the team would be home for nine days after spending the last nine on the road. Johnny hoped that a little home cooking could right the ship.

In any case, he was happy to see his family. Somehow that always helped him put things into the proper perspective. He also hoped that the phone calls he made regarding Luke and his dad had helped solve their problem. That was actually more important to Johnny than the four losses the team just suffered at Nantucket's hand.

It was Independence Day morning and Johnny had forgotten it was a holiday. He'd learned that holidays during baseball season can be easily forgotten. He, Catherine, and Kat were having an early cookout with Bernie, Rachel and the kids. They arrived at Bernie's house where he was already wearing his, It's Thrillin' to be Grillin apron, which Rachel objected to with a personal, deep-seated hate.

With a plethora of grilled meats and side dishes to choose from, the family filled their plates.

Before digging in, Johnny asked, "Bern, did you make that call for me?"

Bernie tapped the side of his head. "Geez, I completely forgot. We have to be at the stadium by three."

Johnny put some ketchup and mustard on his burger. "So you got in touch with him then?"

Bernie pulled some steaks from the grill. "Yep. I think this is all going to work out, too."

Rachel was confused by the cryptic conversation.

"What are you two talking about?"

Bernie said, "Nothing. You'll find out later."

Rachel put a fresh bib on Lizzie. "Can't you just tell us now?"

Bernie waved his grill fork. "I don't want to jinx anything."

The family ate, then Bernie and Johnny headed to the stadium. Luke showed up shortly after.

"Thanks for coming early, Luke. Have a seat. We'd like to talk to you,"

Luke hung his head and sat. "Coach, I know I haven't been very good lately. I'm sorry about that, but please don't cut me. I'll be better. It's just this thing with my father..."

Bernie stopped him. "Luke, we aren't cutting you. We just want you to see someone who we think can help. He'll be here in a few minutes."

Luke couldn't imagine how seeing anyone would help, however, Bernie and Johnny had given him a chance, so he was willing to try.

As Luke buttoned his jersey, he heard a deep voice behind him singing, "Three. It's a magic number."

Luke turned around. Standing there with a smile on his face and just the hint of a stray tear in the corner of his eye, was his father.

"Dad! What are you doing here?"

"Your coach and owner thought it might be a good idea."

Luke jumped up and hugged his father.

"Dad, I'm so sorry about the shop."

"It's fine, son. Really. That shop gave us a nice living for a long time. The world is moving on, and it's time I did too."

Luke wiped a tear from his eye. "What are you going to do?"

"Luke, I'm your father..."

Luke interrupted. "Dad, if you mention 'The Force' I swear I'm going to lose it."

Paul laughed. "What I'm saying is, that you need to trust me. Bernie has offered me a job and I'm taking it."

All of a sudden Luke had a smile from ear to ear. "You're going to work for the team?"

"Yep. They're making me head of the Maintenance Department. I'll get to fix things and keep this place running, plus I can teach these youngster's a few things or two. Heck, I might learn something too."

"It sounds great but what about the house?"

Paul swallowed hard. "I'm selling it. Bernie found me a rental until I can find a new place up here."

"Are you sure you want to do this?"

Paul nodded. "I'm sure. It'll be a fresh start. Also, I get to watch you pitch. I haven't had a chance to do that in a long time. Stop worrying about me already. Everything is going to be fine now."

Luke hugged his dad again. "Yeah. Yeah, it is. I'd better finish getting dressed and then head down to the bullpen. I'm starting tonight. Are you staying to watch?"

Paul put his hand on Luke's cheek. "Damn right I am."

"Great! I'll make you proud."

"Son, you always have."

Luke gave his dad one last hug, grabbed his glove and headed to the bullpen. Johnny and Bernie met with Paul.

Johnny said, "Thanks for coming. Sometimes a guy just needs to know his dad is all right."

Paul took Johnny's hand then Bernie's. "Thank you both for what you've done for us. I don't know what I can do to repay you."

"You can start by fixing the freezer in the visitor's clubhouse." Bernie said, laughing a little.

Paul smiled. "Okay, Boss, I'll get right on it."

"It can wait until tomorrow. You've got something more important to do tonight."

Bernie offered Paul a seat in his suite to give him a bird's eye view for his son's start.

As Luke took the mound, he saw his father in Bernie's suite. He gave his father a 'thumbs up' sign, which his father returned. Luke threw a curveball, a changeup and finally a fastball to strike out the first batter of the game.

"How fast was that?" Johnny asked Jimmy.

"Ninety-eight."

Johnny then yelled for the entire dugout to hear, "Gentlemen, I think we're in for a good night!"

Luke then proceeded to strike out the next two hitters to finish off the inning, then the next three in the second and three more in the third. No one had touched him.

Mark lead off the bottom of the third with a line drive single into left field. Freddie followed with a perfectly executed hit and run single to right. Runners were now on first and third with no one out, and Luke stepping to the plate.

The Albany third and first basemen were both anticipating a bunt. The pitcher threw a high fastball, hoping Luke would pop up any bunt attempt. Problem for the Albany pitcher was that Luke had no intention to bunt. Luke swung, and launched the ball towards the left field foul pole. Everyone watched and held their collective breath until the ball hit the pole with a thud. It was Luke's first professional home run and he'd hit it with his father watching.

Paul hollered, "Nice rip, son! Nice rip!"

On the mound, Luke continued his mastery. The leadoff hitter in the fourth inning tried bunting his way on base, but Luke fielded the ball and threw him out by a step. He finished the inning with a strike out and by inducing a pop up to Pete. In the fifth, he struck out two of the three hitters and remained perfect. While Luke's confidence grew, Paul's tension mounted.

The Pride added a run in the bottom of the fifth when, with two outs, Hideki hit his first home run with the Pride, a line drive over the left field fence. Now up 4-0, Luke took the mound to start the sixth inning. In between a fly ball to Derek in right and a ground out to Miguel at shortstop, he recorded his thirteenth strikeout of the game. He picked up two more strikeouts in the seventh; yet another perfect inning.

No one in the dugout would talk to Luke. They didn't want to jinx him. A nervous Luke said, "Come on, guys. Talk to me. It's all right. I won't blame you if I blow it."

The Pride carried a 4-0 lead into the eighth inning. Luke was still as sharp as he was at first pitch. As a matter of fact, he seemed stronger. He struck out the side for the fourth time on the night. That made sixteen strikeouts and only three outs away from a perfect game.

Now Paul wasn't the only one in Bernie's suite who was nervous.

"Oh God I hope he can do it," Catherine said.

"He's so close," Rachel added.

The ninth inning began. Luke took a deep breath, feeling surprisingly calm. He faced the first hitter of the ninth inning and struck him out with two changeups and a blazing fastball to finish him off.

Johnny asked, "How fast, Jimmy?"

Jimmy looked up from his radar gun. "Ninety-nine."

Luke came at the next batter with a two fastballs for a quick two strikes. He fired the third pitch. It looked like another fastball grooved over the middle. This time the batter had it timed. As he swung, however, the ball darted away from him and he missed for strike three.

Johnny was pleasantly surprised.

"When the hell did he come up with a slider?"

Jimmy shrugged, a bit mystified. "Must have been working on that one by himself."

One out stood between Luke and perfection. He'd struck out eighteen hitters in the game on top of it. The capacity crowd that had been so raucous to this point suddenly became almost silent.

With adrenaline pumping through him in full force, Luke threw his next two fastballs by the batter. Ricky first signaled for another fastball then the change up. Luke shook him off each time. He wanted to throw his curveball.

There's no way he's looking for a curve, Luke thought, looking in the batters eyes.

Ricky finally gave Luke the signal he'd been waiting for. Here it comes, he said quietly to himself as he released the ball.

It spun towards the plate but not with the break Luke wanted.

Aw shit! was the first thought that came to his mind.

The batter swung and smoked a line drive towards the third base line. The perfect game was as good as gone...or so everyone thought.

Hank dove towards the foul line, glove fully extended. The ball took a hard bounce up into the webbing. Hank scrambled to his feet and fired the ball towards first base with almost the same speed as Luke's fastball. Stretching out fully, Pete caught the ball a fraction of a second before the batter hit the bag. Luke had done it! A perfect game!

His teammates mobbed him on the mound and celebrated. Malcolm and Joey dumped the team water bucket over his head. Ice cold water had never felt so good. After struggling in his past few starts worrying about his father, everything now felt amazing. Heck, it felt perfect!

As the celebration died down, the fireworks show began. The entire Endino family and Paul descended from the suite to the field where Bernie lead them to watch the show from the infield grass. Paul sought out his son and when he found him, the tears of joy began to flow.

"Son, that was just incredible. I'm so proud of you."

"Thanks, Dad, but geez, will you stop crying already?"

Paul stepped back and gave his son a playful smack. "That's a deal."

Luke brought his dad to where Hank was standing.

"Dad, I have someone I want you to meet."

Luke tapped Hank's shoulder. "Hank, I'd like you to meet my dad, Paul Simms."

"Pleasure to meet you, sir."

Luke grinned. "You really saved my bacon tonight."

"Thanks, but I owed you one."

Luke was on top of the world. Less than twenty-four hours ago, he thought he'd be giving up baseball and going home to his father. Now, he'd just thrown a perfect game and his father had come to him.

[19]

GIMME A BREAK

LUKE'S PERFECT GAME SPARKED the Pride. The team won seven of its final eleven games before the All-Star Break for a 52-47 record. It still left them fourteen games behind Nantucket for first place, but the gap between them and Quakertown for the wild card spot was trimmed to three games.

The team members all had different plans for their break. Hank was off to represent the Pride in the All-Star Game. Many of the players were going home to visit their families, while a few were taking short trips to forget about baseball for a while. The Endinos were heading to the beach. With the girls already there, Bernie and Johnny drove together from Albany to meet them.

"Looks like we're in a playoff chase, huh Dad?"

"Still a long way to go, Bern. I'm not thinking playoffs yet." Johnny was lying. He'd been thinking more and more about the playoffs with each passing day.

Bernie continued the conversation.

"Charlie's been great with Connecticut. Who else do you think might get called up?"

Johnny stretched out in the passenger seat and folded his arms. "I'm surprised we still have Hank. I think we're going to lose him soon. We could see Clark go up too. He's been doing a nice job with that knuckleball."

He really had. He was 12-6 at the break with a respectable 3.37 earned run average. Not only was he pitching well, but he had become a big help to Jimmy in coaching the younger players. In all honesty, Clark should have made on the All-Star team.

Bernie and Johnny arrived at the beach house. Walking in, Johnny yelled, "Is Anna Banana here?"

In seconds, Anna ran to the door carrying her sand bucket and pail.

"Poppie! Daddy! Can we go to the beach now?" she yelled with the excitement only a 3-year-old can generate.

Bernie said, "We just got here, kiddo. Let Daddy and Poppie unpack first. We'll go in a little bit, okay?"

The Endinos had a peaceful day at the beach. So peaceful, in fact, that Johnny actually napped while sitting in a lounge chair.

"This is the best rest your father has had in a little while," Catherine said to Bernie.

Bernie squinted into the sun as he looked to his mother. "Mom, is Dad all right doing this?"

Catherine put some sun block on her already red shoulders. "I think he's fine. It's just a little tougher than he thought. It isn't like coaching a Pony League team."

Bernie drew in the sand with his finger. "He's doing great, Mom. I wish he'd just understand that. I feel like he doesn't believe us because we're his family."

Suddenly Bernie had an idea. Catherine was right. Johnny needed to hear from someone not related to him. He went into the house and grabbed his phone. It was a call he hoped would help Johnny to relax.

It was almost ten o'clock by the time everyone was ready to call it a night. Bernie climbed into bed and closed his eyes when Rachel softly asked, "So...who did you call?"

With his head buried in a pillow Bernie responded, "Really, Rae? Right now...you need to know?"

"I won't be able to sleep until you tell me and if I don't sleep, you don't sleep."

Bernie rolled over and sat up.

"All right. I called Jerry."

Rachel whacked him with her pillow. "Jerry? Why did you need to call him? We're on vacation. What is it about 'vacation' that makes you feel you need to call Jerry?"

Bernie shook the stun out of his head. "Because my dad still doesn't think he's doing a good job. We all tell him he is, but he doesn't listen. He needs to hear it from someone else. I thought Jerry was a good choice. Can we sleep now?"

Rachel gave Bernie a kiss. "Yep. Good night."

Bernie nestled his head back into the pillow and began drifting off to sleep. Just as he'd nearly achieved peaceful slumber, Rachel asked, "B., when is Jerry going to tell him?"

"Huh? Oh, he said he'd tell Dad sometime tomorrow. I guess he'll give him a call in the afternoon or something. 'Night."

Satisfied with Bernie's response, Rachel ended her questions for the night.

After a good night's rest, the Endinos gathered around the breakfast table for a feast. While everyone was enjoying the meal, the doorbell rang. A confused Bernie answered it.

"Good morning, Endinos! I brought you some pastries from this great, little bakery in Connecticut!"

Jerry had come all the way from Connecticut. Everyone but Bernie was shocked to see him.

Mary called Rachel over and whispered, "Who is that man?"

Rachel whispered back, "That's Jerry Benjamin, the pizza mogul. He sold Bernie the baseball team. Jerry owns another team too. He and Bernie sort of work together."

"How do they work together?"

"It's complicated, Ma. They just do."

Mary asked Jerry if he'd like some breakfast. Jerry quickly pulled up a chair next to Bernie and his dad.

Bernie said, "So, Jerry, I didn't expect to see you at my house. What's up?"

Jerry tied a napkin around his neck. "Just in the area for a little R&R since we're on the break and figured I'd stop by."

"Any plans while you're in town?" Rachel asked.

Jerry seized the opportunity to segue into the real reason for his visit.

"Nothing in particular. Just taking a break from the hectic season. Speaking of which, how are you holding up there, Johnny?"

Johnny took a sip of coffee. "Okay, Jerry. A little tough getting used to the grind and the travel, but it's been an experience so far."

After loading his plate with bacon and eggs, Jerry had a few things to tell Johnny.

"You know, Endino, I've had a few managers for this team and I've never had one quite like you. I can't really figure out your style, but I like it. You throw caution to the wind. I mean, that move you pulled with the pitchers in the outfield was crazy. You're getting a lot out of those boys, more than I thought you could. Keep doing what you're doing. You're just what this team needs."

Johnny was speechless. For the entire first half of the season he had thought Jerry saw him as a joke.

Jerry took one last forkful of eggs and piece of bacon then got up from the table.

"Thank you folks for the hospitality. I'll leave you to enjoy the rest of your vacation."

He shook Johnny's hand. "I'll see you soon. Can't wait to see what other tricks you've go up your sleeve."

Bernie walked with Jerry to the front porch.

"I didn't expect you to come all the way here to talk to my dad, but thanks, Jerry. He needed that."

"No problem, Endino. Needed to get out of Connecticut for a few days, anyway. Weather's been awful."

At the table, Johnny was still in disbelief.

"Jerry came here. Unreal."

"Yeah Dad, how about that?"

Johnny took his last sip of coffee. "Yeah, how about it?"

Maybe Johnny knew Bernie had something to do with Jerry showing up at the house. It didn't matter to Bernie. Someone that wasn't family or friend said Johnny was doing a good job. That's what really mattered.

[20] CALIFORNIA DREAMING

WITH ONLY FORTY-FIVE GAMES left, overtaking Nantucket for the division title was a near impossibility, but knocking off Quakertown for the wild card spot was a reachable goal.

The post-break schedule began with eight home games, split between Lexington and Akron. The Pride had won six of the eight games. It was a great start but Quakertown matched it, maintaining a three-game edge over the Pride.

The remaining eight July games were all on the road, divided between Lexington and Fort Wayne. Johnny had by now started to adjust to the schedule after several months of it. Unfortunately, someone else wasn't.

"Hey, Johnny, can I talk to you for a minute?" Coach Phil asked, entering his office.

"Yeah sure, Phil, but can we make it quick? We've got a bus to catch for the airport in a few minutes."

Phil sat down. "Johnny, I'm not going with you to Lexington. I'm...man this is tough...I'm resigning as a coach."

Johnny leaned forward on his desk. "Why now, Phil? Things are coming together."

"I know, but I can't do this anymore. I thought I could, but it's been tougher than I expected, especially the road trips. Plus, I miss my customers."

Johnny understood. It had been tough on him too, but then again, he'd always had a passion for this. He made his plea.

"Are you sure you won't finish out this season?"

"No, I'm done. I've thought about it for a long time. I should have come to you sooner. My heart just isn't in it."

Johnny sighed. "We'll miss you. You've been a big part of getting us to where we are. Check in on us once in a while. You're always welcome in the clubhouse."

"I will. I'm reopening the barber shop, so if you or any of the guys need a cut, I'll take care of you."

Johnny gave his friend a quick hug and boarded the bus to the airport.

At the stadium, questions were flying around the locker room about Coach Phil. They hoped to get answers during the pre-game meeting. Johnny obliged. "Last night, Phil resigned as a coach for personal reasons. Frank, you'll take over as first base coach. That's it tonight. Lineup is posted, gentlemen. See you on the field."

The Pride broke a scoreless tie in the top of the third inning when Mark lead off with a double and Malcolm singled him home.

Clark's knuckleball was dancing like Fred Astaire. He cruised through the first four innings, allowing just one hit and striking out three. As the Pride came to bat in the top of the fourth inning, the clubhouse boy delivered a message to Johnny:

Endino,
I need you to take Gresham out of the game as soon as you get this message. I traded him to San Diego for a young starter. Sorry about the late notice.
Jerry

Johnny was stunned. First his friend and first base coach, and now a veteran pitcher who'd become a mentor to the younger players.

Johnny yelled, "Jimmy, get down to the bullpen and start warming up!"

"Now? Why? Clark is cruising."

"I'll explain later, but you've got to get your ass to the bullpen!"

Johnny called Clark into the tunnel leading back to the clubhouse.

"What's wrong, Skip? I'm feeling great tonight. Why'd you pull me?"

"Jerry sent me a message. You've been traded to San Diego. Looks like you're back in the big leagues." Every word was painful for Johnny.

Clark tried lightening the mood. "California dreamin', huh?"

Johnny forced a smile. "You've earned it. Just sorry it has to be somewhere else."

"Yeah, me too. Really appreciate what you and Jimmy have done for me, Coach. You guys saved my career. I'll never forget it."

"Our pleasure. Now go win games for San Diego. Pack your stuff, and get the hell out of my clubhouse."

Clark gave Johnny a handshake. "You're a hell of a manager. Take care and tell Jimmy I said thanks and goodbye."

There were two outs and a runner on first with Clark's spot in the order up. Coach Art was in a complete panic. "Geez, Johnny, what the hell happened to you...and where's Clark? He's up!"

"Joey, grab a bat! You're hitting for Clark!" Johnny hollered.

Johnny instructed Joey to work the count as long as he could. He needed to give Jimmy as much time as possible to warm up.

Joey took the first pitch for strike one then watched a curveball for strike two.

"Protect the plate!" Johnny yelled, not having anything better come to mind at the moment.

The next pitch was a rising fastball that Joey tipped foul into the catcher's mitt for strike three. So much for working the count. Ready or not, Jimmy was coming into the game.

Jimmy gave up three hard singles to the first three Lexington hitters and the game was tied at one. Jimmy clearly didn't have it, but Johnny was stuck, thanks to Jerry's note. The fourth batter of the inning ripped a two-run single and the Pride trailed, 3-1. Johnny went out to talk with Jimmy.

"All right, Jimmy, minimize the damage the best you can. Sorry I had to do this to you but..." Johnny hesitated for a second. "Clark's been traded to San Diego. Just do what you can, for as long as you can."

Jimmy couldn't believe it. He'd worked so hard to get Clark's respect and now that he'd gotten it, Clark was gone.

Jimmy's mind wasn't on the game. He'd completely forgotten about the runner on first base, allowing him to steal second easily. Jimmy tried focusing but the batter lined the next pitch back at Jimmy's head. Somehow, he got his glove up just in time and snagged the drive for the second out of the inning, then turned and threw to second to catch the runner straying too far from the bag for an inning-ending double play.

As the team entered the dugout, Johnny yelled, "Way to get out of it, Jimmy!"

"It was either catch it or eat dinner through a straw for a while."

In the end, the Pride dropped the game 5-1 and more importantly, lost a game in the standings to both Nantucket and Quakertown.

Back at the hotel, Johnny called Bernie. Bernie whispered as he answered the phone.

"Aw geez, Bern, were you asleep?"

"No, Dad, I'm up but everyone else is asleep. Let me go out onto the porch so we can talk."

With Bernie safely outside, the conversation continued.

"What's up?"

"Phil quit, Clark got traded to San Diego and we lost to damn Lexington tonight. I just need to vent."

Bernie looked up at the clear, moonlit sky. "I heard about Phil and Clark. You've just gotta let it go, Dad. Heck, you're the one who told me that getting guys ready for the Majors is the main job of a triple-A manager.

"We're supposed to get them ready for our big league team, not to be traded."

Bernie reminded his father that San Diego may be Clark's last chance at being in the Majors again. He also told Johnny that the pitcher Jerry got in the trade is named Antonio Feliz. Johnny asked, "Is he any good?"

Bernie was as diplomatic as possible.

"His numbers aren't great, but he might have potential with the right coaching."

"He might have potential? So you're telling me that the kid basically sucks, right?"

It had already been long day for Johnny and tact was no longer in play.

"Right now he's not the best pitcher you've got."

"Just what I need during a playoff race. Another project. Well, this has been one shitty day. I'm going to bed."

After Johnny hung up he thought, *Things are really going well, too. Why did Phil and Jerry have to go and screw it up?*

Johnny knew he was being irrational. If Phil's heart wasn't in the job, then quitting may help the team in the long run. As for trading Clark, Jerry was just trying to make a good business move while helping a guy get one last chance at glory. Johnny was going to tell this to himself over and over again until he fell asleep, hoping that maybe he'd finally believe it.

The Pride won five of the eight games on the road trip. It brought them to 63-52 on the season, but Quakertown had played better since the break and had pushed its wild card lead to five games.

Antonio Feliz debuted in Fort Wayne and wasn't very good. He lasted only four innings and allowed seven runs. If this team was going to make a playoff push, either Antonio had to get better or Johnny needed to find someone else to pitch.

Quakertown was coming to town for two games and the Pride needed a sweep. They also needed their two starting pitchers for the series to last deep into games because the bullpen was running on fumes.

Jorge Santiago got the start in the series opener. It was a hot night with humidity so high that even breathing made you sweat.

Jorge was already dripping after his warm up tosses. Quakertown loaded the bases before Jorge got a strikeout to end the inning. No runs for Quakertown, but Jorge had already thrown thirty-one pitches...about double what Johnny wanted.

The second inning also didn't go smoothly yet Jorge dodged another bullet as Quakertown stranded runners on second and third base without scoring. Jorge had already thrown fifty-four pitches in two innings, a number he normally didn't hit until he'd pitched at least four innings.

Johnny said, "He's struggling, Jimmy. Is there anyone else available tonight?"

"I can go if you need me." The man who reluctantly resumed his career, was now volunteering to pitch.

"You sure?"

"Yeah, but do me a favor hold off as long as you can."

Jorge allowed the first run of the game in the third inning. He'd thrown eighty-two pitches in sweltering heat. Johnny took him aside after the inning.

"You're done for tonight, Jorge. I'm not risking your health."

Jorge wiped his brow with his sleeve. "Coach, I'm okay. I can pitch more."

Johnny patted Jorge on the back. "No more tonight. We need you again in five days."

Jimmy headed to the bullpen. While he got loose, the Pride tried to rally. Miguel drew a walk and Malcolm followed with a bunt single.

Johnny got an idea. Instead of sending up a position player to pinch-hit for Jorge, he sent up Jake Williams. Greg was confused. "Why send up a pitcher to hit for the pitcher?"

Johnny pointed to the field. "Just watch."

Johnny looked like a kid who just found a quarter in the couch cushions.

As the first and third basemen moved in preparing for a bunt, Jake squared. Both corner infielders charged hard. Miguel and Malcolm broke towards third and second. With the runners on the move, Jake pulled the bat back, choked up and swung. The third baseman ducked as the ball whizzed past him into left field. Miguel scored easily while Malcolm scampered to third on Jake's RBI single.

Johnny looked at Greg and winked.

Greg said, "You sneaky son of a bitch."

Johnny sent Joey Phillips in to run for Jake. After Hideki lined out, Johnny pulled the next rabbit out of his hat. Mark looked down at Art in the third base coaching box for a sign. Joey continued increasing his lead at first. As soon as the Quakertown pitcher began his stretch, Joey took off for second.

The Quakertown manager yelled, "He's going!"

Joey was more than halfway to second. The Quakertown pitcher, unnerved by the yell, stopped his delivery to home.

"Balk!" yelled the home plate umpire. Malcolm was awarded home while Joey got second base. The Pride had almost literally stolen the lead away from Quakertown. Jimmy took the mound with a 2-1 lead as the fourth inning began.

Johnny watched as Jimmy warmed up. He looked better than Johnny had ever seen him.

Maybe this will be okay, he thought.

For Jimmy's first inning, everything seemed okay. On only four pitches he got three outs. Everything he'd thrown had worked.

Pete gave Jimmy a little more breathing room in the bottom of the fourth when he hit a long home run over the centerfield fence. Jimmy breezed through the next three innings, allowing just two hits and no runs. As he walked off the mound after the top of the seventh inning, Johnny asked, "How do you feel?"

Jimmy, drenched in sweat, said, "Doing okay. Still some left in the tank. I'm just going to change my t-shirt real fast. It's like wearing a washcloth out there."

By the time he'd changed, Jimmy's spot in the batting order was coming up. As Jimmy rushed to the batter's box, a fan near the Pride dugout yelled, "Hey McConnell, you're a mess! Tuck in your shirt tail, dude!"

Jimmy tucked then stepped into the box 0-3 with three strikeouts in his limited batting experiences. Jimmy dug his back foot into the batter's box. He was guessing fastball all the way and if he didn't get one, he'd look damn stupid. Thankfully for the Pride, he'd guessed right. Jimmy slashed the ball passed the first baseman and into the right field corner.

Malcolm scored all the way from first base. Jimmy slid into second just ahead of the throw for a double. The entire Pride team laughed and pointed towards second base at their coach, who had just gotten his first professional hit and run batted in.

With a 4-1 lead, Jimmy wanted to get three outs then turn the game over to Wil. The eighth inning got off to a bad start as Jimmy hit the first batter. The next batter drew a walk, putting runners on first and second with nobody out. Johnny had Wil get loose in the bullpen. Jimmy got the next batter to line out to Malcolm. It was the first out of the inning but it was a loud-out.

Johnny walked out to talk with Jimmy. "Still feeling okay, Jimmy?" His pitcher looked like he'd just stepped out of the shower.

"Yeah, I'm all right. Give me a chance."

"All right. Go get 'em then."

Jimmy called Ricky out to the mound. "I'm ready."

"You sure?"

"Yeah. Next pitch."

Ricky slammed the ball into Jimmy's glove. "All right, throw it."

In the dugout, Johnny asked Coach Art, "What the hell was that about?"

The batter settled into the box and Jimmy delivered his next pitch—a knuckleball. It fluttered like a gum wrapper in a hurricane. The batter swung and hoped, but hit a ground ball right to Hank. In one fluid motion he fielded the ball, stepped on third and threw to first just in time to nip the runner for a gorgeous, inning-ending double play.

Johnny was happily shocked. "Ho...ly...shit! The son of a bitch has been working on a knuckler!"

Jimmy had pitched five innings of shutout baseball and even had a run-scoring hit. Johnny patted him on the back and said, "You saved our asses out there today. I couldn't have asked for more. Hit the showers. I'll play pitching coach for the rest of this one."

"Thanks, Skip, but I'll stay here. I want to make sure Wil finishes out my win."

Jimmy's worries were short-lived as Wil had no trouble in the ninth. The Pride got a big win and Jimmy was the star and savior.

In the clubhouse, Johnny noticed something tucked inside Jimmy's cap. "Jimmy, what is that?" Johnny asked, pointing to the cap.

Jimmy said, "Go ahead and read it. It was stuck to my locker when I went in to change my shirt."

It read:

Jimmy,
I can't tell you how much help you've been to me. You got me a second chance. Now take your own advice. We've worked on that knuckleball together for months. Throw it. Good luck.
Clark

Johnny took off his cap and rubbed his forehead. "Well I'll be damned."

The team ignited off of the big win, came out swinging in the second game of the series. They put eight runs and fourteen hits on the board in winning it.

The Pride headed into a much-needed day off just three games behind Quakertown for the wild card and still had eight games left against them.

It was the seven games coming up against Nantucket in two weeks that worried Johnny. The key was to focus on what was right in front of them before looking down the road, otherwise, they might fall smack dab into the middle of a deep pothole.

[21]

THE DOG DAYS OF A DOG FIGHT

THE PRIDE FELT GOOD as August marched forward but a 5-5 record over a 10-game stretch tempered it. It was a stretch that realistically ended any chance to win the division and put the team four games behind Quakertown for the wild card. Making matters worse, they now had 15 days of playing only Quakertown and Nantucket.

At the core of the team's recent struggles was its inability to score runs and, unfortunately, a lot of it was due to the guys Johnny brought in.

Mark was mired in a 4-30 batting slump. Ricky had struck out 11 times in his last 19 at-bats. Derek hadn't had a hit in the last four games.

Sitting players was always tough. Sitting players that you've known personally since they were kids was even tougher.

Then there was Antonio. Johnny knew that Feliz was a project when the Pride got him. Little did he know how big a project. He'd made four starts since joining the Pride and had only pitched into the fifth inning once.

Johnny met Bernie for coffee and a much-needed talk.

"My guys haven't been cutting it lately, Bern. I'm not sure what I should do."

"Slumps happen, Dad. Realize that this is probably the most baseball they've played in one season. Think about them out there night in and night out and all the travel and other things that they aren't used to. It has to be tiring."

Johnny knew Bernie was probably right but it still didn't solve his problem.

"Dad, maybe you should play a few of the other guys some more... see what they can do. Maybe they'll surprise you. "

"All right, I'll mix up things with the lineup. Now, what should I do with Feliz? He's been awful."

Bernie picked a piece off the top of his low-fat blueberry muffin. "I did some research. He wasn't bad when he first started pitching in the minors. Actually, he was really good."

Johnny topped off his coffee with some cream. "Well what the hell happened?"

"I'm not sure, but you know who caught for him? Alex Golden."

Alex, Johnny's backup catcher may have held the key to turning Antonio's season around.

"Bern, I think it's time I have a chat with Alex."

Bernie took another bite of muffin and washed it down with some coffee. "You may want to do that soon. Feliz is starting tonight."

Johnny grabbed his coat in a hurry. "Oh shit, I forgot it's his turn. Talk to you later, Bern."

Johnny called Alex from his office.

"Alex, it's Coach. I want to talk about Antonio. You caught for him, right?"

"Yeah. A bunch of times when he first came up."

"And he was pretty good, right?"

"He was when I caught him."

"What about the other times?"

"Well, uh, not so good, I think."

Johnny thanked Alex and hung up. He had the information he needed. With an idea in mind, Johnny called Jimmy, who was watching some game films.

"Hey Jimmy, have you been able to figure out what's wrong with Feliz yet?"

"It's funny. When we're working in the bullpen, he looks good. When he gets into the games, he's not the same pitcher."

"In your sessions Alex is catching him, right?"

"Yeah. Every time."

"That's what I thought. Thanks, Jimmy."

Johnny thought he'd figured out Antonio's problem. If he was right, the upcoming game could go a lot differently that he thought. If not, the Pride could be in for a long one.

Johnny had a rare chance to relax. He had two hours before he had to leave for the stadium and no fires to put out. Family were all doing things and he was actually alone. He grabbed his newspaper, which he got to read only once in a blue moon since taking the manager's job. Just as he sat down with a cup of coffee, the doorbell rang. "Shit. So much for my paper," he said to no one.

Johnny opened the door and there stood Ricky. "Coach, got a minute?"

"Sure, Ricky. Come in. Do you want a coffee or something?"

"Oh no thanks. Coach, I need to talk to you about something." Johnny sat down in his big recliner. He loved that chair.

"Talk to me, Ricky."

"Coach, I haven't slept well lately. I keep thinking about stuff."

Johnny sipped his coffee. "What stuff Ricky?"

"Well screwing up, I guess."

Johnny shook his head. "What the hell are you talking about? Everyone screws up once in a while. For God's sake, Ricky, forget about that."

Ricky stared at the carpet for a second then looked at his manager. "Coach, I just wanna make my dad proud."

Ricky's dad had died years earlier in a car accident. He never saw the drunk driver that t-boned him. It was that accident that made Ricky want to work in law enforcement. His dad had coached Ricky at every level of baseball and had high hopes for him.

"Ricky, look at me."

Ricky lifted his head. "I knew your dad for a long time. When he talked about you, he lit up. He could not have been any prouder of you. I know he's watching over you and I know you are still making him proud."

Ricky broke down and cried. "I miss him every day, Coach."

Johnny got up and hugged the burly catcher.

"I know, Ricky. I know. You just keep playing hard for me every day. You're my catcher and you're doing a great job. Now go home and rest. We've got a big series coming up and I need you ready for it."

Ricky wiped away his tears and smiled. "I will, Coach. Thanks. I've got this."

Johnny smiled as he closed the door behind the burly catcher, remembering the man as a boy and the father who adored him. He returned to his coffee and newspaper.

Game time approached and Johnny addressed his team. "Gentlemen, our season will be made or broken over the next fifteen games. You've all done some great things. I need you to keep it up even more. I know I've demanded a lot of you guys, some more than others. Tonight I'm asking for some other guys to step up. Here is tonight's lineup."

The lineup that everyone had gotten used to was a little different. Mark was sitting this one out and seldom-used, Joey Phillips was starting at second. Surprising as this was, it wasn't the biggest surprise of the night.

"Alex, you're catching tonight."

Johnny had to see if Alex could be the difference for Antonio. It also gave Ricky a rest that was long past due.

Johnny saw right away that Antonio looked more comfortable, especially after starting the first hitter with a knee-high fastball for strike one.

"That's the one, Tony! That's the one!" Alex yelled. He was the only one who ever called him, Tony.

Two more pitches and Antonio had a strikeout. He stayed sharp, setting the boys from Quakertown down in order. He did it again in the second and third innings, but Johnny's altered lineup could only muster one hit and no runs over the first three innings. If the Pride was going to score, Johnny might need to dig deep into his bag of tricks.

Antonio's first tough spot came in the top of the fourth after he gave up back-to-back, one-out singles. This normally lead to big trouble, but not this time. Antonio calmly delivered his next pitch and Miguel turned the ensuing ground ball into an inning-ending, double play.

Miguel started off the bottom of the fourth for the Pride by stroking a single into left field. It was Johnny's first chance to work some magic. The chess match began with Quakertown's manager calling for a pitchout on the first pitch to Hideki. Miguel barely flinched at first base. Undaunted, the Quakertown manager called for a second pitchout but again, Miguel stayed put. The manager put his pitcher in a hole. Not wanting to fall further behind, the Quakertown pitcher threw a big, fat fastball right down the middle and Hideki didn't miss it, hitting a run-scoring double that gave the Pride a 1-0 lead.

Johnny imparted some wisdom to Jimmy. "Sometimes doing nothing is doing something."

Hank and Pete followed with back-to-back home runs and a 4-0 lead for the Pride. Meanwhile, Antonio remained sharp. It was as if Johnny has an entirely different pitcher.

The ninth inning began with the Pride still leading, 4-0. Antonio got two quick outs and was an out away from a complete, game shutout. With a 1-2 count, he threw a sharp-breaking curveball to the Quakertown batter. Although he swung and missed for strike three, Alex couldn't hang on to the baseball and it skipped off the webbing of his mitt to the backstop. By the time Alex ran it down, the batter was safe at first. Alex shook his head, disgusted with himself. The next batter followed with a two-run home run that cut the Pride lead in half.

Johnny instructed Jimmy to have Wil start warming up then headed to the mound to check on his pitcher.

Johnny asked, "How do you feel?"

Before Antonio could answer, Alex said, "He's fine, Coach. This inning is my fault."

Johnny looked at Antonio then Alex. "All right, I'll take your word for it. It's all yours, Antonio."

Johnny was met by Jimmy at the top step of the dugout. Jimmy said, "I don't know how long it's going to take for Wil to get ready."

"Let's just hope we don't need him."

Alex stuck the ball into Antonio's glove. "I won't let you down again tonight."

Alex was a smart catcher who studied the opposition like a college kid cramming for exams. He knew the next Quakertown hitter had a weakness for breaking pitches in the dirt. He called for sliders on the first two pitches. Both broke out of the strike zone, and both were swung at for strikes.

Alex didn't need to put down a signal for the next pitch. Antonio knew what to throw. His slider bit hard. As the ball skipped in the dirt the batter swung for strike three, but for the second time in the inning, the pitch eluded Alex.

This time Alex raced to the ball and while diving, fired a strike to first base, nipping the runner and ending the game. The Pride was now just three games out of the last playoff spot.

As they came off of the field, Antonio grinned and said to Alex. "Thanks, man."

Alex patted his pitcher on the shoulder. "You shouldn't have had to throw that pitch, anyway."

Shortly after the game, Johnny's phone rang. It was Bernie.

"Looks like you got it figured out, Coach."

"It's only one win, Bern. Still three games out."

"You're tough, Dad. Nice job anyway. Talk to you tomorrow."

Johnny felt he had to be tough on himself. He couldn't lose his edge because he and his team still had a long way to go. The offense was still struggling. Tomorrow he'd ask for the opinion of his newest coach.

"Frank, you've been working with the guys for a few weeks now. Tell me what you see."

Frank paused for a second. "I see a lot of potential, but we only have two guys who hit with any consistent power...Hank and Pete. Hideki might be the best all-around hitter on the team next to Hank..."

Johnny said, "I'm with you so far."

"Yeah, but here's where we get to potential that needs to become actual. Like if I were managing, Miguel would hit leadoff. He's quick, hits the ball on the ground, and he can bunt."

Johnny couldn't believe he hadn't considered this move. Frank continued.

"Malcolm would bat second. He hits the fastball well and with Freddie getting on base, he'll see a lot more of them. There's just one thing about Malcolm, Coach."

"What?"

"You have to stop the switch-hitting thing. Let him hit from the right side. I've been working with him strictly from there and he's done great. I'm afraid it'll mess up his progress if he keeps trying to switch-hit."

Johnny nodded. "What else?"

Frank felt more comfortable with each word. "Hideki, Hank and Pete is a decent order, but what if you go with Hideki, Hank, Ricky and Pete? Hank has great plate discipline, Ricky is a free-swinger, but he can murder a mistake and with Pete behind him, pitchers aren't as likely to pitch around him."

This was a conversation Johnny's wanted to have with someone for a while. He picked Frank's brain a little more.

"So who hits behind Pete?"

Frank said, "Derek. Hits the ball pretty well to all fields and knows the strike zone."

"And then Mark hits eighth, right?"

"Yeah, when he plays."

Johnny turned his head as if he had water in his ear. "When he plays?"

Frank stood up and began to pace the office. "Coach, Mark hits lefties, but he's having a heck of a time against the righties. I've been watching Mike Dillon. He's left-handed, runs pretty well and makes decent contact against righties. I think you need to at least give him a chance."

Johnny had been taking notes the entire time. "Anything else, Frank?"

Frank looked to the floor then to Johnny. "Yeah. Thanks for talking to me. I wasn't sure if I was hired out of pity or not until just now."

"Don't ever feel like that. I'm thrilled to have you. Thanks for the insight."

With the talking done, Frank had a list of players he needed to see.

It was a few minutes before game time. Johnny read off the lineup. It didn't sound familiar to anyone except Frank. Johnny was using his lineup. Frank was both excited and scared at the same time. What if this didn't work? Would Johnny ever listen to him again? Frank's nerves hadn't been this bad since his first year in Class A-ball. As the team headed to the field, Frank headed to the restroom, thankful he'd eaten a light lunch. With his nervousness now flushed down the commode, Frank joined the rest of the team on the field.

After a perfect first inning from Luke, Miguel lead off the Pride half of the first, slapping a line drive pass the shortstop for a single. Malcolm followed in his first time back as a full time right-handed batter. Typically this would be a bunt situation but as people are learning, Johnny was not always typical. Rather than calling for a bunt, Johnny had Miguel break for second base while Malcolm poked the pitch into right field for a gorgeous hit-and-run single. The Pride now had runners on the corners. A Hideki sacrifice fly later plated the first Pride run of the game. After a walk to Hank put runners on first and second, Ricky came up with a chance to add to the Pride lead. He swung and hit a laser beam of a line drive over the fence in left centerfield, bumping the Pride lead to 4-0.

The Pride's revamped lineup coupled with Johnny's in-game strategy worked to perfection. In the end, the team scored eleven runs on fifteen hits with Pete and surprisingly, Mike Dillon, also hitting home runs. The 11-0 drubbing put the entire clubhouse in a happy mood.

Johnny said, "Gentlemen, that's a great win tonight! Now we have them worried! Tonight's game ball goes to...Frank Carlson!"

The team went crazy! Frank felt great, even after the team, led by Hideki, picked him up and threw him into the shower in full uniform.

The next two nights would be spent in Quakertown. Win both games and the Pride would tie for the wild card spot. Back in April, no one would have predicted that would even be possible. It was becoming fun. It was exciting. It was getting interesting.

The Pride continued its offensive outburst in the first game at Quakertown. Everyone in the lineup got at least one hit, with Malcolm being the big star, collecting three including two doubles. With an 8-3 win, the Pride was within one game of the wild card.

After a great night's sleep, Johnny planned on meeting Coach Art for breakfast. On his way to the elevator, his phone rang. It was Jerry.

"Endino! How the hell are you doing?"

"I'm doing okay, Jerry. What can I do for you?"

"I'd like your opinion, Endino. We've got September call-ups coming in a couple of weeks. I'd like to bring up Hank, Hideki and maybe Luke. You think they're ready?"

Johnny knew that his role was getting players ready for the next level. Hell, he'd said it time and time again, but now his team was in the middle of a playoff hunt and Jerry wanted to take away his best hitter, his best outfielder, and his best pitcher. Making it worse, the Mantids were mired in last place with the only chance of seeing the playoffs being by buying a ticket. Johnny knew what he had to do but he didn't like it.

"I think all three can help you, Jerry. When are you planning on taking them up?"

"As soon as that calendar reads September."

Not the answer Johnny wanted to hear.

"Jerry, do you really need to bring them up so soon? We're fighting for a playoff spot here. I need those guys."

"I'll make sure you get replacements, Endino. You'll still have a team."

"Replacements? Come on, Jerry, you know the guys you send me won't be anywhere near as good as those three."

"Listen, I need those guys up here and I need them yesterday. You'll just have to make due with what you get."

Johnny had held his tongue long enough. His hot, Italian temper kicked in.

"Yeah well, thanks for screwing me over, Jerry. I'm sure the few at-bats and innings they get to play will be a big help in a more respectable last place finish for the Mantids."

Jerry had reached his boiling point as well. "You're lucky I like a guy will brass balls, Endino or I'd have your ass fired. Good luck, by the way. I hope you find a way to make the playoffs."

Johnny was fuming. If Art wasn't already waiting for him, he'd skip breakfast. He wasn't about to tell anyone about the call from Jerry.

We haven't even made the playoffs yet. No sense to get all worked up about it, Johnny thought to himself.

Johnny was calmer by game time. The new line up was working well. The last two games had been blowout wins for the Pride but this game found them locked in a battle with second place on the line.

The Pride pushed across a run in the third inning then two more in the fifth. Quakertown countered with two of their own in the bottom of the fifth, then tied the game in the bottom of the seventh. The game headed to the ninth knotted at three.

Mark collected a pinch-hit double, yet with no score. Johnny used Christian to pitch the bottom half of the ninth. The first batter singled to left field and got bunted to second. After Christian recorded a key strikeout, the Pride was one out away from taking the game to extra innings.

The next batter hit a ground ball up the middle that looked destined for centerfield, but with a tremendous dive, Miguel stopped the ball just behind second base. He scrambled to his feet, realizing he didn't have a play on the batter. Out of the corner of his eye Miguel noticed the Quakertown third base coach was sending home the runner from second. Getting his feet under him, Miguel made a beautiful throw to Ricky. The ball and the runner arrived at almost the same time. Ricky put down the tag and the umpire yelled, "Show me the ball!"

Ricky held the ball up high in his bare hand, thrilled that the Pride would still have a chance to win this game...or so he thought.

The young home plate umpire hollered, "Safe!"

Ricky was in a near fury at the call. Johnny stormed out of the dugout.

His face beet red, Johnny said, "Are you serious? Are you freaking serious? How the hell can you call him safe? You asked to see the ball, he shows it to you and you call the guy safe?"

"If he'd shown it to me in the glove, I'd have called him out."

Johnny was stunned. He fired his hat to the ground and the tirade was on.

"You call him safe because my catcher shows you the ball in his bare hand? What kind of stupid-ass answer is that? I've never heard anything so damn ridiculous in my life! How did you even get to be an umpire? Did you win a freakin' contest? Is your father in charge of hiring? Seriously, how the hell do you qualify for this job, because I know some people that can use the work who would do the job a hundred times better than your sorry ass! Call him safe because my catcher shows you the ball in his bare hand! That's so freaking idiotic

I can't even comprehend it! You took this one away from us, ump! You freakin' stole it like a common criminal stealing an old lady's purse! Thanks a lot for being an asshole!"

The young umpire stood and took his verbal beat-down. He finally uttered, "Are you done?"

"Yeah, I'm done." He picked up his hat and walked off. His entire team was still in the dugout waiting for him.

"Nice job, Coach. Way to rip him a new one," Ricky said, grinning ear to ear.

"I thought you were going to have a heart attack out there," Art said.

"Let's just get out of here," Johnny grumbled, "We've got Nantucket to deal with next, and thanks to Major Asshole, we're two games out of the wild card and playing a team that we can't seem to beat."

He was right but his timing wasn't. His team had just won three out of four against the team it was trailing. Confidence was high but that one ill-timed comment could ruin everything. Johnny had some damage control to do and the sooner, the better. In the clubhouse, Johnny quickly gathered the team.

"Gentlemen, I know you guys are better now, and you can play with Nantucket. Stay focused...one game at a time. Now let's go home."

It was sincere and heartfelt and seemed to do the trick. Very soon, Johnny would know for sure if it had.

Johnny and the Pride were just about to begin a critical seven-game stretch. Thankfully, it started at home. He had a lineup to prepare but there was something more important to do first.

"Anna Banana, are you here?"

Johnny's voice boomed through Bernie's house.

"Poppie!" Anna yelled as she ran to meet Johnny.

Johnny gave her a hug that made it look like she'd disappeared into his arms as he whispered in her ear, "I missed you."

"Me too, Poppie! What'd ya bring me?"

"Anna, Poppie doesn't always bring you something when he comes to visit," Rachel reminded her.

"No but I did."

He opened a bag and pulled out a stuffed banana with dreadlocks and a Rastafarian hat on top.

"Here you go, sweetheart. A banana for my Anna Banana."

Anna gave it a squeeze.

"I love it!"

Rachel laughed. "Yes, thank you, Poppie."

Bernie heard his father and came from the back room. "Come on into the den, Dad. We'll talk."

Johnny took a seat in his favorite of Bernie's chairs.

Bernie said, "So...tough one last night, huh?"

"Yeah, lost on a garbage call. I thought we were gonna sweep 'em."

"So I hear. It sounded pretty bad."

Johnny leaned back. "It sucked."

"Dad, I got a call from the league office about last night."

Johnny was taken off guard. "A call? What about?"

About your little tirade after the game. The commissioner's fining you $1,000 for it."

Johnny now sat up. "A grand for that? The guy blew the call!" Johnny was almost as furious as he was with the umpire. "He called the guy safe because Ricky held the ball up in his bare hand instead of the glove! A fine for me? That ump should have to pay back his salary for the game for that call!"

Bernie laughed a little, seeing his dad's face going red. "Dad, relax. It's fine. I know it had to be a horrible call for you to blow up like that. You did what you thought was right in the heat of the moment."

Johnny, calmer now, sat back. "Bern, I'm sorry you got a call from the league. I shouldn't have lost my temper like that."

Bernie stood and went to his dad's chair with a serious tone in his voice. "If it ever happens again, I want you to promise me something. I want you to make sure someone records and texts it to me. That had to be hysterical."

Johnny hit Bernie with his cap. "Smart-ass kid."

Bernie laughed. "Get out of here, Dad, you've got work to do. I like what you're doing with the lineup, by the way. It's working."

"I can't take credit for the changes. Frank suggested them."

With that, Johnny left for the field. He really didn't have much to prepare. He just wanted to enjoy the quiet of his office for a while. It was one of his favorite things about the job. During that time, he thought about how crazy everything was and that it couldn't be real. It usually only took the smell of the sweaty laundry bin to remind him that it was.

He felt good about the seven days facing Nantucket despite the season's results to that point. If the Pride kept mistakes to a minimum, Nantucket would be in for a hell of a week.

Johnny gave his regular talk to the team and read off the lineup, which didn't include Mark. He stopped Johnny on the way to the field.

"Coach, you know I left my stunt job for this team, right?"

"Yeah Mark, and I appreciate it, really. You've been a big help but right now I've got to find out what Mike can do. I still need you. We've got some tough lefties coming up and you're going to be my best bat off the bench. I'm also going to use you for defense. Keep working with Frank. If he says you're ready, I'll get you back out there every day. Just give me your best when I use you, all right?"

It wasn't what Mark wanted to hear, but he accepted Johnny's answer and headed to the bench.

The baseball gods were kind to the Pride for the first game as Nantucket played a thirteen-inning game the night before. That coupled with the long bus ride made for one, rough Nantucket night. Led by Hank's two home runs and five runs batted in, the Pride won 9-1. Even better, Quakertown lost its game with Ithaca. The wild card lead was down to one game. Johnny was pleased but knew Nantucket would be well-rested for the next game. He wasn't apologizing for the win, though. The Pride took them any way they could at that point.

The second game of the series went a bit differently than the opener. Nantucket needed just one win to clinch the division. That incentive and a good night's rest were all they needed. Nantucket won, 4-1, setting off a celebration on the Pride's home-field.

Johnny hated seeing this. He knew Nantucket winning the division was inevitable, but doing it against his team on its own field was tough to accept. Adding to his bad mood was news that Quakertown had beaten Ithaca.

Before season's end, the Pride would play Quakertown four more times. If the Pride stayed close, it basically controlled its own fate.

Developments from Nantucket's division clinching win played into the Pride's collective hands. Nantucket had partied hard in celebrating its division title. Luke pitching was an added bonus. It wasn't really a fair fight and the Pride coasted to a much needed 8-0 win, as Quakertown defeated Ithaca to maintain its two-game lead for the coveted wild card playoff spot.

Bernie said, "Good win tonight, Dad."

Johnny said, "Yep. As long as we keep Nantucket tired or hung over, we should have no trouble with them."

Johnny wanted to beat Nantucket once and feel like it had truly been earned.

It was the final home game of the regular season. The sky was still dark gray and it had rained on and off throughout most of the afternoon. The sloppy conditions had an immediate effect, as in the top of the second inning, Derek slipped on the outfield grass chasing after fly ball. Instead of an inning-ending out, the ball rolled to the fence for a two-run triple. The misfortune compounded when the next three batters got singles putting the Pride behind, 4-0. They never recovered, losing 6-1.

After the game, Bernie got an unexpected call from Jerry.

"Hey, Endino! Figured I'd check in on you. So, how's your dad doing?"

"He's doing great, Jerry. The team's battling for a playoff spot."

"I know he's doing a good job coaching, but how's he holding up?"

Bernie was guarded. "Seems fine, Jerry. It's a job he's always wanted."

"You know, Endino, sometimes when we get something we think we want, we wish we'd never gotten it in the first place."

"I don't think my dad feels that way, Jerry. I really think he's doing okay."

Bernie changed the subject, not happy with the discussion.

"So, I hear you're going to take away his best players for September call-ups?"

"I need those guys, Endino. Need to see what they can do."

Bernie took the phone away from his ear and covered the speaker as he hollered. He composed himself. "Can't it wait until after the playoffs?"

"Geez, the team isn't even in the playoffs right now."

Bernie closed his eyes and gripped the phone. "All right, but if they make the playoffs, are you still taking all three of those guys as soon as September gets here?"

"Endino, I really don't give a shit if they make the playoffs. I'm taking what I need."

Bernie had been frustrated since he answered the phone, and the frustration mounted with every word out of Jerry's mouth.

"Come on, Jerry. These kids are going to play every day for my dad and in pressure situations. With you, they get maybe, a few at bats every four or five days in meaningless games. What are they getting out of that?"

Now Jerry was frustrated.

"Endino, no need to worry about a situation that doesn't exist. Go have a cup of tea or something."

"Fine. I'll let this go for now, but I hope you think about it—hard."

Bernie hung up the phone, rubbing his temples. He thought about his dad and what Jerry had said about getting what you want and hoped Jerry was wrong.

[22]

JOHNNY VS. THE UMPIRE, PART TWO

THE OPENER IN NANTUCKET didn't go well. Jorge's best stuff was somewhere back home and Nantucket took full advantage of it. In the end, Jorge gave up eight runs in six innings of work and the Pride lost 8-4. Coupled with Quakertown's win against Albany, the Pride fell three games out of the wild card.

Johnny didn't sleep much that night. He had to work on pulling off a win against Nantucket because if the Pride fell any further behind Quakertown, he wouldn't need to worry about losing his three best players.

Running on little sleep, Johnny took his spot in the dugout. As the umpires made their way to the field, Johnny noticed something different. One of the umpires had been replaced by the young umpire that caused Johnny to lose his cool and collect his first ever fine as a pro manager.

"Son of a bitch," he whispered to himself.

"Don't let it get to you, Coach. It's a new day," Frank said, trying to calm down Johnny.

Tom Eckland was the Pride's starting pitcher for this one. He quickly ran into trouble in the bottom half of the second. With two outs, Nantucket had runners on second and third. With the eighth hitter in the Nantucket lineup due up and the pitcher on deck, Johnny ordered an intentional walk. That's when the 'fun' began.

Tom started his counter with a fastball. The opposing pitcher swung and managed to make enough contact to dribble the ball up the first base line. Tom came off the mound and fielded the ball, making a throw to first for what should have ended the inning.

The batter was running well inside the baseline, and as the throw approached Pete at first it hit his shoulder and ricocheted into right field and down the line. The runners from second and third scored easily, while the runner from first ended up at third. The opposing pitcher hustled his way to second and instead of the inning being over, Nantucket now lead 2-0.

Coach Art yelled from the dugout, "He was out of the baseline!"

Frank screamed, "How can you miss that?"

It was interference, and the young umpire at first base did miss the call. Johnny very calmly and stoically made his way towards first. As he got there, Johnny bent over and dug his finger into the dirt near the bag. He pointed at it and asked the umpire, "Do you know what that is?"

The puzzled umpire answered, "A hole. What's this about?"

Johnny threw up his hands. "Shit. I just lost fifty bucks to a guy I bet in the first row that you didn't know your ass from a hole in the ground."

The umpire's face turned a deep red. "That's it, you're outta here, Endino!"

It was Johnny's turn now.

"That's fantastic! It means I don't have to watch you screw up any more tonight! How the hell did you miss that?" Now Johnny's face was a deep red. "Answer me! My God you're horrible! We're playing our asses off out here, and you're screwing us!"

Johnny kicked dirt on first base before finally walking off of the field. When he got to the dugout he calmly said, "Frank, take over."

Tom gave up a run-scoring single that pushed the Nantucket lead to 3-0. Frank made his first managerial decision.

"Jimmy, see if you can settle Tom down."

After a short talk, Tom got the Nantucket batter to pop up to Pete and end the inning.

"What'd you tell him?" Frank asked.

"I told him to stop screwing around and get the damn out."

Hideki got the top of the fourth off to a good start with a base hit. Hank followed by drawing a walk. With Ricky up, Frank had an idea. He signaled Coach Art who conveyed it to Ricky, Hideki and Hank. As the next pitch reached the plate, Ricky bunted. It was a beauty too. Right down the third base line. It caught everyone by surprise and loaded the bases for the Pride, with nobody out. Pete made Frank's call look even better as he hit a deep fly ball to centerfield that scored Hideki and moved Hank to third. Derek followed by hitting a slow chopper to the Nantucket second baseman. His throw to the shortstop covering the bag at second got the second out of the inning, but Ricky executed a perfect takeout slide ending any chance of a throw to first to complete a double play. His hustle had just helped the Pride to cut the Nantucket lead to 3-2.

Hank lead off the top of the sixth inning and on a three ball, one strike pitch he blasted one towards the left field wall. It looked for sure like the game would be tied, but a strong wind was blowing in and the Nantucket left fielder caught the ball at the wall for the first out. As Ricky stepped into the box, Frank perused the field. He yelled, "Ricky, take a look out there!"

Ricky stepped into the batter's box, while glancing around the field. As the pitch neared the plate, Ricky amazingly bunted again for another hit.

"I'll be damned," Jimmy said.

Frank shrugged. "Well it worked once,"

In the clubhouse, Johnny was watching the game on closed-circuit television. "That smart son of a bitch," he said to himself, shaking his head.

The tying run was now on first base with one out. A double by Pete and a Derek sacrifice fly later tied the game at three.

As the bottom of the sixth started, Frank turned to Jimmy. "You'd better go warm up. You're going in next inning."

Jimmy did a double take. "I'm what? You're nuts, you know that?"

"Maybe, but I still want you to go and warm up."

Johnny noticed Jimmy warming up in the bullpen.

"What the hell is Frank doing?" He said aloud to nobody.

Frank's interesting coaching choices continued in the top of the seventh.

"Joey, grab a bat! You're hitting for Tom!"

Greg was puzzled. "Joey? Why Joey? He's hitting .211 this year."

"Joey can hit this guy. I've seen him."

Joey stepped into the batter's box and watched as the first pitch crossed the outside corner for strike one. Joey dug in and waited for the next pitch. His eyes got as big as pie plates when he saw a hanging curveball headed his way. Joey swung hard. By the sound of the bat, Frank knew Joey had made great contact. The ball was hit like a shell out of a rifle as it hooked towards the right field foul pole. It cleared the fence in the nick of time, staying fair for a home run. The Pride had taken a 4-3 lead.

Greg looked at Frank.

Frank grinned. "I told you."

In the empty clubhouse, Johnny yelled, "Good call, Frankie! Good call!"

With the lead, Frank hoped Jimmy could give him two good innings before turning it over to Wil. Frank's hopes ended on Jimmy's first pitch as the Nantucket batter drove it deep over the centerfield fence to tie the game. Thankfully it was the only damage done, but the game was tied heading to the eighth inning.

Hank got hit with a pitch to start the inning, putting the go ahead run on first base with Ricky stepping to the plate. Frank flashed signals to Art. The third baseman who had already been burned twice by Ricky's bunts, moved closer. No way was he getting burned again.

As the pitcher delivered, Ricky squared to bunt. The third baseman charged hard. Suddenly, Ricky pulled the bat back. He was swinging away. Ricky drilled the fastball down the left field line and into the corner. Had the third baseman been in his normal position, it may have been a double play ground ball. As it stood, Hank ended up on third base and Ricky cruised into second with a double.

"Atta boy, Ricky!" Johnny yelled from his clubhouse office.

After an intentional walk to Pete, the bases were loaded for Derek. For the third time in the game, Derek delivered with a fly ball to right, deep enough to score Hank and move Ricky to third. With runners on the corners, Mark was due up. He'd been hitless in three at bats thus far. Nantucket's manager had his corner infielders in tight just in case Frank had another bunt up his sleeve. Mark wasn't bunting. On a 2-0 pitch, he scorched a line drive up the middle for what looked like a run-scoring single. Unfortunately for Mark, the Nantucket pitcher's reflexes worked perfectly. He stabbed the ball out of the air and threw on to first to get Pete who had strayed too far completing the easy inning-ending double play. Mark fired his bat towards the dugout in disgust but the Pride had taken the lead at 5-4.

Frank sent Jimmy back to the mound, hoping he had one good inning left in him.

Jimmy found himself in trouble with one out in the eighth as Nantucket had runners on first and third. Wil started warming up as Frank went to the mound to chat with Jimmy.

Frank said, "Tough spot, huh?"

Jimmy said, "Yeah, no shit."

Frank peered out to the bullpen. "Wil's getting ready, so I just need you to get out of this mess so he can come in next inning and get all the credit."

Jimmy couldn't help but laugh. He thought back to his first game on the mound with the Pride. He had an idea. His first pitch to the next hitter was a fastball, high and inside. The batter jumped out of the box. Ricky saw the ruse and played along. Ricky said, "Uh oh. That's not good."

The Nantucket hitter's curiosity took over. "What's not good?"

"He's got no idea where the ball's going. It's happened before. Almost put a guy in the hospital last time."

Ricky had gotten into the batter's head. Jimmy's next pitch began in tight to the batter. While the batter bailed out, the ball broke over the inside corner. Strictly on reflex, he swung and hit a slow ground ball to Miguel who charged hard and started a sweet 6-4-3 double play to end the inning with the Pride still ahead.

"Beautiful, Jimmy! Beautiful!" Johnny yelled, still not caring that he was the only one there to hear it.

The double play had taken the wind out of Nantucket's sails. Wil had no problem putting them away in the ninth and the Pride had come from behind to win with Johnny sitting in his office. It was a needed win, too, as Quakertown also won, maintaining its three-game lead for the wild card spot.

As the team entered the clubhouse, Johnny was there to greet them all with a handshake and slap on the back. Frank was the last one in. Johnny pulled him aside and said, "I knew you had it in you. Thanks."

Frank managed a smile. "I'm glad you did because I was scared shitless out there."

"I'll try not to do that to you again."

That night, Bernie called Johnny.

"I hear you got tossed again. Sounds like Frank did a good job in your place tonight. Huge win."

"Yeah, he saved us for sure."

"So. Dad, what did you say to that guy this time?"

Johnny recounted the entire story. When he finished, Bernie laughed hard, although he knew he shouldn't. Bernie composed himself. "Dad, I know I said I want you to defend the guys, but you can't keep pissing that guy off. He may have a few more of our games, and right now they are all important."

"I know, Bern, but damn he sucks."

"I don't think he's out there trying to screw you."

"All right, Bern, I hear you. I'll try to make nice with him tomorrow."

In the end, it was a wild day but a good one. Johnny had taught Bernie for his entire life. Bernie just turned the tables. It was a lesson Johnny was sure he'd use again.

Johnny hoped the team could ride the momentum of its comeback win in the final regular season game of the year scheduled against Nantucket. Antonio was the scheduled starter. He'd been great ever since Johnny made Alex his personal catcher. This game however, Johnny was starting Ricky. He wanted his best hitters playing in such a key game.

"Are you sure about this, Coach?" Frank asked.

"I have to do it, Frank. Antonio shouldn't need a personal catcher to pitch anymore."

The Pride got off to a good start with Hideki driving Miguel home from second for a 1-0 lead before Nantucket got a chance to hit.

Antonio walked the first two batters on eight pitches. He got a break when the next batter hit a line drive to Pete, who stepped on first and turned it into a double play. It didn't get him out of the woods however, as he gave up a run-scoring double followed by a single that gave Nantucket a 2-1 lead. The inning ended with Hideki making a running catch at the fence.

The Nantucket lead was short-lived as Ricky belted a home run in the second to tie the game at two. When Frank came in from the first base coaching box, Johnny said, "See? We need his bat."

Frank began, "I guess but still…"

Johnny put up his hand. "Stop." He was in no mood for the 'but.'

Antonio's struggle continued as he allowed a single then a run-scoring triple to the first two batters of the inning. He got another break when the opposing pitcher popped up a suicide squeeze bunt that Ricky caught, then tagged the runner coming from third for a double play. Miguel followed with a great diving catch to end the inning. Nantucket had taken back the lead, 3-2 and Antonio wasn't exactly fooling anyone. It got worse. Nantucket's first four batters in the third inning all reached base with the last one hitting a two-run home run to push the lead to 7-2.

"Should I get someone up in the pen?" Jimmy asked.

"Not yet. Let me talk to him. I don't want to burn the bullpen."

Johnny asked for a time out and met Ricky and Antonio on the mound.

"What's up, Antonio?"

"I…I'm just not comfortable, Coach. I work better with Alex."

"You know what, son? You're going to have to get comfortable with other catchers, because Alex isn't always going to be there to catch for you. If you can't get comfortable with someone else, you're going to have a short career. It's time for you to grow up, because this is big-boy baseball. Now cut the shit, and wise up."

Johnny couldn't believe what he'd just done. *What is my problem?* he thought to himself.

He got back to the dugout, where Jimmy asked, "What did you say to him?"

Johnny sat back and stared at the field. "I told him to grow up."

Johnny wished that was all he'd said.

The 'pep talk' did no good, Antonio gave up two more runs before Johnny took him out. As Antonio walked off, Johnny simply said, "I'm sorry."

Despite the 11-3 loss, the Pride lost no ground in the standings.

There were only four regular-season games left; all against Quakertown. The Pride had to win them all to make the playoffs. After the Nantucket game, Johnny wasn't sure that his team could do it and more importantly to him, he wasn't sure he was the man to lead them there.

[23]

A GIFT FROM MOTHER NATURE

A DRUBBING AT THE hands of Nantucket, followed by an all-night bus ride, made for a miserable start to Johnny's day. He got home to Catherine who was cooking breakfast. She paused and gave him a kiss.

Catherine said, "Welcome home. I thought you might be hungry."

Johnny smiled a very weary smile.

"Save it for me. I need to sleep right now."

He fell asleep almost immediately after his head hit the pillow.

About four hours into his slumber, the telephone rang, waking him up. A few minutes later, Catherine came into the bedroom.

"Johnny, are you awake?"

He was still groggy. "Yeah. What's up?"

"That was Bernie. The game tonight is rained out."

Johnny had been sleeping so deeply that he had no idea it had been raining for hours. Catherine told Johnny that they'd be playing twice tomorrow with the first game at noon and a second at seven o'clock that night. It was welcomed news. Johnny didn't mind the double header. He was running on fumes at this point. He also realized how little time he'd spent with his wife since the season began.

"Hey, Cath, let's go out to dinner tonight, and maybe a movie. What do you think?"

She smiled with a love that was unbroken. "Sure. That sounds great."

Normally, when Johnny and Catherine went out they grabbed a burger. That time Johnny wanted it to be different. He took his wife of twenty-seven years to one of the best steakhouses in the area. They each order filet mignon...and why not? They could afford it, and Johnny wanted to give his wife the best night he could. He felt he owed it to her for his being on the road so much the past few months. While waiting for their meal, they talked and for the most part it wasn't about baseball, but about their kids; their grandkids, and Catherine's childhood friends that Johnny didn't know well...but it didn't really matter.

Johnny looked at her. "Cath, are you all right with me managing this team? I mean, it has to be tough not having me around for over a week at a time."

She took a forkful of asparagus. "Sometimes it's hard, but I know it's something you always wanted to do."

Then she took Johnny's hand. "Are you all right managing this team?"

That was the million-dollar question. It had been a long season. There were some amazing moments, as well as some that Johnny chose to forget. He enjoyed coaching his old players, but sometimes it was so damn hard separating his personal feelings from what he knew was right for the success of the team. It was also tough dealing with players coming and going because, for him, it disrupted the chemistry of the team. Managing a Triple-A team was clearly worlds apart from managing in the Pony League. He looked at Catherine and the warm smile on her face.

"Yeah, Cath. I'm all right managing this team."

"Then manage them as best as you can. I'm fine. Let's finish dinner. We don't want to be late for the movie."

It was just what Johnny needed to hear. He just wanted to be sure Catherine was fine. As long as she was, he could continue doing his job.

The Endinos finished their meal and made it to the movie on time. Thanks to Catherine, Johnny was ready for the four-game fight to the playoffs that he and the Pride faced.

DOUBLEHEADER

The skies cleared, and the Pride and Quakertown had a long day of baseball ahead. Luke was starting the afternoon game. He'd been phenomenal all season, and there was no reason to think that would change. Johnny gathered the troops.

"Gentlemen, it may not say so on the schedule, but today, our playoff season begins and for us—it's sudden death. You guys have achieved a lot this year, probably more than you or I thought. No one expected us to be here. We've got nothing to lose. Go out there and play full out for the next three days. Just remember, we can't win four until we win one."

Luke started the game by striking out the lead hitter on three pitches. Johnny turned to Jimmy, "I've got a good feeling about this one."

Luke was scintillating. His fastballs were lively, his sliders were sharp, and his changeups were mesmerizing. On the offensive side, Hank, Pete, and Ricky all hit home runs as the Pride won 5-0, with Luke going the distance allowing just three hits. One down, three to go.

There were still a few hours until the second game. Bernie checked in with Rachel at home.

"How's everything at the homestead, Rae?"

"Jerry called here. He wants you to call him as soon as you can."

Bernie sent goodnight kisses over the phone and called Jerry, wondering what he wanted.

"Thanks for getting back to me so soon, Endino."

"No problem. So, what's up?"

"I'm not taking Luke for September call-ups. I can't use him until next week anyway, so he may as well stay with you guys until your season ends."

Bernie closed his eyes a moment, relieved.

"Might not be for a while if we make the playoffs, Jerry."

Unfortunately for Bernie, Jerry wasn't finished.

"Yeah well, I'm about to make that tougher, Endino. I'm taking Hank and Hideki up tomorrow, so they won't be joining you in Quakertown."

Bernie groaned. "Jerry, come on, do you need them both right now?"

"Geez, quit whining. I told you about this. I've booked them on a flight here tomorrow."

"Damn it!" Bernie was a like a hornet buzzed out of its nest. "You could have at least bought me dinner before screwing me like this! Who are we getting to replace them, anyway?"

"That's going to be a problem, Endino. I can't get anyone to Quakertown in time for the two games there. You're gonna have to play short-handed."

"You've got to be kidding me." At that point he had a death grip on the phone.

Jerry said, "I'm sorry Endino, but there's no way I can get you anyone right away. You'll just have to make due."

"This sucks, Jerry. It really sucks."

Sometimes getting pissed off can lead to an idea.

"Jerry, if I can find two guys to replace them, is it all right with you if I use them?"

"I'm not paying new players for a few games, Endino."

"You're already paying one of them."

"What are you talking about, Endino?"

"Let me activate Frank. I don't even know if he'll play, but at least he'll be an available body."

Jerry paused. "All right, you can activate Frank. Who's the other guy?"

"Greg."

"Jeffers? You're the guy who cut him."

"Yeah, when I had a full roster. He's still a good outfielder and base runner and again, he probably won't even get used. I'll pay the stupid salary, if it helps."

Jerry sighed. "Sign him to a contract. I'll pay it, but keep it short-term...I'm not running a charity here. Get them signed for your second game today. I don't want Hank and Hideki playing tonight."

It was Bernie's turn to screw Jerry a bit.

"What was that, Jerry? I...I'm losing...connection...I...hear...you... Thanks...I'll...you soon."

Jerry was not amused. "Endino? Endino? Endino! Those two guys had better not be in that lineup tonight!"

Bernie didn't care. He was going to make sure Johnny had one more game with his very best players.

The nightcap got off to a rough start for the Pride. Jake gave up a two-run home run in the top of the first putting the Pride in a quick 2-0 hole. Hideki got one of those back in the bottom of the fourth when he singled Malcolm home from second. Neither team would score again until the sixth inning, when Quakertown got back-to-back two-out doubles to push the lead to 3-1.

Bernie was watching from his box seat near the field. He called Johnny over just before the ninth inning started.

"What do you need, Bern? I'm sort of busy."

"Hideki and Hank are joining the Mantids after the game."

Johnny's response to the news was stoic. "They're still mine for one more inning."

Christian's pitched a perfect top half of the ninth to keep the game at a 3-1 deficit for the Pride. As the players came in from the field, Johnny called over Hank, Hideki and Yosh.

"Guys, you're both going to Connecticut tomorrow. Congratulations." He could only smile.

Yosh interpreted the news to Hideki. He didn't need to interpret Hideki's nod of thanks to Johnny. Hank's response was a little more vocal.

"No shit! I'm going to the bigs?"

It was what Hank has wanted for what seemed like forever. He embraced his manager. "Thanks, Coach. You helped me get there."

"Hank, you didn't need me."

"Bullshit. I owe you one."

Johnny had one request. "Just help me win this ball game."

Quakertown's closer, Heath Smallcomb, got the task of finishing off the Pride and its playoff hopes. Miguel worked a hard-fought walk to start the inning after falling behind in the count 0-2. Hideki followed with another walk on nine pitches.

Smallcomb had already thrown twenty pitches in the inning, and he'd only faced two batters. Hank's turn to bat came up and Smallcomb's arm was already fatigued.

Hank took advantage and crushed the first pitch. Before the ball had landed, Hank's teammates were already heading to home plate to greet him. Hank had kept the Pride's playoff hopes alive with a walk-off, game-winning three-run home run! The Pride had swept the double header and pulled to within one game of the playoffs.

Hank was mobbed at the plate. During the celebration, Johnny hollered, "Don't hurt him! He's going to Connecticut!"

That prompted more congratulations. Johnny then yelled, "And Hideki's going with him!"

Ricky and Pete grabbed Hideki and lifted him into the air. The Pride hadn't qualified for the playoffs yet, but the atmosphere sure made it seem that way. Everyone was happy for Hank and Hideki, and no one was worried about playing without them. Right now, it was about feeling good and confident that they could win, no matter who was in the lineup.

The Pride had a bus ride to Quakertown ahead of them. Johnny asked Greg and Frank to arrive forty-five minutes ahead of the rest of the team for a chat.

"Guys, you know that Hideki and Hank were called up to Connecticut last night."

"Yeah. Good for them," Greg said.

"They earned it," added Frank.

"You're right, guys, but here's the problem. Jerry can't get us replacements, so right now, we're down two guys for tonight."

Frank said, "Man that sucks."

Greg asked, "He can't get us anyone?"

Johnny shook his head. "No, but Bernie and I had an idea. We talked to Jerry, and he's okay with us putting you and Frank back on the roster. Whadda 'ya think?

Greg said, "We tried this already, remember Coach? It didn't work out so well."

"Greg, I'd like to have your glove and speed available, if I need it."

Greg hesitated. "I don't know, Coach."

"Come on. I'm in a bind. Help me out."

Greg took a few steps in a circle. "I don't know what help I'll be but all right, Coach. Put me on the roster."

Johnny then asked Frank, "What about you?"

Without hesitation, Frank answered, "Hell, yeah!"

"All right, guys. Thanks. Grab your gear and get on the bus."

Game time approached and after Johnny let the team know that Greg and Frank were playing again, he offered strategic advice.

"Gentlemen, we need to get creative to score runs tonight. Justin Parker is pitching for Quakertown. Work the count on this guy. He has trouble pitching out of the stretch. All right, kids, let's even this thing up!"

Johnny's strategy didn't work right away. Three innings into the game, Parker hadn't allowed a hit and had four strikeouts. Thankfully, Jorge had been almost as sharp and the score was knotted at zero.

Jimmy looked to Johnny and said, "We may have to get more aggressive."

Johnny shook his head. "Not yet. He hasn't allowed a base runner, but he's thrown a lot of pitches. He's gonna get tired and when he does, we'll be ready."

Miguel drew a walk to start the fourth inning. With someone finally on base, it was time to play a little small ball. Malcolm bunted Miguel to second, giving Pete a chance to put the Pride ahead. Johnny grabbed Pete. "Remember, Pete. Patience."

The normally free-swinging Pete took his manager's advice and drew the second walk of the inning. The Pride now had two on and one out for Ricky. Johnny's advice here was simple.

"Ricky, look fastball on the first pitch. If it's good, rip it."

Jimmy asked Johnny, "What happened to patience?"

"We did that. Now, it's time to get aggressive."

Ricky had his sights set on a fastball and Parker gave him one, belt high. Ricky swung and smashed a line drive over the shortstop's head and into the left centerfield gap. Miguel scored easily, Pete cruised into third and Ricky pulled into second with a stand up double.

Johnny felt the building momentum. *He's ours*, was his thought.

Derek and Freddie followed with back-to-back walks for the second Pride run of the inning. Mike hit a sacrifice fly to drive in the third and final run of a productive fourth, and Parker's last inning. Johnny's 'selective aggressiveness' strategy as he called it, paid off in a big way. In all the Pride drew nine walks and collected four hits, parlaying them into six runs. Meanwhile, Jorge cruised and the Pride won, 6-1, setting up a one-game showdown for the final playoff spot. Johnny knew he couldn't stand on patience in the finale. Bud Fisher was pitching for Quakertown and he had impeccable control. The Pride would need to find a new way to scrape together runs, and Johnny had less than twenty-four hours to figure out how.

It was the last day of the regular season and a few hours before the bus left for the stadium. Johnny asked Tom Eckland, Antonio, and Ricky to meet him in the lobby.

"Guys, have a seat. Tom, I'm starting Antonio tonight. You've been great for us, but Quakertown hasn't seen him as much as they've seen you. I'm going with a gut move here."

Tom wasn't expecting this news, and he wasn't not thrilled to hear it. His rotation mate didn't like what Johnny said next.

"Antonio, Ricky's catching tonight. I know you like pitching to Alex, but we can't afford to have Ricky's bat out of the lineup with Hank and Hideki gone."

Antonio looked at Ricky and Johnny. "Remember what happened last time?"

"Yeah, I remember. Do you remember what I told you?"

"You said I have to learn to pitch to someone else if I want to be a professional pitcher."

Johnny was still sorry for how he talked to Antonio but he knew it was true. He needed Antonio at his best.

"Trust your stuff. You know you have it. Ricky's a great catcher. He'll help you out if you get into trouble."

Ricky said, "I've got your back, man. We can do this."

Johnny offered Antonio one more piece of advice.

"Talk to Luke. He may be able to help you relax out there."

It was a bold move by Johnny, still, this whole season had been filled with bold moves. He just hoped this one wouldn't cost him a shot at the playoffs.

The team prepared hoping this wouldn't be the last game of the season. While they dressed, Johnny noticed that Pete looked pale.

"Pete, come here for a minute."

Pete pulled himself from the stool in front of his locker and went into Johnny's office.

Johnny said, "Are you all right?"

Pete was drenched in sweat.

"Sure, Coach. I'm fine."

"You don't look fine. Tell me what's up."

"All right, I sort of threw up once or twice before I got on the bus, but it's probably just nerves."

"Nerves? Pete, you're white as a ghost and you're sweating like a thief at a police convention. I don't think this is just nerves."

"Coach, I'll be fine. Just let me get..." Pete couldn't finish. He ran into the bathroom barely making it in time to throw up once again.

When Pete came out Johnny said, "Pete, you aren't playing tonight."

Pete pleaded to play, telling Johnny there was nothing wrong.

Johnny went from manager-mode to father-mode. "The hell you are. Stay in the clubhouse tonight. Drink fluids, and I'll have someone get you some flu medicine. I just hope this isn't contagious."

Pete didn't argue as he was busy running back into the bathroom.

Johnny was already down Hideki's and Hank's bats and now he'd lost Pete. Johnny addressed the team.

"Gentlemen, Pete can't go tonight. Frank's starting in his place. If I'm going to be down one of my best players, I can't imagine a better replacement. Gimme your best, gentlemen. That's all I ask."

The Pride went down in order to start the game. Johnny and Jimmy held their breath as Antonio took the mound. Last time he worked with Ricky, things didn't go well at all.

Antonio paced anxiously around the mound before facing his first batter. Ricky called for a fastball but Antonio shook him off. He threw his curveball instead, and the Quakertown leadoff hitter smacked it into the right field corner for a double.

Johnny said, "Aw shit! This can't happen."

Antonio's confidence was shaken just one pitch into the game. He walked the next hitter, then gave up a run-scoring single. He'd faced three batters, gotten none out, and trailed 1-0.

Johnny said, "Jimmy, go talk to him."

Luke quickly chimed in. "Coach, let me do it. I think I can help."

"What the hell. Okay Luke, go do your thing."

Luke strolled to the mound. "What's going on out here, man?"

"Just a little nervous, I guess. I wish Alex was back there."

"Yeah well, he's not and you've got to get over it. Remember what we talked about on the bus?"

Antonio kicked the dirt. "Yeah."

Luke patted him on the back. "All right then, just do it."

Antonio said, "I'll feel stupid."

Luke looked him in the eye. "Just do it."

After another stroll around the mound, Antonio was ready to try Luke's advice. He began humming to himself then quietly sang,

Arroz con leche me quiero casar con una señorita de la capital...

It was a Spanish lullaby that his mother sang to him when he was a child to calm him. Luke suggested Antonio sing it to himself any time he felt overwhelmed and right now, he definitely felt overwhelmed.

Antonio threw a slider to the Quakertown hitter, who hit a one-hopper to Mark. He flipped the ball to Miguel who stepped on second then threw on to first to complete the double play.

"That's the way, Antonio!" Ricky yelled from behind the plate.

Antonio's next three pitches were all strikes and the inning ended.

"What the hell did you say to him?" Johnny asked Luke.

"Just told him to sing."

"Well shit, we may need to form a friggin' choir next season!"

Antonio continued humming along...literally. He hadn't allowed a base runner since the third hitter of the game and heading into the top of the sixth, it was still 1-0, Quakertown.

With one out, Ricky crushed a double into the left field corner. Frank struck out, leaving it up to Derek to keep the inning alive.

The Quakertown pitcher got ahead in the count, 1-2, and threw Derek a hard-breaking slider out of the strike zone. Derek tried but couldn't hold up on his swing.

The Pride and Derek, however, got a huge break. Somehow Derek managed to make contact and hit a hump back line drive towards third base. With the third baseman shifted away from the line, the ball fell just inside the third base bag. By the time the left fielder ran it down, Ricky had scored, and Derek was standing on second base with a double.

Freddie had been red-hot and Quakertown's manager knew it. He had Freddie walked bringing Mike up with a chance to break the tie. Mike swung at the first pitch and barely tapped the ball between the pitcher and first base. By the time the first baseman fielded it, Mike was on first and the bases were loaded.

For as hot as Freddie had been, Mark was that much colder. He'd hit the ball hard; he was just hitting it right at people.

Mark was anxious to help out his team, maybe too anxious. He swung at the first pitch and hit right on top of the ball, bouncing it high off of home plate. The Quakertown catcher hopped out of his stance to field the ball while Derek charged hard towards the plate. The ball descended into the catcher's mitt and he turned to tag Derek. As he lunged to make the tag, Derek dove head first towards the back corner of the plate. It was a perfect slide. Derek had put the Pride ahead, 2-1.

Frank yelled to Mark, "Nice rip, baby! You crushed that one!"

With one out in the bottom of the sixth, Antonio allowed a single, which the runner turned into two bases after he stole second. In the past, this situation would have derailed Antonio. He took a step back and again sang to himself,

Arroz con leche me quiero casar con una senorita de la capital...

Stepping back to the pitching rubber, he struck out the next batter for the second out. Now relaxed, Antonio got the next batter to hit a routine ground ball towards Frank. The inning should have been over, but Frank allowed the ball to roll between his legs and into right field, allowing the tying run to score from second base. Before the next pitch, Frank said to Antonio. "Sorry, man. I don't know how I missed it. I'm really sorry."

The new Antonio simply replied, "It's okay, Frank. I'll get this one."

He retook the mound, sang himself the lullaby, and put the inning to bed with a strikeout. The game headed to the seventh inning, now tied at two.

Quakertown's pitcher got two quick outs to start the seventh inning before Ricky singled to left, keeping the inning alive. With the goahead run at first, Johnny hollered, "Greg, grab a helmet! You're running for Ricky!"

Frank was getting a chance to redeem himself. Just before he stepped to the plate, Johnny pulled Frank aside. He handed Frank Greg's bat.

"Frank, I want you to use this."

Frank looked puzzled. "This toothpick? Why?"

"Because, you've been late on the fastball all day. He knows it and he's going to keep pumping them up there. You'll get this bat around quicker. Trust me."

Having no good argument, Frank took the bat and headed to the plate.

Greg led off of first base far enough to draw a throw from the Quakertown pitcher. Greg dove back into first, just barely beating the tag. Undaunted, Greg dusted himself off and lead even further from the bag. He drew another throw and it got by the first baseman. Greg scrambled to his feet and took off, safely reaching second.

The first pitch Frank saw was a fastball. He swung and with Greg's bat, smacked a single into centerfield. Greg scored from second and the Pride took back the lead. When Greg got to the dugout, and held his bat, saying, "Glad someone knows how to use this damn thing."

Alex replaced Ricky behind the plate but in this game, it didn't seem to matter who was catching. Antonio retired the next six Quakertown hitters in order. He'd thrown one hundred and three pitches in eight innings, but didn't look tired. He struck out the first batter of the ninth but it took him ten pitches to do so. Seven pitches after the strikeout, he put the tying run on base with a walk. Now up to one hundred and twenty pitches, Antonio was showing signs of fatigue.

"Get Wil up," Johnny said to Jimmy.

Reluctantly, Jimmy called the bullpen. Wil's had been used a lot lately, and Jimmy was worried that he wouldn't be effective.

The third batter of the inning drove a ball deep into centerfield. Malcolm got a great jump and ran the ball down just in front of the fence for the second out. Johnny thought he might not need Wil after all. Antonio shook his arm, hoping to get a few more pitches out of it. It didn't help as the next batter whistled a double into the left field corner. Quakertown had the tying run on third and the winning run on second. Johnny emerged from the dugout.

"You gave us all you have, Antonio. Let's see if Wil can bring it home. Good job, son."

When Wil got to the mound, Johnny asked him how he felt. Wil took a deep breath. "I'll give you what I've got."

Johnny hoped what Wil had was the final out of the game.

Wil knew from his warm ups that he had no zip on his fastball. If he was closing this one out, he'd have to do it with smarts.

The Quakertown hitter was Teddy Bridges, their biggest home run threat. Teddy ate fastballs for breakfast and with Wil not having his good one, it looked like another satisfying meal was in store. Alex gave Wil the sign for a fastball. Wil nodded, stretched, and threw a changeup. Bridges, who was looking for a fastball all the way, swung and was well out in front of the pitch. He hit a harmless pop up towards third. The ball nestled into Mike's glove for the third out and a win for the Pride.

They'd won four in a row over Quakertown and were headed to the playoffs.

Bernie met Johnny by the fence.

"Congratulations, Dad."

"Thanks, Bern, but we haven't done anything yet."

Bernie just shook his head. "You're something, Dad. You just made the playoffs with a team that finished dead last a year ago. Enjoy yourself for just a minute, will ya?"

Johnny said, "Awright but just for a minute. We've got Fayetteville in two days."

Bernie knew his father would relax only when he was ready. At the moment it was on to Fayetteville to see just how long the crazy season would continue.

[24]

ON TO THE PLAYOFFS!

THE TEAM WAS ABOUT an hour away from heading to Fayetteville. Bernie was along for the ride.

"Ready to go, Dad?"

"I guess. Still not sure how we'll do this without Hideki and Hank."

Then the two mean heard, "Did someone mention me?"

Standing in front of them was Hank Rundle with his bat, glove and suitcase in hand.

Johnny hugged him. "What the hell are you doing here?" Bernie said, "Yeah, Hank, why aren't you in Connecticut?"

"When I saw you guys made the playoffs, I asked Mr. Benjamin if I could come back and help out. I want to finish what we'd started."

Johnny just shook his head. "I can't believe you're doing this, but I'm damn glad you are. Welcome back, son."

Johnny turned to Bernie. "How about that?"

"He's gonna be a big help. Who's roster spot does he get?"

Bernie quickly got a response from an eavesdropper.

"Don't worry about it. He can have my spot," Frank said.

"Hey, Frank. Guess you've seen Hank already."

"Yep. Saw him at his locker. Nice to have him back."

Bernie shook Frank's hand. "Frank, thanks for filling in for the past few days and thanks for giving up your roster spot for him."

"When I had to use Greg's bat, just to get a ball by the second baseman, I knew it was time to call it a career. I'm the past. Hank's the future."

Johnny said, "You're still my hitting coach."

Frank sat back in his seat. "Wouldn't dream of leaving now."

Getting Hank back was a boost for the Pride, but there was another surprise on the way. Jimmy came into the clubhouse and he wasn't alone. "Look who I found wandering the concourse."

Next to Jimmy was Clark Gresham.

"Shit, Gresham, you're supposed to be in San Diego? Why the hell are you here?"

"Turns out they were just trying to boost attendance. Figured my name would draw a few fans. Stuck me in the bullpen and trotted me out once a week to pitch. That got old fast, so I asked them to release me. Called Jerry to see if he'd let me come back to pitch here and he said okay, so here I am."

"Damn Clark I'm glad you thought of me, but I'm not sure how I can use you."

Jimmy had the solution.

"Give him my roster spot. I need to concentrate on coaching anyway. Move Tom and Jorge to the bullpen and have Clark pitch right after Luke."

"Yeah, I like that. All right, Clark you're in. Welcome back."

All of a sudden Johnny had his power hitter, and a great veteran pitcher back on his team. He believed the Pride had a real chance now to win this series and he knew the rest of the team would feel that way too.

With Clark back, Johnny also had his playoff rotation plan figured out. Jake would start the first game with Clark set for game two. Johnny would save Luke for the third game at home. He wanted

Luke's father to see him pitch. After that would be Antonio, and if the series went five games, Johnny guessed he'd figure something out.

He let his pitching staff know his plan. Just about everyone was on board. Only Tom and Jorge had issues. Johnny talked to them both.

"Jorge, Tom, I need you guys in the bullpen. We need some strong guys to help get to Wil. I'm counting on you both and I know you can do it."

At that point, Clark chimed in, "Hey guys, I'm sorry about this, but my old ass can only pitch once every four games or the AARP might cut my benefits."

Clark's wit helped. Tom and Jorge laughed and finally were all in with Johnny's decision.

It was clear, crisp, and cool, a perfect night for baseball. Everyone was riding high from the four game sweep of Quakertown and the return of Hank and Clark. The Pride came out swinging in the first inning, scoring three times thanks to a run-scoring double from Hank and Ricky's two-run single. They added two more runs in the third on Pete's two-run home run.

The defense was just as good, highlighted by Malcolm's diving catch to end the third inning, and Pete's leap to rob a potential two-run double in the bottom of the sixth. Jake gave Johnny six innings, allowing just two runs on five hits. Malcolm drove home a run in the seventh and Hank capped off the scoring with a two-run blast right after. Tom pitched three perfect innings in relief and the Pride won the first game, 8-2. Johnny couldn't be happier with his first playoff game.

Back at the hotel, Johnny and Bernie stopped by the downstairs café for a coffee.

"Nice start, huh Dad?"

"Always take a win on the road, Bern."

Bernie put two sugar packets in his coffee. "The guys look more confident every day."

"Yeah. I just don't want them getting cocky."

Bernie laughed. "I don't think you'll let that happen."

Johnny pointed his finger at Bernie. "Damn right, I won't."

Father and son looked up at the sports news on the Café's TV, hoping to catch an update on how Nantucket made out in its first playoff game against Dayton. They'd also won easily in a 10-1 rout.

"Damn!" They each said at the same time.

"Well, it is what it is, Bern. Before we worry about Nantucket, the Pride needs to put away Fayetteville."

Clark hadn't pitched in eight days but he felt more rested than rusty. It was a beautiful night for baseball as the skies were crystal clear and there was a cool, steady breeze blowing in from left field. If anyone was hitting a home run tonight, they'd need to earn it.

The Pride didn't hit in this game like it did in the opener. Through four innings, the only hit was a bloop single from Ricky. Good thing Clark was also shutting down Fayetteville.

Ricky lead off the fifth inning with a single and was bunted to second by Freddie. Derek struck out then Mike was walked intentionally, bringing Clark to the plate with a chance to help himself. Clark wasn't exactly a strong hitter. As a matter of fact, he pretty much sucked at it. Johnny offered this advice. "If it's over the plate, swing and pray."

The Fayetteville pitcher threw a fastball right down the middle. Clark swung in the spot where he expected the ball to cross the plate. As things turned out, he picked the right spot. Clark made solid contact, slicing the ball hard just beyond the reach of the Fayetteville first baseman and into the right field corner. Ricky scored easily from second and Mike followed, just beating the throw. Clark was perfectly content to stay at first base on a ball that most guys, including the slow-footed Ricky would have turned into an easy double. The Pride had taken a 2-0 lead.

Clark mesmerized Fayetteville with his knuckleball, shutting them out through eight innings. Hank lead off the ninth in fabulous style, hitting a home run deep into the Fayetteville night, putting the Pride ahead, 3-0. Johnny called Clark over. He already had Wil loosening up in the bullpen.

Johnny said, "Wil's ready. Whaddaya think?"

"Coach, I haven't had a complete game shutout in four years. It's gonna take this entire team to get me out of there now."

Clark faced the top of the Fayetteville lineup in the ninth. The first batter of the inning dragged a bunt, one of Clark's knuckleballs just by him for a single.

Chicken shit hit, Clark thought.

Fayetteville's next batter stepped in and he also bunted. By the time, Hank got to the ball both runners were safe, and Fayetteville had the tying run at the plate with nobody out.

Jimmy said, "Should I talk to him, Coach?"

"Nothing to say. Let's see what he does."

Clark was stewing. In his mind, Fayetteville was playing pansy baseball. Still fuming, Clark decided to send a message to the next batter. His first pitch was a fastball, chin high and inside. The batter spun out of the way just in time, sprawling in the dirt. As he got up, he pointed his bat towards Clark. Clark just smirked and muttered,

"Bunt that one, asshole." Feeling better, Clark threw another fastball.

The Fayetteville batter hit a groundball to Miguel who started a 6-4-3 double play. Fayetteville's clean up batter was its last hope, and he hadn't touched Clark's knuckleball all day. Unfortunately, Clark let his ego take over. Thinking he could sneak a fastball by the hitter, Clark dealt. The mediocre fastball left the yard in a hurry and now, the Pride clung to a 3-2 lead.

Johnny quickly headed to the mound.

"Great game, Clark. Wil's going to finish this one off for you."

"Shit, Johnny, I just need one more out. I can get it."

Johnny was not willing to risk losing this game.

"No, you're done for tonight."

Clark was pissed, big time. He slammed the ball hard into Johnny's hand as he walked off. Under his breath, Clark muttered, "Can't believe he hit that fastball."

Wil finished warm ups and prepared to close out the game. He'd been dominant for the past few months and that continued. Three fastballs were all it took for him to strike out the batter he faced and to give the Pride a win. The Pride would head home in the morning just one win away from advancing to the Championship Series.

"Coffee tonight, Dad?" Bernie asked Johnny as they left the stadium.

"Yeah. I can go for a cup."

They found an all-night doughnut shop and grabbed a table.

"You're in the driver's seat now, Dad."

Johnny sipped his coffee. "Nothing's done until it's done."

Bernie poured some cream into his cup. "Sorry. I forgot. No enjoying anything."

Johnny threw a napkin at his son. "Don't be a smart ass. I'm still your father."

Bernie started to smile but noticed the concern on his father's face.

Bernie said, "All right, what's up?"

Johnny voiced his concern.

"I hated taking Clark out tonight. Why did he throw that fastball?"

Bernie said, "I don't know. I guess he still thinks he can dial it up when he has to."

Johnny stirred another sugar into his coffee. He said, "That's what I'm afraid of."

Bernie pulled out his cell phone and checked the scores for Nantucket, showing the results to Johnny. They'd won, and were also a win away from the Championship Series, much to Bernie's dismay. The two teams were on a collision course.

"Is everything all right, Dad? You're kind of quiet. Still worried about Clark?"

Johnny tapped on his coffee cup. "What? Oh, I'm fine. The Clark thing will work out. Just thinking. You know, Bern, we really shouldn't be here."

Bernie had grown tired of Johnny's 'were just lucky' attitude. He wanted to end it.

"Every team needs some luck once in a while. We've had some bad things happen too, Dad. It all evens out. Can we just let this go?"

"We don't have to talk about it but that doesn't mean I won't think about it."

Bernie took a bite of his donut. "Fine. I just don't want to hear it anymore."

It had been a while since the Pride played a home playoff game. Luke took the mound and looked around the stadium. It was packed to the rafters. He noticed his father watching from Bernie's box. His dad shot him a fist pump and Luke returned it.

Luke's first two pitches of the game weren't good as both sailed high. A look of concern came across Johnny's face. Luke's third pitch, another fastball bounced about four feet in front of home plate for ball three. Pitch number four was high and wide and Fayetteville's leadoff hitter drew a four-pitch walk.

Johnny said, "I'm going out to talk with him."

Jimmy said, "He's only thrown four pitches."

Johnny got up from the bench. "Yep, and none of them were even close. Need to nip this in the bud. Jimmy, what's the gun been reading for him anyway?"

"Two of 'em hit triple digits; the other two just missed."

Johnny arrived at the mound much to Luke's surprise. "Something wrong, Coach?"

"Throwing the ball pretty hard today, huh Luke?"

Luke shrugged. "Yeah, I guess so."

Johnny took of his cap and scratched his head. "Maybe a little bit too hard."

Luke nodded. "Guess I'm kinda excited. Playoffs, full house, dad watching; just pumped up."

"Sing your song, calm down and throw strikes. Trust me, you throw plenty hard." Johnny left the mound hearing Luke softly sing to himself, "Three is a magic number".

He delivered a fastball at the knees at 98 miles per hour. The Fayetteville base runner took off for second, figuring Luke had forgotten about him. Luke's velocity and a quick catch and release by Ricky cut him down for the first out of the inning. Luke kept singing and firing fastballs by the next two Fayetteville hitters to end the inning.

As he came off of the field, Luke tapped Johnny on the shoulder. "Thanks for the tip, Coach."

The Pride scored the first run of the game in the bottom of the second inning. After Pete led off with a double, Ricky brought him home with a single into centerfield. Luke was on cruise control mowing down Fayetteville hitter after Fayetteville hitter. Through six innings, he'd allowed only one hit on a slow ground ball to Miguel. The Pride offense had gotten him three more runs along the way, including yet another home run from Hank.

Before the top of the seventh began, Johnny asked Luke, "How are you feeling?"

"Actually, Coach, I'm kinda hungry. Let's see if I can get this thing over so we can hit that post-game spread."

Luke made quick work of Fayetteville in the seventh and eighth innings as the Pride carried a 4-0 lead into the ninth.

Luke got the first batter of the ninth inning looking at a slider for the first out and the second on a fly out to Derek. Luke knew what he wanted to do. Ricky didn't need signs now. He simply took his position, nodded, and let Luke work.

The first pitch was a fastball swung through for strike one. The second pitch was a duplicate with the same result.

Johnny said, "He's still throwing hard. What's the gun say, Jimmy?" "Last one touched 99, Coach."

Luke's next fastball had a rise on it, moving from the batter's chest at release to around neck high by the time it reached home. The batter swung and missed horribly for strike three. The Pride had advanced to the Championship Round.

Ricky met Luke at the mound. "A one-hitter in the play offs! A one-hitter!"

Johnny assembled the team in the clubhouse.

"Gentlemen, nice work! This is where we wanted to be. Not sure who we'll be playing yet..."

Frank interrupted, "Nantucket, Coach. They won tonight, 7-3."

Johnny clapped his hands vigorously. "Okay. You guys can beat them. The series doesn't start for three days. Get some rest."

Playing in the Championship Series!

Bernie still couldn't get over the fact that this bunch had a chance to play for the championship. If it was a dream, Bernie didn't want to wake up.

[25]

HERE WE GO!

THE PLANE TO NANTUCKET taxied down the runway. Bernie and Johnny talked pitching rotations and lineups for the series, although Johnny was pretty tight-lipped about it all even to his son and team owner. Privately, Johnny was concerned that the team may be too comfortable since things were going so well. At the same time, he didn't want to make changes for the sake of making changes.

Bernie was already in the hotel restaurant for his customary road trip breakfast with Johnny. He couldn't remember the last time he'd been the first one to arrive. A few minutes later, his father joined him. He looked like a bus had driven over him then backed up to finish the job.

"Hey, Bern. Did you order yet? I need coffee, extra strong."

"No. I just got here. What time did you get to sleep last night...or should I say this morning?"

Johnny sat down hard. "I finally settled in around 2:30...and don't worry about it."

Just then, the waitress came to take their order.

"Good morning, boys. What can I get for you today?" She stopped and perked up. "Hey, you manage that team from Pennsylvania, don't you? We have to play you guys tonight!"

"Yes, ma'am. I hope you don't hold it against me."

She smiled politely then took their orders. Shortly after, she returned with two cups and a pot of coffee.

"It just finished brewing," she said, filling their cups.

Johnny took a sip of his coffee. "We have to beat these guys, Bern. We've come too far."

"I think having Hank and Clark is going to make a big difference, Pop."

The two men said very little for the remainder of breakfast. Johnny was too tired to talk anyway. As they finished, their waitress returned.

"Anything else, boys?"

Johnny wiped his lips with his napkin. "No ma'am. That was great. Just the check and give it to me."

"This one's on the house. My manager's a baseball fan."

"Would you mind asking him to come out to the table? I'd like to thank him."

In a minute, the manager of the hotel restaurant came to the table.

"Was everything all right, gentlemen?"

Johnny shook his hand. "It was great. Thanks, but you didn't need to do that."

"It was my pleasure. You're quite a story, Coach."

"Me? A story? Nah, I'm just a guy doing a job."

"Well, for a guy who's never done this professionally before, you're doing a hell of a job."

"Thanks. I appreciate that. Make sure you take care of this lady here."

"I will, Mr. Endino. Hey, would you mind signing an autograph for my son? He'll love it."

Johnny took the index card and pen. "Sure. Just tell him not to try selling it. He'll get more for a pack of gum." He signed the card, making sure his penmanship was perfect. He never liked signatures that couldn't be read.

The manager looked at the card and shook Johnny's hand again. "Thank you so much and good luck, but not too much."

Johnny and Bernie laughed, then got up to leave.

Bernie said, "They were nice, huh?"

"Yeah they were. I can't believe he asked for my autograph, though."

"See, Dad? Someone else thinks you're doing a great job, too."

Johnny felt somewhat satisfied. That breakfast was just the nourishment he needed.

The players were both excited and nervous, particularly 'Johnny's guys.' They'd won championships before, but at a time when their moms and dads were driving them to the park.

Johnny had set his pitching rotation. He had Antonio pitching the first game with Clark following in game two. Jake was scheduled for game three, and Luke for the fourth game. If it went five, anyone and everyone might have to pitch.

Satisfied with the rotation, Johnny started his pre-game talk.

"Circle up, gentlemen! Can't win three until we win one. I just ask that you continue giving me your best. I'm sticking with the lineup that got us here. Antonio, you're good with Ricky, right?"

Antonio nodded.

"Well then, let's hit the field boys!"

It was chilly and overcast in Nantucket for the series opener, and the weather had kept attendance down. They'd only get about four thousand fans for the game and that was a plus for the Pride, who had played in front of ten thousand Nantucket fans several times this season. Nantucket took the field to sparse applause.

Johnny said to Jimmy, "So much for the home crowd."

Jimmy pointed towards the field. "Yeah, but do you see who's working the plate tonight?"

Johnny hadn't paid attention as Coach Art normally took the lineup to the plate prior to the game. Johnny noticed the young umpire that had screwed him twice during the season.

"Son of a bitch! Not here! Not now!"

"Better keep calm, Coach. Just hope he's learned from his mistakes."

Miguel stepped to the plate and took the first pitch for strike one.

The Championship Series was underway.

Two pitches later, the Nantucket starter grooved a fastball that Miguel drove into the right centerfield gap for a leadoff double. After Malcolm bunted him to third, Hank stepped to the plate. Playing it cautiously, the Nantucket pitcher walked him. Now, Pete would get his chance.

Johnny yelled, "Make 'em pay, Pete!"

The excitement of the situation made Pete overanxious. He hit a ground ball to the shortstop on the first pitch he saw. It looked like a sure inning-ending double play. The shortstop flipped the ball to second for the first out, but Hank made a clean, hard slide into the second baseman flipping him before he could make the throw to first. Miguel scored from third giving the Pride the early lead.

It didn't take long for Johnny to see that the combination of Antonio and Ricky was going to be fine. Antonio set Nantucket down in order on nine pitches, all strikes.

The Pride lead extended to 2-0 in the fourth inning when Pete led off with a booming home run.

With a two-run lead, Antonio continued to mow down the Nantucket hitters. In five innings of work, he'd allowed just two hits and no runs.

The Pride tacked on another run in the sixth when Malcolm walked, stole second, and scored on a single by Hank. Another perfect inning from Antonio followed and after six, it was 3-0 Pride.

After cruising through six innings, Antonio ran into some trouble in the seventh. On a three ball, two strike pitch, he threw what looked like a perfect curveball for strike three. It was so good that it fooled the umpire, who called it ball four.

Immediately Jimmy said, "Calm, Coach. Calm."

Johnny wanted to verbally rip the guy apart but resisted the temptation. Antonio, however, had lost his focus. On the very next pitch he threw a room service fastball that turned into a Nantucket two-run home run. The Pride lead was now just one run, and there was still nobody out.

Johnny said, "Jimmy, you'd better go talk to him. If I go out there, I'll probably get tossed."

Jimmy walked out, waving his hand for a time.

"Coach wanted me to check on you. How're you doin'?"

"I had that guy. It was strike three."

Jimmy spit. "Yeah, well you've got to forget about it and get this guy."

Suddenly Antonio got louder.

"It's hard to forget about it when the ump screws you!"

His timing couldn't be worse as the umpire was heading towards the mound to end the conference at that very moment.

"If you don't agree with how I umpire, then you can enjoy the rest of this game from the bench. You're outta here!"

Jimmy was almost begging. "Aw shit, really?"

"Yeah, Coach, he's gone, and if you're not careful, you can join him."

Johnny, realizing what had happened, came out to protect his pitching coach.

"What's the problem?"

"You're pitcher doesn't agree with how I'm umpiring tonight and I tossed him."

Johnny threw up his arms. "Come on. It's the Championship Series, for God's sake."

The young umpire just shook his head. "He cussed, Coach."

Johnny took his hat off and scratched his head. "He cussed? Seriously? Son, you have to get a thicker skin."

The young umpire pointed at Johnny. "That's enough, Coach."

Johnny turned away. "I'm done here, anyway."

Johnny signaled for Tom to come into the game. His only advice was, "I need six outs, then we'll let Wil finish this."

Johnny took a slow walk back to the dugout. When he got there, he turned to Jimmy. 'That kid is going to kill me."

As it turned out, Tom was up to the challenge. Two ground balls and a fly out to Freddie later, the seventh inning ended with the Pride clinging to a 3-2 lead.

After striking out the first batter of the eighth inning, Tom ran into trouble when the second hitter doubled into the right field corner.

Johnny said, "Get Wil up."

"Already?" Jimmy asked.

"We can't wait to be behind. Get him ready."

Malcolm caught a line drive in center for the second out. Maybe Johnny wouldn't need Wil just yet. That feeling didn't last as the next Nantucket batter walked, putting runners on first and second with two outs. Johnny made a double switch, sending Greg to replace Derek in right field and calling Wil from the bullpen. Wil got to the mound where Johnny had a request.

"I need an extra out from you tonight."

"Hey as long as it's only one, no problem."

Wil had a confidence now that was nonexistent when he first joined the team. He promptly threw three pitches, striking out the batter and ending the inning with the Pride still up 3-2.

The Pride didn't score in the ninth, but Wil didn't really need the insurance. In one of the most amazing displays of relief pitching Johnny could remember, Wil retired Nantucket in the ninth by striking out all three hitters and using just nine pitches. That meant in total, Wil had struck out four batters on twelve pitches. The Pride took game one from Nantucket in its own building.

In the clubhouse Johnny nodded to his team. "That's one, gentlemen. Tomorrow we play again. Get a good night's sleep."

He said it with very little emotion. Johnny didn't want the team to get complacent, himself included. Game two was in less than a day and everyone needed to be ready.

After winning the first game, every member of the Pride began to feel invincible. Johnny didn't like it one bit. On the bus to the stadium he said to Bernie, "You know Bern, it's a fine line between confident and cocky, and right now, we're walking it."

Johnny addressed his troops.

"Okay gentlemen, it's that time! Let's treat this one as if we'd lost last night. I want you to feel every game is a must-win at this point. Maintain your focus."

The weather and the crowd were both better for game two. Through four innings, neither team had scored. In the top of the fifth, the Pride had two outs with Pete on second. Malcolm had a chance to break the scoreless tie, but with Clark on deck, seeing a good pitch to hit was probably a pipedream. The first two pitches were fastballs, just off the plate. Malcolm stepped out of the batter's box and rubbed some dirt on his hands. He got back into the box, moving just a hair closer to the plate. It was barely noticeable. Sure enough the next pitch was another fastball just off the outside corner of the plate. This time, Malcolm reached out and poked it over the first baseman's head and into the right field corner. Pete scored easily from second on Malcolm's double, giving the Pride a 1-0 lead. It was a short-lived lead, however, as Nantucket tied the game in the bottom of the inning on a home run over the right field wall.

The game stayed tied until the top of the ninth. Mark was scheduled to lead off the inning and thus far he'd had a miserable day, going 0-3 with three strikeouts. Johnny prepared to send up a pinch-hitter when he noticed the Nantucket pitcher calling his manager out to the mound. During warm ups, his foot had landed awkwardly in a hole on the mound and he'd twisted his ankle. The pain was too much to bear. The Nantucket manager signaled to the bullpen and brought in his only left-handed relief pitcher. The turn of events changed Johnny's mind. Instead of pulling Mark from the game, he gave him some advice.

"Look for the slider early. He lives and dies by it."

It was the perfect advice. The first pitch was a slider. Mark swung and belted the ball deep down the left field line. As the ball hooked, Mark contorted his body, hoping somehow it would keep the ball fair. In Mark's mind, his gyrations worked as the ball grazed the foul pole for a home run.

Johnny yelled, "Well I'll be a son of a bitch!"

Johnny was starting to believe in the mystical luck that seemed to surround his team. If not for the freak injury to the Nantucket pitcher, Mark wasn't even batting. Not only did Johnny leave him in, but Mark hit a home run, only his third one of the season and it just nicked the foul pole.

Meanwhile, Jimmy snapped Johnny back to reality. "Think we should get Wil up now?"

"Yeah. Have him get loose."

The Pride went down quickly after the home run; too quickly for Wil to be ready.

Johnny had no choice. "Clark, do what you can until Wil gets warm."

Clark had done a great job but he'd already thrown ninety-seven pitches and at thirty-six, with a rebuilt arm, there wasn't much left for him to give. The first batter of the inning smacked Clark's first knuckleball by Miguel for a single. Johnny nervously looked to the bullpen, hoping for the signal that Wil was ready.

After a bunt to move the runner to second, Clark fell behind 3-1 to the next batter. Just as the signal came from the bullpen that Wil was ready, the Nantucket hitter scorched a ground ball towards the hole at second base. Mark dove to his right, came up with the ball and fired to first just in time for the second out as the tying run moved to third base. That was all Johnny needed to see. He went to the mound and said, "Great game, Clark. Let's see if Wil can finish it for you."

"Again, Coach? One more out. I can get it."

Johnny, attempting to diffuse any issue brewing, said, "I might need you again. Can't risk an injury."

Johnny and Clark both knew it was complete bullshit. Clark handed Johnny the ball, again unhappy. When Wil got to the mound, Johnny put the ball in his glove. "Just need one tonight."

Wil nodded. "Piece of cake."

If only it was that easy. Wil walked his first batter on four pitches. Frustrated over the walk, Wil lost focus and allowed the runner to steal second base easily. Now not only was the tying run on third but the winning run had moved up to second. On Wil's next pitch, the Nantucket batter hit a ground ball between the pitcher's mound and first. Pete ranged far to his right and fielded the ball, while Wil broke from the mound to cover first. The ball, Wil, and the Nantucket batter all reached first base at virtually the same time. Wil's foot came down first near the corner of the bag. As the Nantucket batter crossed the bag, the umpire yelled, "Safe!"

Wil couldn't believe it. He immediately began yelling and cursing at the young umpire, forgetting that the play was still going on. The runner from second base never stopped and headed home. By the time Wil realized what was happening, his throw to the plate was too late and Nantucket had won the game, 3-2. Johnny raced from the dugout over to first base to continue the argument but wasn't ranting and raving. He calmly asked the young umpire, "What do you have against us?"

"What are you talking about, Coach?"

"He was out. My guy beat him to the bag."

"Coach, I always watch the bases. Your pitcher missed the corner of the bag."

Johnny walked away, dissatisfied with the answer. The Pride was that close to being ahead two games to none and going home for game three. Now they were going home with a split and momentum shifting to Nantucket in a heartbeat.

Johnny and Bernie talked in the hotel lobby.

"We got the split, Dad. That's all you can ask for on the road."

Johnny shook his head then said, "We had 'em, Bern. That game was ours."

Bernie said, "We've had our share of games go that way. Just have to get over it."

Johnny said, "Yeah, but it still sucks."

It was a tough way to lose a game. Both Johnny and Bernie were interested to see how the team would react to something they hadn't dealt with in a few weeks.

[26]

HOME FOR A PAIR

The atmosphere in the locker room before game three had a pall still hanging in the air. There was a noticeable lack of spark in the team as the game got underway. It was a near sell-out crowd and the noise level was almost deafening; a stark contrast to what this team heard less than a season ago. Even that great fan response failed to boost the team's spirit.

As Jake warmed up, Jimmy said to Johnny, "He looks off tonight; I'm a little worried."

Jimmy's observation was dead on. The first three batters of the game singled and before everyone in the stands even sat down, it was 1-0 Nantucket. They'd add one more run, making the score 2-0 before the Pride had a chance to bat.

In the second inning, Jake allowed a home run to the leadoff hitter. In the third, he'd give up a two-run home run, pushing the Nantucket lead to 5-0. Johnny took off his hat, wiped his brow and wondered what the hell to do. He had Jimmy signal for Tom to warm up.

Jimmy said, "What about Jorge?"

Johnny was firm. "No. It's gotta be Tom."

Jimmy didn't know why it had to be Tom, but made the signal. In the stands, the crowd that had been so loud and supportive early sounded more like the crowds the Pride had heard a season ago.

'Get him the hell out of there, Endino!" ... and ... "I came here tonight for this?" echoed throughout the stadium. Johnny hated hearing it, but he understood as someone who had seen things from the fan's side. All he could do was take his medicine.

Three full innings into the game and the Pride not only trailed, but hadn't had a single hit. Johnny pulled Jake from the game and had Tom take over. In no uncertain terms, Johnny told Tom that he'd need to take one for the team. Tom held Nantucket in check for the next two innings, but the Pride offense mustered just a single by Hank.

Tom allowed a one-out walk in the top of the sixth however got a ground ball to Miguel that should have been an inning-ending double play. The bad day for the Pride continued, however, as Miguel skipped his throw to second into right field. Nantucket now had runners on second and third with one out. The boo-birds continued.

"Nice throw, Beniquez! I hope you killed that worm!"

"I knew it was too good to last!"

Nantucket took advantage of the mistake with a sacrifice fly to push the lead to 6-0. The Pride had very little life coming into the game, and now there was practically none. The Pride never mounted a threat and lost, 7-0. The team had gone from an out away from being in the driver's seat to one loss away from losing the championship.

As the team entered the clubhouse, Johnny hollered, "Everyone together...right now!"

They couldn't remember the last time he sounded that angry. His tone became more somber once everyone was assembled.

"First, great job, Tom. You saved the bullpen. Gentlemen, I know you're better than you played. Now, I need you to show me. Forget the fans out there heckling you. Know how to shut them up? Win. Put this game behind you. Tomorrow, we come back and get another chance. It's the last game you'll play here this year, and for some, it may be the last time you play here ever, so go out on a high note. Get some rest. See you tomorrow."

Just like always, Bernie was outside the clubhouse, waiting for his father. "Just not our day, Dad."

"Nope."

"Last home game of the season tomorrow. No matter what happens, it's been a good year."

Johnny reflected for a moment. "Yeah it was, wasn't it?"

Bernie was glad his father finally realized what had been accomplished. The Pride was again a playoff team. At the start of the season, no one outside the team believed this could happen. Still, no one was ready for it to end. Win or be done for the season. It was this simple. Of course, doing it wouldn't be so easy.

Johnny was still in his office, struggling with a lineup for the critical fourth game of the series. He crumpled four lineups and tossed them in the wastebasket before finally settling on one.

As the team took the field for pre-game warm ups, Johnny saw his players were intense and focused, more than he'd seen them all year. He looked to Jimmy. "I think we're going back to Nantucket."

Luke was ready to begin the most important start in his short pro-career. The first batter chopped the ball just over Luke's head.

Mike charged hard, bare handed the ball and threw to first just after the runner had crossed the bag. Nantucket had its leadoff hitter on. Luke took the ball from Pete and kicked the dirt in frustration.

Luke started the next hitter with a fastball. As he delivered the runner broke from first. The batter hit what normally would have been a double play ground ball.

Mike, however, was covering second base and the ball bounced by him into right field. Nantucket had executed a perfect hit and run, putting runners on the corners with nobody out.

Now Luke paced the mound. He threw a slider that jammed the next batter who hit a pop fly into foul territory down the first base line.

Pete made a beautiful over-the-shoulder catch for the first out, but both runners tagged up and advanced. Nantucket had a 1-0 lead and a runner on second with one out. The odd inning continued when the Nantucket clean up batter struck out but ended up on first when the ball skipped by Ricky to the backstop. Compounding the issue, the runner from second advanced to third.

Luke couldn't believe what was happening. The next batter hit a fly ball to shallow centerfield. As Malcolm made the catch, the runner from third broke for the plate.

Ricky yelled, "He's coming!"

Malcolm's throw was strong, but off line. The runner from third scored, while the runner from first took second base.

The fans got restless.

"Awww, not this again!"

"I can't believe this!"

It was like reliving a bad dream for Johnny.

Luke fooled the next batter with a slider, getting him to hit the ball off the end of his bat towards third base. The ball had a funny side spin on it and eluded Hank, turning into a run-scoring double. In one of the strangest innings Johnny could remember, his team now trailed 3-0.

Jimmy said, "I'd better go talk to him."

Johnny stopped him. "No, I'll do it."

When Johnny got to the mound Luke asked, "What the hell am I doing wrong?"

"What do you think you're doing wrong?"

Luke thought for a second. "Nothing. I'm making good pitches out here."

Johnny put his hand on Luke's shoulder. "Exactly. It's just been one of those innings. Relax, and keep doing what you're doing. We'll get 'em back for you."

His confidence now restored, Luke made quick work of the next Nantucket batter, striking him out with three consecutive blazing fastballs.

Johnny rallied the rest of the team. "All right now it's our turn! Let's get those back!"

For as lucky as Nantucket got in the top of the first, the Pride was as unlucky in the bottom half. Miguel began the inning by hitting a line drive right to the first baseman. Malcolm followed by scorching a one-hop ground ball that the shortstop deftly back-handed, then threw to first for the second out. Freddie then stepped in and hit a ball over the third base bag that the third baseman fielded with a dive, got up and threw to first just in time for the third out.

Luke's second inning went much smoother as he set Nantucket down in order. The bottom of the inning saw the Pride get three more hard-hit balls that resulted in three outs.

The first inning was a distant memory as Luke breezed through the third inning without allowing a base runner. Derek, Mike and Luke all made good contact in the bottom of the third and all three were put out. Three innings were in the books and Nantucket was still ahead, 3-0.

The Pride finally broke into the hit column when Miguel started off the bottom of the fourth inning by grounding a single passed the shortstop.

Johnny ordered Malcolm to bunt.

Jimmy said, "Coach, we're down three runs."

Johnny offered Jimmy a math lesson. "Yeah, and if we move Miguel to second and score him, we'll be down two runs."

Almost on cue, Freddie smacked a single up the middle, scoring Miguel easily from second base.

Johnny smiled at Jimmy. "See?"

The score remained 3-1 as the game headed to the bottom of the sixth. Johnny had a decision to make. Luke was due to lead off and while he'd been cruising since the first inning, the Pride needed runs. Johnny made the tough decision. "Great job Luke. You're done for tonight."

"But Coach, I'm rolling now! Let me finish."

Johnny just patted him on the back. "Joey, grab a bat! You're hitting for Luke!"

Upon hearing this, Jimmy asked, "Should I get Jorge up now?"

"No, not Jorge."

"Shit, Coach! Why not? He hasn't pitched at all in the playoffs and..."

Johnny stopped him. "Jerry shut him down for the year. Doesn't want to ruin the kid's arm."

"So, who should I get up?"

Johnny looked Jimmy in the eyes. "You."

"Say what?"

"You. I want you to warm up. You're going in."

"Me? I'm not even on the roster...or am I?"

"When Jerry shut Jorge down, I added you to the roster. I didn't know what else to do."

Jimmy's voice got louder with every word. "Well shit, why the hell didn't you tell me?"

Johnny shrugged. "I didn't think I'd use you."

"So you figured you'd just tell me two minutes before you send me to warm up?"

"Yeah...pretty much."

Jimmy grabbed his glove. "You're serious about this?"

Johnny smiled. "Yeah. Get your ass to the bullpen."

Jimmy reluctantly went to warm up while Joey stepped to the plate. He put up a heck of a fight and worked a leadoff walk. In textbook Johnny fashion, Miguel bunted him to second for Malcolm. Malcolm singled to left, putting runners on the corners and Freddie did his job hitting a sacrifice fly to center.

The Pride was now only down a run. After Hank walked, Ricky had an opportunity to help out his old buddy, Jimmy. He picked on a first pitch curveball and lined it over the second baseman's head to the centerfield wall. Malcolm scored easily from second to tie the game.

Hank was barreling around second and was headed for third when he saw Coach Art frantically waving him home. The second baseman took the cutoff throw, wheeled, and fired towards the plate.

Hank had a full head of steam going as the throw reached the catcher. He collided full force with the catcher, knocking him to the ground, and dislodging the ball from his mitt. Hank touched the plate with his hand and the Pride took the lead.

The jubilation was short-lived.

Hank remained on the ground writhing in pain and clutching his knee. Johnny and the trainer ran out of the dugout. As they arrived at home Hank, grimacing, moaned with his eyes closed tightly. "It's my knee! Oh shit, my knee!"

The trainer did a quick examination. A somber look came over his face. "I think he tore his ACL."

The ACL is the anterior cruciate ligament of the knee. Tears can take nine months to heal, and there are no guarantees that it would heal well enough for Hank to play again.

Johnny looked at Hank and could barely speak. "Great play, Hank. You got us the lead." It took everything he had in him for Johnny to hide his devastation. Had Hank stayed in Connecticut, this would have never happened.

The trainer said, "Let's get him off the field and into the clubhouse. We've got to ice and elevate it."

Pete and Derek helped Hank off the field. On the way to the clubhouse, Hank said, "Stop here. Put me on the bench. I want to stay for this."

"Hank, go back to the clubhouse so the trainer can take care of you." Johnny frowned and put his hand on the player's shoulder.

Hank, looking at Johnny, asked the trainer, "Can I hurt it any more by staying on the bench?"

The trainer began, "No but..."

Hank interrupted, "Then get me some damn ice, wrap up the knee, and leave me right here."

The trainer looked to Johnny.

"If he can't hurt it anymore and he wants to stay, let him."

As instructed, the trainer got an ice pack.

Johnny said, "Damn it, Hank, I'm sorry."

Hank grinned through the pain. "For what? I'm the dumb ass who barreled into the catcher."

The game moved to the top of the seventh. Several weeks of rust became apparent as Jimmy walked the first two batters he faced.

Johnny went out to calm him. "All right, Jimmy, just relax out here."

Jimmy looked around the stadium. "I still can't believe you put me out here. What the hell are you thinking?"

"I'm thinking you're the guy I want out here to get us to, Wil."

"Well, no offense, but I think you're bat shit crazy."

Johnny laughed. "Just pitch the damn ball, will ya?"

Nantucket's strategy was to bunt the runners over to put the go ahead run on second. Jimmy just wanted to throw a strike. He let go with a fastball, chest high. The batter bunted and popped the ball straight up. As the ball hung in the air, Ricky dove at it. The ball landed in his mitt for the first out. In the meantime, the runner from second had strayed too far from the bag. Ricky scrambled to his feet and gunned a throw to second base, just in time to complete the brilliant double play. A potential rally was now just one out from being extinguished. Riding the energy, Jimmy struck out the next batter preserving the lead.

Johnny met Jimmy on the top step of the dugout.

"Not bad. Now how about one more?"

Jimmy raised his eyes. "Never satisfied are you, Coach?"

The bad luck that plagued Luke in the first inning turned itself around for Jimmy in the top of the eighth. The first batter of the inning hit a line drive that looked destined for right field, but Mike made a perfectly timed leap for the first out. The next Nantucket hitter ripped a ball down the first base line as Pete dove to his left, then flipped the ball to Jimmy covering first for the second out.

He hadn't fooled anyone, however Jimmy had gotten two outs. He fell behind 2-0 to the next hitter before grooving a fastball that the batter crushed towards the left centerfield gap. The ball had double written all over it. Freddie and Malcolm both sprang into the chase, hoping to at least keep it in front of them. As they closed in, Freddie dove. Malcolm had no option but to jump over Freddie like a sprinter over a high hurdle. Somehow while all this was happening, Freddie came up with a sensational catch to end the inning. Three more outs and the Pride would tie the series!

Jimmy came off the field and about panted to Johnny. "Well I sucked out there."

"Looks like two no-hit innings of relief in the score book."

Jimmy laughed. "And there won't be another one, right?"

"Nope. You're done. Wil's going to finish this one. Nice work, kid."

It was all up to Wil to keep the series alive. He retired the first two hitters on a strikeout and a fly ball to centerfield then got ahead of the next batter, 0-2. The crowd was at a fever pitch now. One more strike and the series would head back to Nantucket. The rush of adrenaline got in the way as Wil's next pitch came too far inside and hit the batter. Nantucket was still alive and after its next hitter singled to left, it had a two-out threat.

Johnny yelled from the dugout, "It's all right, Wil! No damage!"

Wil wiped his brow, took a deep breath and stepped back onto the pitching rubber looking to get the final out. The batter hit a pop fly towards the right field foul line. Pete, Mike and Derek all laid chase. Mike had the only chance at making the catch. He took one last step and dove. While in mid-air, the ball hit the webbing of his glove however the impact upon landing jarred the ball loose. It kicked into foul territory and by the time Derek ran it down, the two runners on base had scored and the batter was standing on third base with a triple. It appeared as though Nantucket had taken a 5-4 lead.

While Nantucket celebrated, Hank yelled from the far end of the Pride bench, "Coach, he missed third! He missed third!"

Johnny cupped his hand over his ear. "What, Hank?"

Hank yelled again, "The lead runner missed third base. I watched him! He wasn't even close! Missed it by a mile. You have to appeal."

"You're sure?"

"Hell, yeah he missed it!"

Johnny quickly yelled, "Wil, appeal the first runner! He missed third!"

Wil nodded and once the ball was signaled in play, he made the appeal. The third base umpire, who until now had been the bane of Johnny's existence, yelled, "Out!"

It was the third out and none of the runs counted.

Thanks to Hank's observation and the young umpire at third being true to his word that he 'always watches the runners,' the Pride had won game four and was going to Nantucket to decide the championship. No one in the stadium could believe it.

Johnny shook Hank's hand. "Nice job. You saved our asses tonight."

Hank winced. "My manager always told me that even when you aren't in the game, stay in the game."

Johnny smiled and tapped Hank gently on the cheek.

In two days, the Pride had a chance to be league champions. It didn't matter how they got there. It just mattered that they'd made it. Johnny wondered how anything could top what just happened. He was about to find out.

[27]

THIS ONE'S FOR ALL THE MARBLES

IT WAS A FEW hours before the team was scheduled to leave for Nantucket. Johnny was normally the first one to arrive but when he pulled up, there was already a car waiting in the parking lot. Out of the driver's side stepped a beautiful brunette. She walked around to the passenger's side, opened the door and Hank emerged with a heavily wrapped leg and a pair of crutches.

"Coach, I want you to meet my fiancée, Heather."

Johnny shook her hand. "Pleasure to meet you, Heather."

"Nice meeting you too, Coach. Hank's told me a lot about you." Heather gave Hank a kiss and returned to the car.

"All right, Hank. What gives?"

"I just want to wish you and the guys luck. The doc says if I stick to my rehab program, I should be ready for spring training but I shouldn't move around too much and long bus rides aren't a good idea."

"I didn't expect you even to show up here this morning."

Hank took a deep breath. "Coach, I've gotten away with a lot of shit in my life because I'm a pretty good ballplayer. Teachers, coaches and even my parents sometimes would let me be...well an asshole, just because I was good. Then I met you and you didn't take any of

327

my shit, not an ounce of it. I want to thank you for that. You made me grow up. I appreciate it…a lot."

"Son, even with everything this team has accomplished this year, hearing that from you is more rewarding than anything. You are the best player I've ever had the pleasure to manage. Do what the doctor tells you. I want to see you playing in Connecticut next season."

"Yeah well, just let me warn you that I'll probably be doing some rehab with you guys next season and being a pain in your ass."

"Just take care of that leg and that girl of yours, all right?"

"I will, Coach. Good luck tomorrow. Bring home the title."

As Heather helped Hank back into the car, Johnny called out, "Make sure he's good to you. If he isn't, you tell me."

Johnny watched them pull away.

I made a difference, Johnny thought. He smiled and shouted, "YES!!" into the empty lot.

The last game of the season, win or lose, was moments away. There was a warm breeze blowing and not a cloud in the sky. For as long as the year has been, it felt like only yesterday that Bernie asked Johnny to manage the team. Johnny gazed at the team gathered for one last pre-game speech.

"Gentlemen, this is what we wanted from day one. No matter what happens tonight, I'm damn proud of what we've accomplished. We've not only made it to the final game of the Championship Series, but we've sent some guys up to the Big Leagues and that's what this is really about. You've all made progress this year."

He paused, looking at them as they looked back to him. He saw in each of their eyes, the young 12-year-old boys, hopeful and expectant, trusting and ready to take on the world. His throat hitched, suddenly dry, but he cleared it and continued .

"I hope that tonight doesn't end up being the greatest moment in your baseball lives, but I'd like it to at least be a great moment in your baseball lives. Go out, play hard, and what the hell, let's win this thing!"

Johnny took to the top step of the dugout and looked around the stadium, still not believing he was there. Johnny had chosen Clark to pitch this most important game.

Jimmy came into the dugout from the bullpen where he'd watched Clark's pre-game warm up pitches.

Johnny said, "How's he looking tonight, Jimmy?"

Jimmy hesitated to answer. "I'm not sure what to expect tonight. It wasn't a great bullpen session."

Johnny just gave a slight head shake. All he could do now was hope for the best.

Miguel led off and struck out on three pitches. Johnny hoped it wasn't a sign of worse things to come. Malcolm flied out to left field and Freddie grounded out to shortstop giving the Nantucket pitcher an easy inning.

Now it was time to find out what Clark had. He started the Nantucket lead off hitter with a knuckleball that missed the outside corner. His next three pitches were all knuckleballs, and all missed the strike zone, giving Nantucket a base runner to start the game. Things didn't get any better as the first pitch from Clark to the next hitter was a knuckleball that got away from him for a wild pitch. Nantucket had a man on second with nobody out.

Jimmy said, "Maybe I should talk to him."

Johnny put out his arm, holding Jimmy back. "No. Let him work this out."

Clark gathered himself and delivered another knuckleball, his sixth in a row. The batter grounded out to second as the runner moved to third. Getting out of the inning without allowing a run would be tough and Clark didn't make things any easier when he walked the next batter. Runners were on the corners now, with just one out and Fowler stepping to the plate. He'd thrown eleven pitches in the inning and all of them knuckleballs.

Johnny said to Jimmy, "Why the hell isn't he using his other pitches?"

Jimmy shrugged. "I wish I knew."

Clark continued struggling with his control. The count had gone to 3-1 on Fowler. Surely, Clark would throw his fastball now. Clark went into the stretch and delivered another knuckleball. The Nantucket cleanup batter was looking for the fastball, and was out in front of Clark's pitch as it fluttered towards the plate. It resulted in a perfect double play ball to Miguel that ended the inning with no damage done.

The second inning for Clark was no smoother than the first. He ran the count full to the first batter of the second inning before getting him to fly out to the wall in centerfield. The next batter singled and Clark still had thrown nothing but knuckleballs. A six-pitch walk, already his third walk of the game, put runners on first and second with just one out.

Under his breath Jimmy said, "Damn it, throw some of your other pitches."

Clark fell behind 3-1 in the count to the next batter. His knuckleball didn't come as a surprise this time as the batter launched a deep fly to the wall in right. Derek made the catch with his back against the fence as the runner from second tagged up and went to third. Luckily for Clark, Nantucket's pitcher was up next and he was a terrible hitter. Clark struck him out and again escaped trouble. He'd thrown twenty-four more knuckleballs and kept the game scoreless.

Jimmy spoke to Johnny privately. "Coach he's already at forty pitches. If he keeps this up, we're going to need the bullpen early."

Johnny knew the pitch count but at that point wasn't going to worry about it.

Clark took the mound to start the third with the game still knotted at zero. He began the inning with his fourth walk of the game. After a sacrifice bunt moved the runner to second, Clark fell behind in the count 2-0 to the next batter before he lined a knuckleball towards third base. Mark, now given the task of playing third, was perfectly positioned and caught the ball for the second out. Clark worked carefully to Fowler and issued his fifth walk of the game. Jimmy paced the dugout while Johnny remained firmly in place on the top step. Clark rallied yet again, striking out the next Nantucket batter and keeping the game tied.

Clark got the first two outs of the fourth inning without incident but walked the third batter. The baseball gods were again kind to him as the Nantucket pitcher came up and swung miserably at three knuckleballs, striking out to end the inning. Four innings pitched and seventy-eight pitches thrown; each of them a knuckleball. As the Pride players came off of the field, Johnny finally talked with Clark.

"How are you feeling?"

"Feeling great, Coach. No problems."

Johnny wasn't thoroughly convinced that Clark was being honest.

Ricky lined out and Derek struck out to start the fifth. With two outs and nobody on, another inning appeared to be going by the wayside until Mike kept it alive with a single.

Mark stepped to the plate. His second game home run had gotten him into a groove. He swung and slammed the pitch into the right centerfield gap. Mike was running full-tilt towards third, fully expecting to score. As he approached third, however, he saw Coach Art frantically waving for him to stop.

Johnny said, "Why is he stopping him?"

Jimmy said, "He could have made it! The second baseman is just getting the ball!"

The Pride now had runners on second and third with two outs, but Clark struck out to end the threat. Johnny calmly talked with Coach Art.

"What made you hold Mike?"

Art's response was barely audible.

"I was thinking about what happened to Hank and I didn't want to see another kid get hurt in a collision. I can't have that on my conscience."

Johnny was sympathetic to his friend. "It's okay, Art. I understand."

Clark got the first out of the fifth easily but issued his seventh walk of the game to the next batter with the heart of the Nantucket order on the horizon. A single put runners on the corners with one out.

Jimmy said, "Johnny, we've got to get someone up in the bullpen now."

Johnny was reluctant. "All right. Get Antonio up."

Clark grabbed the rosin bag and out of the corner of his eye noticed Antonio throwing in the bullpen. He threw it hard to the ground. Clark fell behind Fowler, 3-0. Fowler got the green light to swing, a courtesy given to most good hitters, and hit a hard ground ball headed towards centerfield. It looked like Nantucket would be first on the scoreboard.

Mike had other ideas. He dove as the ball bounced over second base, fielded it and flipped to Miguel. With his bare hand, Miguel caught the toss and in a fluid motion threw on to first just in time to complete the double play, ending the inning in spectacular fashion. Fowler slammed his helmet as the game headed into the sixth inning still tied at zero.

Johnny motioned to the bullpen to have Antonio sit down.

Jimmy was practically begging Johnny to take Clark out of the game. "Johnny he's at ninety-one pitches. You can't leave him out there."

"Jimmy I love you, but let it go. I'll let you know when I'm ready to get him out of there."

Even Johnny couldn't believe what he'd just told his pitching coach. He just had a gut feeling and he was riding it.

Clark started the bottom of the sixth in a scoreless deadlock. For the moment, Johnny's hunch seemed to be right. Clark got through the inning without incident for the first time in the game and used only ten pitches to do it.

Both Pete and Ricky lined out hard to centerfield starting the seventh inning before Derek came to bat. Nantucket's pitcher hadn't made many mistakes in the game but he made one to Derek, who drove his first pitch deep the opposite way into the left centerfield gap. The ball bounced off of the base of the fence and by the time the centerfielder came up with it, Derek was standing on second base with a double. Johnny yelled, "Greg, grab a helmet! You're running for Derek!"

Greg was much faster than Derek and with still no score, Johnny wanted to make the most of any scoring chances that came his way. Mike hoped to get something he could drive to get home the run. He quickly got ahead in the count, 2-0. Now he could focus on getting a pitch he could drive. As the pitcher looked in for a sign, Greg extended his lead from second base. The pitcher quickly spun and threw to the second baseman sneaking in behind Greg. The throw arrived in plenty of time and Greg got picked off to end the inning. He came off of the field with his head hanging.

Johnny grabbed him. "Shake it off, get your glove, and go to right. I need you out there."

Greg nodded and grabbed his glove. It wasn't the time to feel sorry for himself.

Clark's troubles resurfaced when he issued his eighth walk of the game to start the seventh. After the pitcher bunted, Nantucket had the go ahead run at second, with one out.

Jimmy asked, "Get Antonio up again?"

Johnny crossed his arms. "No. Not yet."

Clark looked to the dugout then to the bullpen, noticing that no one was warming up. Focused, he struck out the next batter. Just one more and Clark would dodge yet another bullet. The Nantucket batters were now all sitting on Clark's knuckleball. With the runner on second, Nantucket's batter grounded Clark's pitch passed Pete into right field. The runner from second rounded third and headed for the plate as Greg fielded the ball and threw home. It was a perfect throw, probably the best throw Greg had ever made. Ricky caught it chest high and dropped the tag in plenty of time to cut down the runner and maintain the 0-0 tie into the eighth inning.

"Great throw, Greg! Great throw!" Johnny yelled as the team came into the dugout.

Johnny took Clark aside. "Clark, I'm sending up a pinch hitter. You're done tonight. Great job."

Clark's tone wasn't an angry one. It was more a plea.

"Don't take me out, Johnny. Please."

"Clark, what's up?"

Clark swallowed hard. "This is it for me, Johnny. This is my last game."

"Why?"

Clark took a deep breath. "The other day I felt a twinge in my arm. I didn't think much of it, but it turns out my old injury is flaring up. At this stage, I can't go through another surgery and rehab. The only thing I can throw without much pain is my knuckleball."

"Well that explains the one hundred and eleven of them you've thrown tonight. You should have told me."

Johnny motioned for Antonio to get loose.

Clark begged. "Don't, Johnny. I can do this. They haven't scored on me yet."

Johnny was torn. As Johnny contemplated his move Clark said, "Look, if I get into trouble next inning I'll come out. Heck, I'll take myself out. Just give me a chance to finish. That's all I ask."

Johnny scratched his head. "Okay, but you're on a short leash."

Mike walked and Mark followed with a single to start the eighth. The Pride had a real threat going. Clark bunted the runners to second and third with one out.

Nantucket's manager made a strategic move and had Miguel walked to set up a force play at home. Malcolm had a chance to give the Pride the lead. After getting ahead in the count 2-0, Malcolm dug into the box deeper. He was looking for a fastball and got one, right down the middle. He swung hard and lined a ball up the middle. Unfortunately for the Pride, quick reflexes by the Nantucket pitcher turned a potential RBI hit into a home-to-first double play to end the inning. Clark headed back to the mound.

"I can't believe you left him in," Jimmy said.

"Have faith, Jimmy."

Clark was facing the heart of the order and he had no room for error. The first batter hit a hard line drive to Freddie in left for the first out of the inning. Next up was Fowler who had hit the ball hard all night long with nothing to show for it. The count went to 3-2 on Fowler with Clark fully aware that he was one mistake from being taken out. He threw his knuckler, but it didn't turn over as it should have. Fowler drove it high and deep into centerfield as Malcolm took off towards the fence. Mother Nature again played friend to Clark as the wind kept the ball in the stadium. Malcolm made the catch at the base of the wall for out number two.

Jimmy said, "Johnny..."

Johnny quickly interrupted. "No, Jimmy."

Clark took a deep breath and said to himself, One more and you're out of the inning.

Clark continued his knuckleball regimen, again falling behind in the count. The batter took a big swing and made solid contact as the ball headed into the left field corner. Freddie chased as the ball came down and landed just barely into foul territory for the second strike. Clark breathed a sigh of relief as the count went to 3-2. He took a new ball from the umpire and let fly with a knuckleball that started well into the left hand batter's box. It looked like ball four for sure. As the batter prepared to take his base, however, the wind helped the pitch to dart quickly over the outside corner of the plate for strike three. Clark had only his second 1-2-3 inning of the game, and more importantly to him, he didn't have to come out as the incredible pitchers' duel headed to the ninth inning.

Johnny hollered, "Come on, fellas! One may be all we need!"

Freddie got the ninth off to a great start by doubling just beyond the reach of the first baseman. Pete launched a drive to the deepest part of the ballpark. This time the wind helped Nantucket as the ball was caught, but Freddie alertly tagged up and moved to third. Ricky had a chance to break the scoreless tie but he'd have to do it against Nantucket's dominating closer, Sam Bowers.

Ricky was far from nervous about facing Bowers. He was a fastball hitter and Bowers threw heat. Ricky rubbed a little dirt on his bat handle, stared down Bowers, and settled into the batter's box.

Bowers threw his first pitch and Ricky's eyes got huge. He was going to drive that fastball through that wind. There was just one problem; Bowers had thrown Ricky a changeup. Bowers threw changeups about as often as February 29th was be found on a calendar. All Ricky could do was pop up harmlessly to the third baseman for the second out.

The Pride's hopes for breaking the tie rested on Greg's shoulders. Since being resigned, Greg hadn't taken advantage of the few times he batted and a confrontation with Bowers looked to be a mismatch.

Johnny said, "Just try to put the ball in play, Greg. Use that speed."

Greg awaited the first pitch from Bowers. It was a fastball over the outside corner for strike one. Greg shook his head. Making contact would be difficult to say the least.

Bowers delivered another fastball. Greg swung and was nowhere close to making contact. Greg was down to his last strike. He stepped out and looked first at Johnny, then at his dad coaching third. He took off his helmet and wiped the sweat from his brow. Finally, Greg stepped back into the box, looking more determined than ever. Bowers was almost cocky knowing he had Greg right where he wanted him. Bowers began his windup and shockingly Freddie broke from third base. The pitch reached home plate and Greg did the unthinkable...he bunted! It was a beautiful bunt that rolled up the third base line.

The Nantucket third baseman never expected a two-strike bunt. Who would? Freddie had already crossed the plate as the ball rolled on the dirt just inside the third base line. The third baseman's only choice was to let the ball roll. When it finally came to rest on the third base line, Greg was standing on first with a bunt single and the Pride had a 1-0 lead.

Freddie got back to the dugout and went right to his manager. He said, "That was one hell of a gutsy move, Coach."

Johnny said, "It was Greg's idea." What looked like a stall tactic was actually Greg signaling his idea to Johnny, Coach Art, and Freddie.

Bowers was fit to be tied on the mound. Under his breath he mumbled, "That lousy, little son of a bitch!"

Greg was walking on air. He'd redeemed himself both in the field and on the bases.

Johnny said to Jimmy, "Get Wil up."

"Are you sure?"

Johnny nodded. "I want him ready just in case."

The Pride was three outs away from being champions.

Johnny stopped Clark as he headed to the mound. "All right, finish this thing."

Clark tucked his cap on and took the mound. The first batter of the ninth hit a ball just in front of the left field fence where Freddie made the catch for the first out.

Jimmy said, "Wil's ready."

Johnny looked to the mound then at the scoreboard. "Just tell him to sit tight."

Clark flipped his knuckleball to the next batter but it came in flat. The batter swung and hit a line drive down the third base line. Mark dove, taking a mouthful of dirt and fielded the ball on one hop, throwing to first from his knees. Pete stretched and made the scoop on a short hop for the second out. It was a great play on both ends. Two down and just one to go.

Clark looked to the bench but Johnny wasn't moving. Clark's heart was racing...so much so that he walked the next batter on four pitches. Nantucket's manager sent up a pinch-hitter for Bowers and Clark walked him too.

Jimmy pleaded, "Johnny, you have to take him out now. You have to."

Johnny was firm. "Not yet."

He didn't know why he was waiting to make the move, but he'd give Clark every chance he could to finish the game.

Nantucket was back at the top of its batting order with two outs, the tying run on second and the winning run on first. Clark's first knuckleball moved a bit too much and got by Ricky, moving the runners to second and third.

Before Jimmy could utter a syllable, Johnny said, "I'm going to talk to him." Johnny took a slow walk from the dugout. He got to the mound. "Wil's ready out there."

Clark's jersey and hat were drenched in sweat. "I'm fine. Let me finish this one off."

The Pride was one out away from completing an incredible season. Wil was rested and had done a great job closing since Jimmy and Johnny worked with him. It should have been an easy baseball decision. Johnny was just about to signal to the bullpen when Clark put a hand on his shoulder.

As tears welled up in his eyes, Clark very deliberately made his final plea.

"Please, Johnny. Let me finish this."

Johnny sighed and nodded. "It's all yours."

When Johnny got back to the dugout, Jimmy said, "You left him in."

"I'm playing a hunch, Jimmy."

Clark looked in for a sign, but everyone knew what he was throwing. Clark's next knuckleball found its way over the outside corner for a called strike to even the count. He felt his energy being sapped with every pitch, but there was no way he was quitting. His next pitch was hit solidly towards first base. It went over Pete's head and into the right field corner. As the runners rounded the bases, however, the first base umpire yelled, "Foul ball!"

It was foul by the slimmest of margins. The count was 1-2 to the batter but Clark's knuckleball had become like batting practice to the Nantucket hitters. Everyone on the Pride was just hoping that the ball would be hit at someone to end the game.

Clark asked the umpire for a new baseball. He rubbed until it felt right to him. Clark stretched and threw his 142nd pitch of the night. The first one hundred and forty-one had all been knuckleballs. Pitch number one hundred and forty-two was a fastball. It took everything

Clark had left in him to throw as hard as he possibly could. When he released, Clark felt the sting in his arm. It was a sting he anticipated, but things had gone on long enough and he was ending them one way or another.

The batter was caught off guard. The ball was almost in Ricky's glove when the batter swung and missed.

The ballgame and championship belonged to the Pride.

Clark knelt on the mound and cried. He cried because of the pain in his arm. He cried because he'd just helped his team win the title. He cried because that title-winning pitch would be the last one he'd ever throw. Mostly he cried because someone had shown enough faith in him one last time to let him finish what he'd started.

Clark's teammates gathered near the mound. They shook hands, hugged, and hollered for several minutes.

Johnny and the coaches stayed in the dugout, also celebrating as they watched their players acting like little boys, and they loved every minute of it.

Jimmy shook Johnny's hand. "Hell of a season, Coach."

Johnny could barely speak. "Yeah, it was."

From the seats Johnny heard, "Coach! Hey, Coach!"

It was Bernie. Johnny headed to the stands and embraced his son. Bernie said into Johnny's ear, "I knew you were the right guy for this job."

With a twinkle in his eye, and maybe a glimmer of moisture, Johnny answered, "Thanks for believing in me."

Bernie hopped the fence and headed to the clubhouse with his father. As the players finished their on-field celebration, they came into the clubhouse where sparkling grape juice was waiting. It was all the league would allow them to have.

Players began grabbing bottles, shaking them, and popping them open to pour over anyone's head that happened to be there, including Johnny and Bernie. It was a great celebration that lasted about an hour before things died down. It was then that Johnny spoke to his team.

"Gentlemen, it's been quite a journey. You all fought hard for this, and I thank every one of you for helping us to win this thing. I could not have asked for a better bunch. Thank you for everything."

Johnny barely got the last three words out. He'd had the perfect ending to an amazing season but in the aftermath, Johnny started thinking about the future.

It was late October, about five weeks since the Pride had won the title. Bernie's family was at the beach house along with Johnny and Catherine. The weather was still warm and they were all enjoying the peace. Rachel, Kat and Catherine were making lunch while Bernie fed Lizzie and Johnny helped Anna build a block castle on the floor. Bernie's cell phone rang breaking the peace.

"Hello?" Bernie just listened and smiled for a second to the voice on the phone before saying, "Dad, it's for you."

He paused in his castle building and promising Anna he wouldn't be long, took the phone.

"Johnny, Jerry Benjamin here! How're you doing?"

"Great, Jerry. What can I do for you?"

"Johnny, what you did with that team this year was something else. I didn't think you had a chance bringing in the guys that you did but son of a bitch, you pulled it off. You did some crazy shit out there but damn, it worked for you..."

342 | Dad, wanna be our Manager?

There was a long silence. Johnny waited for the owner to get to the point and just as he took a breath to speak up, Jerry continued.

"Johnny, I just fired the Mantids manager. He wasn't getting anything out of the guys. How'd you like to be my manager?"

This time, the long silence was on Johnny's end. He pondered the question and the unexpected offer. He took in the family spread out before him, his eyes resting finally on his grandaughter continuing to work on the castle they were building together. And he knew that there was no decision to make, not really.

"Thanks for the offer, Jerry. I'm flattered, but I'm retiring from managing. It was a great experience, and I would not change a moment of this past year. But I want to spend more time with my family."

"You're a damn good manager, Johnny. If I give you a week, will you reconsider?"

Johnny couldn't believe his ears. A guy who six months ago thought it was crazy for Bernie to hire his father to manage was now offering him a Major League job.

Johnny continued to look at Anna, who was patiently waiting for her Poppie. "Thanks, but I've got another job lined up already. My granddaughter and I are going into construction. Keep in touch, Jerry."

Johnny handed the phone back to Bernie.

Bernie asked, "What did Jerry want?"

"He offered me the Mantids' manager job. I turned him down."

Bernie smiled. "For what it's worth, Dad, I think you'd have done a great job."

"Thanks, Bern. You gave me a chance to do something I'd always wanted to do. It was amazing, but one year of it was enough and hey, I went out on top."

"No one else could have done what you did."

"I'm sure someone could have but thanks for saying that, Bern."

This reminded Bernie that he had a call to make. Bernie handed Lizzie over to his sister and went outside to make his call.

"Hey, Frank, it's Bernie Endino.

Frank, wanna be our manager?"

Cast of Characters

Bernie's Guys

Name	Position	Previously
Derek Figlione	Player	Financial Advisor
RickyBenetti	Catcher	Prison Guard
Greg Jeffers	Player	Gym Teacher
Mark Benfanti	Player	Stunt Man

The Coaches

Name	Position	Previously
Mickey Dowdell	Former Manager	Coal Barons
Johnny Endino	Manager	Warehouse Manager
Phil Figlione	Batting Coach	Barber
Art Jeffers	Base Coach	Grocery Manager
Jimmy McConnell	Pitching Coach	Accountant

The Players

Name	Position	Previously
Jerry Benjamin	Owner Mantids	Major League Franchisee
Hank Rundle	Third Baseman	Pride
Malcolm Jackson	Outfielder	Pride
Frank Carlson	First Baseman	Pride
Miguel Beniquez	Infielder	Pride
Alex Golden	Backup Catcher	Pride
Freddie Martinez	Outfielder	Pride
Jake Williams	Pitcher	Pride
Charlie Vanholdt	Pitcher	Pride
Clark Gresham	Pitcher	Pride
Joey Phillips	Utility Player	Pride
Christian Perez	Relief Pitcher	Pride
Mike Dillon	Utility Player	Pride
Luke Simms	Pitcher	Pride
Pete Robinski	First Baseman	Pride
Wil Robinson	Relief Pitcher	Pride
Hideki Mariyama	Outfielder	Pride
Jorge Santiago	Starting Pitcher	Pride
Tim Mathis	Relief Pitcher	Pride
Casey Francis	Relief Pitcher	Pride

FAMILY

Bernie Endino	Husband / Father / Son / Lottery Winner / Owner of the Pride
Rachel Endino	Wife / Mother / Fundraiser
Anna Endino	Bernie & Rachel's older daughter
Lizzie Endino	Bernie & Rachel's younger daughter
Catherine Endino	Bernie's mother / Johnny's wife
Kat Endino	Bernie's sister
Paul Simms	Luke's Father
Yoshinori Ito	Hideki Mariyama's interpreter

About the Author

J.B. LIVES IN DUNMORE, Pennsylvania. He has two children, Maria and Abby. He continues to enjoy baseball and hopes someday that the Atlanta Braves will win another World Series.

www.ingramcontent.com/pod-product-compliance
Lightning Source LLC
Chambersburg PA
CBHW032030090426
42733CB00029B/73